The secret life of romantic comedy

MANCHESTER
1824

Manchester University Press

The secret life of romantic comedy

Celestino Deleyto

Manchester University Press
Manchester and New York
distributed in the United States exclusively by Palgrave Macmillan

Published by Manchester University Press
Oxford Road, Manchester M13 9NR, UK
and Room 400, 175 Fifth Avenue, New York, NY 10010, USA
www.manchesteruniversitypress.co.uk

Distributed in the United States exclusively by
Palgrave Macmillan, 175 Fifth Avenue, New York,
NY 10010, USA

Distributed in Canada exclusively by
UBC Press, University of British Columbia, 2029 West Mall,
Vancouver, BC, Canada V6T 1Z2

British Library Cataloguing-in-Publication Data
A catalogue record for this book is available from the British Library

Library of Congress Cataloging-in-Publication Data applied for

ISBN   978 0 7190 7674 9   hardback

First published 2009

18 17 16 15 14 13 12 11 10 09   10 9 8 7 6 5 4 3 2 1

Mixed Sources
Product group from well-managed
forests and other controlled sources
www.fsc.org Cert no. TT-COC-2082
© 1996 Forest Stewardship Council

Typeset
by SNP Best-set Typesetter Ltd., Hong Kong
Printed in Great Britain
by Cromwell Press Ltd, Trowbridge

For Anita

Contents

List of illustrations   *page* ix
Acknowledgements   xi

Introduction   1

1 **The theory of romantic comedy**   18
  Romantic comedy and laughter   19
  Happy endings, forgotten middles and the ideology
    of romantic comedy   24
  The space of romantic comedy   30
  The Sydney issue   38
  Genres and films   45

2 **Comic negotiations**   55
  I Laughter, love and World War II:
      To Be or Not to Be   55
    Love and the invasion of Poland   59
    A table for three: the love triangle   62
    Lubitsch meets screwball royalty   66
    That great, great Polish actor   72
    Performing love, performing war   75
  II Romantic comedy in no man's land:
      Kiss Me, Stupid   81
    Romantic comedy in the 1950s   82
    Satire and comedy   85
    Moral standards and character identification   89
    Climaxing in Climax   91
    Bang, bang   96
    Comic combinations   100

3 **Romantic comedy on the dark side**   **103**
  I The other thrills of *Rear Window*   103
     Look at me   105
     Society calling   111
     It started with a kiss   118
     The neverending story   124
  II The space of comedy and beyond:
     Crimes and Misdemeanors   128
     Love, faith and the comic space   131
     Inside the Statue of Liberty or love in the time of
      cholera   134
     Splitting genres   139
     The fisher king and the future generations   143

4 **Contemporary romantic comedy and the discourse**
  of independence   **148**
  Love in real time: *Before Sunset*   157
     The realities of love   158
     Walking and talking   163
     Sex and the city   167

References   **177**
Index   **185**

List of illustrations

1 'Search me, sheriff'. John Wayne and Angie Dickinson
in *Rio Bravo* (dir. Howard Hawks, 1959,
Warner Bros.)   *page* 5
2 'There's always something': love in the workplace.
Michael Douglas and Annette Bening in *The
American President* (dir. Rob Reiner, 1995,
Columbia, Universal)   41
3 Love between prima donnas: performing marriage
in *To Be or Not to Be*, starring Carole Lombard
and Jack Benny (dir. Ernst Lubitsch, 1942,
United Artists)   70
4 'Quite a bomber': Maria Tura takes the lead in
the performance of desire. Carole Lombard in
To Be or Not to Be (dir. Ernst Lubitsch, 1942,
United Artists)   79
5 'Coming Mrs. Spooner?': marriage as fantasy
in *Kiss Me, Stupid*, starring Kim Novak and
Ray Walston (dir. Billy Wilder, 1964, Lopert, MGM)   92
6 'Kiss me, stupid': Zelda's face and the comic space.
Felicia Farr in *Kiss Me, Stupid* (dir. Billy Wilder,
1964, Lopert, MGM)   99
7 'Is that normal?': Stella questions Jeff's masculinity.
Thelma Ritter and James Stewart in *Rear Window*
(dir. Alfred Hitchcock, 1954, Paramount)   115
8 'Anything bothering you?': Lisa starts her campaign
to subdue the fortress of reluctant 1950s masculinity.
Grace Kelly and James Stewart in *Rear Window*
(dir. Alfred Hitchcock, 1954, Paramount)   121

9 The *mise en scène* of the end of love: Women take
the blame. Woody Allen and Joanna Gleason in
Crimes and Misdemeanors (dir. Woody Allen, 1989,
Orion)   136

10 Alternatives to romance: Jenny widens the space of
romantic comedy. Woody Allen and Jenny Nichols
in *Crimes and Misdemeanors* (dir. Woody Allen, 1989,
Orion)   146

11 Love as fantasy and reality: Céline and Jesse
fictionalise their past. Julie Delpy and Ethan Hawke
in *Before Sunset* (dir. Richard Linklater, 2004,
Warner Bros.)   160

12 Will Nina make them stop talking? The open ending
and the future of relationships. Julie Delpy in
Before Sunset (dir. Richard Linklater, 2004,
Warner Bros.)   174

Acknowledgements

Research towards this book was funded by the Spanish Ministerio de Educación y Ciencia (research project no. HUM2004-00418) and the Diputación General de Aragón (re. H12). Part of this research was carried out at the libraries of the British Film Institute and the University of Zaragoza. I would also like to thank the following people for their help at various stages of the process: Peter W. Evans, for providing the initial inspiration to write about romantic comedy; Christine Holmlund, for her encouragement and ideas during our preparation of the panel on genre at the Chicago SCMS conference; Kelly McWilliam, for sharing with me her unpublished material on lesbian romantic comedy; Chantal Cornut-Gentille, for her help, friendship and encouragement and for introducing me to the basics of chaos theory; and the staff of Manchester University Press, for always making things easy for me. My thinking about genre has been shaped through lengthy discussions with my colleagues in the 'Cinema, culture and society' research group and I am greatly indebted to all of them. My most special thanks go to Constanza del Río, my most demanding critic, from whose academic acumen and personal involvement in my work I continue to benefit shamelessly; Frank Krutnik, whose work I have admired for years and who generously helped me when I most needed him; and Marimar Azcona, who has discussed with me the theory of romantic comedy for hours on end and has collaborated in this project as if it was her own. As usual, I owe most to my wife Anita, for her constant love and affection, and to my daughters Elena, who keeps me abreast with the new affective protocols, and Esther, the person with the clearest notion of what is and is not a romantic comedy.

Introduction

Jack, a bank robber, and Karen, a cop, meet in the boot of a car when he breaks out of jail. They become attracted to one another as they discuss Faye Dunaway movies. Their romance develops and intensifies as one chases after the other, in more ways than one. The ambiguous ending suggests that sex may have become more important than the (federal) law. This is one way of describing the plot of Steven Soderbergh's *Out of Sight* (1998) and it is a description that makes the film sound very much like a romantic comedy, whether we take our definition from accounts of the genre's classical antecedents in Greek and Roman New Comedy (for example, Miola, 2002), from Northrop Frye's theorisation of Shakespearean *green world* comedies (1957), or from more recent approaches, like Steve Neale's discussion of romantic comedy's conventions (1992) or Tamar Jeffers McDonald's 'master definition' of the genre (2007: 9). The meet cute, the wrong partners, the learning process and other features listed by Neale, or the quest for love, the light-hearted way and (arguably) the successful conclusion required by Jeffers McDonald are in place, as are romance, desire, gender difference and social pressure, all easily identifiable as some of the genre's central thematic concerns.

The film was released at a time of maximum popularity of the genre and, while it can just as accurately be described as a caper movie, a crime film or a thriller, the cultural importance of romantic comedy at the end of the 1990s facilitated the genre's appearance in this and other unexpected places – films like *Scream* (1997), *Starship Troopers* (1997), *Play It to the Bone* (1999) or *Entrapment* (1999), to name a few. Yet, since it has not been seen as a 'conventional' romantic comedy, *Out of Sight* does not figure in recent accounts of the genre. Romantic comedy being the most superficial of mainstream genres, boundary patrolling on the part of the critical institution has been necessary to guarantee its purity and to preserve its superficiality, and Soderbergh's film has been conveniently kept out of the recent canon. Movies like *Pretty Woman* (1990), *Sleepless in Seattle* (1993), *The Runaway Bride* (1998), *Maid in Manhattan* (2002), *Love Actually* (2003) or *The Holiday* (2006) are easier to fit into a remarkably inflexible but critically successful generic mould than a text directed by a contemporary *auteur* and characterised by generic instability. When Nick James, in a recent *Sight & Sound* editorial, describes the most crassly commercial type of product of contemporary cinema as 'a conviction-free romantic comedy aimed at the teen market' (2005: 3), he is clearly tapping into a critical consensus about the genre and is most certainly not thinking of a film like *Out of Sight*. The same critic, in an appreciative and very perceptive discussion of *Before Sunset* (2004), refers to the centrality of sex, the notion of the ideal partner, the characters' talk of love, romance, relationships and idealism, the discourse of relationship theory and other topics which generally find their home in the fictional space of romantic comedy, yet never once mentions romantic comedy, the mere idea of Richard Linklater's film belonging to this genre being antithetical with the critic's admiration for the movie. For James, *Before Sunset*, with its heightened realism, its naturalistic performances, its real-time chronology and its self-effacing fluid camerawork, is an example of 'pure cinema', belonging to the tradition of Jacques Rivette and Eric Rohmer (2004: 14–15), a type of film inhabiting a totally different universe from that of popular film genres.

It is not my intention to argue that films like *Out of Sight* and *Before Sunset* belong to the genre of romantic comedy – that they are romantic comedies. Rather, I would contend that our understanding of these and many other movies would benefit from considering them in relation to romantic comedy and, conversely, that any discussion of these and similar films that does not take on board their generic participation, however imperfect or problematic it may be, will not do them full justice. I will also be arguing that the history of the genre is formed not only by those films around whose generic ascription there is a critical consensus – those that can comfortably be defined as 'genre films' – but also by more problematic texts like these two, and, further, that it is often films like these that make the genre evolve in more interesting directions.

Critics' general reluctance to think along generic parameters in cases such as these, as well as the problems and hesitations they face when having to deal with the generic ascription of many other individual texts, stem from critical allegiance to a traditional concept of genre which includes both the idea of belonging and the still powerful and derogatory link between genre and popular culture. This link has had as a result an ideological and aesthetic determinism in the consideration of genres. Within this climate, romantic comedy, more than other genres, has not fared well. A circular argument has been more or less universally accepted whereby only those films that include certain conventions and a certain 'conservative' perspective on relationships are romantic comedies and, therefore, romantic comedies are the most conventional and conservative of all genres. If a film threatens to be mildly interesting in cinematic, narrative or ideological terms then it cannot possibly be a romantic comedy. It is a very popular argument and one that manages to contain the genre within very strict and narrow parameters, which is, after all, what genre critics have traditionally sought to achieve (Altman, 1999: 17, 99). In contrast with this line of reasoning, I suggest that it is partly the proximity of these two films to the conventions of romantic comedy that makes them interesting and worthy of cultural analysis and, simultaneously, that the genre's history is as much indebted to films like *Out of Sight* or *Before Sunset* as to those more routinely considered as romantic comedies. My aim in this book is therefore double: on the one hand, as far as generic theory is concerned, I will be taking issue with the notion of belonging as the most appropriate way to talk about film genre; on the other, I will be arguing that there is more to romantic comedy than meets the eye, that the genre's presence in films is richer, more complex and less ideologically determined than it has generally been taken to be, and that it can often be found in the most unexpected places. In short, I propose to explore the secret life of romantic comedy.

Let us consider another example, in this case a more classical and, apparently, more clearly generic film. In an early scene of Howard Hawks's *Rio Bravo* (1958), Chance (John Wayne) goes into Feathers's (Angie Dickinson) bedroom at the hotel where she is staying in order to arrest her for cheating at cards. She denies his accusation and, taking advantage of his sexual curiosity, challenges him to search her for the missing cards. A power relationship is established between the two characters, within which Chance's social mastery as sheriff over the female adventuress is reversed as she takes the upper hand in this and ensuing dialogues. Again, it would appear from my description that this is yet another conventional scene in a romantic comedy. But *Rio Bravo* is a western, and not just any western but one of the most celebrated films in the history of the genre. Since this genre is, to a large extent, defined by its characteristic *mise en scène*, even the most cursory look at the scene described here will immediately convince the spectator that it is indeed a western. Yet the romantic comedy-inspired relationship between the two characters is by no means a negligible element and similar scenes to this one can be found not only in *Rio Bravo* but also in such adventure films directed by Hawks as *Only Angels Have Wings* (1939), *To Have and Have Not* (1944) or *Hatari!* (1962). A habitual director of romantic comedies, Hawks often allowed scenarios of the battle of the sexes, heterosexual desire and male humiliation at the hands of the aggressive female character to crop up in his 'non-comic' films. His 'comic' worldview and his very personal perspective on the ideal heterosexual relationship crucially affected his work in other genres. For a genre criticism concerned with generic ascription, *Rio Bravo* then poses a certain problem of impurity. Is the film a western? Or does Hawks's authorial intervention in the genre turn it into something else? Is this a case of a film artist's subverting the conventions of the genre? Or would we dare to say that, because of Hawks's presence as director, the movie provides an original blend of western and romantic comedy?

Critics have offered different solutions to this generic problem. Steve Neale, who does not refer to this film in particular, argues that the influence of *auteur* criticism in the formation of most film genres has done great disservice to genre theory. The dominance of films like *Rio Bravo* in the 'official' canon of the western distorts the genre's history since these are 'exceptional' texts which do not reflect the genre's functioning as accurately as more mediocre, less well-known films do (2000: 10–11). *Rio Bravo* would not be the most representative of westerns, because of Hawks's manipulation, even transcendence, of generic conventions. For John Belton, writing in *The BFI Companion to the Western*, the film's generic ascription is problematic because it has a 'non-western' plot: it abandons the wide open exteriors of traditional westerns and its story is not

1 'Search me, sheriff'. John Wayne and Angie Dickinson in *Rio Bravo*
(dir. Howard Hawks, 1959, Warner Bros.)

about conquering the West but about keeping what has been con-
quered. The only thing that he finds western-like about it is the
iconic presence of John Wayne and Walter Brennan (1988: 294).
Robin Wood, using the very approach that Neale criticises, finds
the film both the most traditional of westerns and 'essential Hawks'.
For this author, the value of generic conventions is that they provide
a firm basis from which the director can build his own perspective,
his own personal approach. *Rio Bravo*, therefore, presents an
extremely productive tension between background and foreground,
between genre and *auteur* (1983: 35–40). It goes without saying
that neither these critics nor anybody else has stopped to consider
that the film may be, at least to some extent, also a romantic
comedy.

In his theoretical work on genre, Neale has attempted to shift
the emphasis from the texts themselves to the systems of communication and expectation within which they operate. Genres are not
only situated in the texts but also, crucially, in the industry that
produces them and markets them and in the audiences that consume
them (2000). Thus, while it may be argued theoretically that *Rio
Bravo* is not just a western, the industry marketed and continues
to market it as a western, and most spectators would more or less
intuitively consume it as a western. In those important cultural
senses, the movie is indeed a western. However, while the expan-
sion of genre theory beyond the texts, especially by theorists like
Neale and Rick Altman (1999), is a welcome move and such

resources as promotional material, trade press descriptions of the films, contemporary reviews, etc., have proved invaluable to understand the workings of film genre, there remains room for consideration of the ways in which the texts themselves function generically. While acknowledging the importance of what could be described as the genericity of cinema (the cinema as a system of communication and as an industry), my main focus here is on the genericity of films as texts and, consequently, also as cultural products. As a point of departure, the three accounts of the western and *Rio Bravo* briefly summarised above have one thing in common: the idea of belonging. Genres are groups of films that share a series of conventions. Generic films are films which belong to specific genres and these, in some cases, are inflected in crucial ways by individual directors. The history of a genre is formed by the movies which critics have agreed on as forming part of the canon of that genre. Generically mixed films pose a minor problem since, in this formulation, they belong simultaneously to at least two different genres, but they do not significantly alter the underlying premise of separate spheres for different genres, even though they may occasionally intersect. Contemporary critics have adapted quite smoothly to the proliferation of movies which use conventions from various genres by arguing that a certain text is a cross between, say, an action film, a buddy film and a comedy (*Play It to the Bone*), or a big spectacle film and a romantic melodrama (*Titanic*). Film artists who worked within the genre system, like Hawks, Douglas Sirk, Vincente Minnelli or Fritz Lang, often subverted the genres, parodied them or took them in unexpected directions, but, in spite of the relevance of their films, they were, from a generic viewpoint, no more than exceptions that confirmed the existence of genres and their essential purity. As with Renaissance prodigies, these hybrids, crossbreeds and other monstrosities do nothing but confirm the unchangeable law of the genre. Rick Altman's contention that, in Hollywood cinema, most films are generically mixed, that film producers were not interested in making films within established genres, but rather constantly sought novelty by creating new cycles through the transformation of existing ones, and that studio publicists often tried to sell major films by associating them with several genres at the same time in order to appeal to different sectors of the public (1999), has gone largely unheeded in recent academic genre writing, which is still centrally concerned with whether a film belongs to a genre or not. Jeffers McDonald, for example, compares two similarly titled Kirsten Dunst vehicles and concludes that *Get Over It* (2001) is a romantic comedy while *Bring It On* (2000) is not (2007: 9).

A notable exception is James Naremore's study of *film noir*, which is less interested in providing a list of more or less pure *noir* films than in the concept and the history of the term, and with the light that such an exploration may cast on the films themselves. Taking his cue from George Lakoff's cognitive theory of categories (1987), Naremore argues that every movie is 'transgeneric' and polyvalent and that movie conventions have always mixed, and sees genres as social and historical chains rather than groups of films, a perspective which makes it impossible ever to establish boundaries or categorical definitions for any given genre (1998: 5–6). Lakoff's cognitive theory derives from Ludwig Wittgenstein's attack on categorical thinking. There is no essential feature to any given category; only, as Wittgenstein explains, family resemblances. Some members of a family may share some features with some of its members but not with others (Lakoff 1987: 16–17). As Wittgenstein emphatically begs, 'For if you look at [games] you will not see something that is common to *all*, but similarities, relationships, and a whole series of them at that. Don't think, but look' (1963: 31e). Hence the concept of 'chaining', that is, of categories as chains which develop historically or sequentially and within which certain elements are related to those close to them but not to those in further regions of the chain. It follows that, since the chain constantly acquires new links, genre boundaries are never fixed. At the very most, we can draw a boundary for a special purpose, but that does not ensure that such a boundary will remain in place when our objective changes, or that the boundary drawn by one person will be accepted by another one with a different agenda (33e–36e). This approach rejects the existence of an immovable organising principle for any given category and underlines the constantly changing nature of the relationships which are established between any given components at any point in the chain (or in the complex system).

Lakoff, Naremore and Altman inscribe their approaches within an intellectual tradition of critique of Aristotelian categorisation and Newtonian mechanism. According to this tradition, film genres, like their literary counterparts, are one more system of categories, a way of explaining the world, which is believed to function like a predictable machine that the human being will be able to wholly control one day. Categories are powerful, if illusory, manifestations of this desire to control natural and human patterns of behaviour. Aristotelian philosophy and Newtonian physics have become some of the main targets of poststructuralist theories, and recent approaches to film genres should be seen as one more manifestation of a new intellectual and cultural climate. Within this context, chaos theory provides an appropriate template for the functioning of film genres.

For chaos theorists, human beings, natural phenomena, the physical world, the financial market or mathematical structures are all part of chaotic systems, governed by unpredictability and impossible to control in the long run. These systems, called complex systems, are governed by an unstable balance between order and chaos, always on the edge of chaos, but generating a dynamic evolution out of their instability and spontaneity. Like a river stream, complex systems are in constant flux and their elements are never identical to each other or even to themselves. The internal structure of complex systems is fractal, that is, made up of elements which recall or resemble in themselves the structure of larger systems but are, at the same time, endlessly evolving, mutating and establishing complex relationships with other elements. At any given point, a series of bifurcation points may lead any one of these elements to become 'strange attractors' and make the structure of the system converge around them, change its trajectory, create new systems and, occasionally, threaten to destroy the whole structure, which then may or may not reorganise itself in a different way (Briggs and Peat, 1999). This theory describes with striking accuracy the way genres function. Against the more linear approach, according to which genres, like other categories, work in simple, predictable ways which can be investigated, known, classified and controlled, the chaotic view of genres underlines their instability, the impossibility to establish clear lines of demarcation, and the non-linearity, unpredictability and complexity of their evolution. As Morson and Emerson argue in their account of Mikhail Bakhtin's views on genre, they form not by legislation but by accretion, resembling a jumbled structure rather than a preconceived design (1990: 292). Like fractals, individual films, scenes or even shots often reproduce in themselves the structure and characteristics of the general system while, at the same time, as in the examples mentioned above, often existing at the intersection between different generic systems. As with attractors, genres are often pulled in unexpected ways, bifurcate, generate new genres or disappear (although not necessarily forever) when a combination of circumstances (both external and internal) bring about turning points in their evolution. Ireneusz Opacki's concept of the 'royal genre', the one that best renders the aspirations of a given period, seems apt here. The power of attraction of this genre draws towards itself all the remaining genres, entering in close relations with them and transforming them and the general context in which they operate (2000: 120–2). Genres are not discrete units, or categories, but are part of a complex system which works chaotically but in unison and which is constantly mutating through the films themselves and other discourses, both internal and external to the industry.

Chaos theory, Wittgenstein's critique of Aristotelian categories and Lakoff's cognitive appropriation of it go a long way towards dismantling traditional film genre criticism: the impossibility to isolate one essential property which is shared by all the members of one given class; the idea that the boundaries between classes are changing all the time; and above all, the fact that genres are not uniform categories defined by a collection of properties that all the category members share, but, in Wittgenstein's formulation, chains of relationships and similarities (1963: 31e–33e). These are all empirically observable phenomena that contradict traditional genre thinking. However, one important aspect of generic functioning seems to have been overlooked by Lakoff's theory. For him groups of texts are unstable, fluid and unrelated to many other members of the same category, but the idea of membership, or belonging to a certain category (or, perhaps, several categories) remains safely in place. The groups are looser and interact with one another in more intricate ways than before but remain, however vaguely defined and however provisional, still groups. In this sense, Jacques Derrida's theory of genre goes one step further.

In his article 'La loi du genre/The Law of Genre', Derrida argues that genericity is inescapable, that all texts are generic and that they all bear the imprint of their own genericity. For him genre criticism has always been concerned with norms to be respected, with lines of demarcation, with purity. Mixing genres is a dangerous game because it threatens the purity of the genre and the very concept of

genre. In his own words, 'one owes it to oneself not to get mixed
up in mixing genres' (1980: 204), but even when genres do inter-
mix, the very fact that we speak of 'mixing' guarantees the essential
purity of their identity. The law of genre is, therefore, a norm of
purity, a certificate of guarantee, and the occasional transgression
of the law only serves to reinforce its validity. But what, asks
Derrida, if at the heart of the law, were lodged its opposite: 'a law
of impurity, or a principle of contamination?' (204). What if it were
impossible not to mix genres? What if contamination, the necessary
presence of convention mixing, turned out to be as constitutive of
genericity as generic purity? Before going on to discuss at large the
inherent generic self-consciousness of texts, the French philosopher
offers a conclusion of sorts to this conundrum: 'a text cannot
belong to no genre, it cannot be without or less a genre. Every text
participates in one or several genres, there is no genreless text; there
is always a genre and genres, yet such participation never amounts
to belonging' (212). His reformulated law of genre is both more
pervasive – all texts are generic, there is no text outside the law of
genre – and more ambiguous than the law of generic purity which
he sets out to deconstruct. The opposite of not belonging to any
genre is not, as one could perhaps expect, belonging to one or
several genres, but rather, a participation which 'never amounts to
belonging'. In his view, texts participate in genres but do not belong
to them, or rather, they both belong, insofar as they participate,
and do not belong, because they never go beyond participating. The
Derridean law of genre, with, in chaos theory terms, its constitutive
'fuzziness', separates itself both from the Aristotelian notion of
categories as groups of elements, from Horatian genre prescriptiv-
ism, according to which the poet should follow previously established generic norms, and from the traditional concept of genres as
closed and stable corpora according to which each text belongs to
only one category (with the exception of generic hybrids). Derrida's
critique of generic purity and his implicit espousing of chaotic fuzziness follow on from Wittgenstein's exploration of the contradictions in categorical thinking. Derrida's insight that genericity – the
necessary existence in all texts of marks of categorical thinking – is
inescapable but that categorisation does not describe accurately
the way genres work solves some of the contradictions found by
Wittgenstein because it changes the point of view from belonging
to participating.

Derrida does not go into the details of the specific nature of this participation but the relevance of his theory for the study of film genre cannot be underestimated. Altman's Derrida-inspired defence of the constitutive impurity not only of Hollywood films but also of its genres satisfactorily solves traditional problems of 'genre belonging' – whether *Oklahoma!* (1955) is a western or a musical, whether *Mildred Pierce* (1945) is melodrama or *film noir* – while it also emphasises the industrial and internal nature of generic evolution. For Altman genres are not only part of an intricate system of relationships but they also exist simultaneously at various levels. He describes this as a generic cartography, that is, a series of maps superimposed on one another. Familiar problems – whether a film belongs to one genre or another, whether the term genre should be reserved for comedy and tragedy or be also applied to epic, lyrical poetry and drama, or whether *film noir* is a genre or a style – are solved in one stroke or cease to be problems since a film can relate to various genres at the same time because the frame of reference used to define each one of them is different. Epic, comedy, the musical or the western are not mutually exclusive since they represent categories defined from different perspectives and can therefore all coincide in a single text. This does not invalidate the generic system or its analytical usefulness, but it does reveal that most film critics assume that they are working with a set of stable, fixed terms even though genres, like any other complex systems, are, in fact, constantly changing, not only due to their intrinsic evolution but also to the specific interests of those who create them: the producers, the studios, the directors or the critics themselves (1999: 117–22). However, Altman's focus on contextual factors and on programmatic hypotheses that counteract traditional critical tenets prevents him from dealing with the specific workings of generic texts. His account of the film *Cocktail* (1988) in the chapter 'The Hollywood Cocktail' and the inset 'The Genre Mixing Game' usefully explain the reasons why genre mixing is not only extremely easy but practically inevitable in Hollywood films, but the Tom Cruise film is used here as proof of the pervasiveness of the 'mixing game' rather than as a case study in the textual consequences of genre mixing (1999: 130–9). Similarly, Steve Neale proposes a useful theory of generic evolution but his otherwise inflexible list of genres that *are* and genres that *are not* (melodrama, *film noir*), of films which belong to genres and films which do not, represents one more version of the traditional view of genres as groups of films (2000). But if we insist on asserting that genres are not groups of films, not even chains of members, we need to establish the nature of the relationship between films and genres. How exactly do conventions move from one to the other? Does the movement work in both directions or only in one?

Thomas Schatz has suggested that film genres can be studied, like languages, as sign systems, following Ferdinand de Saussure's distinction between *langue* and *parole*. A film genre would work like a system of rules and individual genre films would be specific manifestations of those rules (1981: 19). However, the static quality of Saussure's concepts does not correspond to the constantly shifting nature of the generic system, in which genres are in a process of constant evolution (and, sometimes, dissolution) and filmic texts operate within this chaotic system, reshaping it every time, sometimes in crucial ways. In chaos terms, a given film could convert itself into a positive attractor, exerting a subtle influence which, in the long run, could affect through self-similar repetition (later films that resemble it) the trajectory of the whole complex system (in our case, romantic comedy). Derrida's insight, therefore, suggests a more radical relationship of mutual and fluid interdependence than that proposed by Schatz. Film genres are sets of conventions which are created, constantly altered and occasionally made to disappear within texts. Film texts use conventions from different genres, and combine them in ways which are not only textually but also historically and culturally specific. Certain combinations, that is, the impact of certain genres upon others within texts, affect the evolution of the genres. Films are independent of genres insofar as they never swear allegiance to any of them, they never *belong* to any of them, but are never fully independent from them because they are always generic: they always use generic conventions and formulae. Although changing linguistic habits is no easy task, it would nevertheless not be completely accurate to say that a certain film belongs to a specific genre, say, that *Rio Bravo* is a western. Rather, *Rio Bravo* uses the conventions of the western in a certain way, one which is not exactly the same as that employed by other films; yet its genericity is not exhausted by this usage. Its participation in the western means that it would not exist as it is without this genre, and the genre would not be the same without its existence. At the same time, it does not exist solely as a western. Genres are not groups of films but abstract systems formed by elements taken from many films. The generic bag contains conventions, structures, narrative patterns, but no films. In a different sense, it is legitimate to say that *Rio Bravo is* a western because it participates in the history of the genre, it is affected by its conventions and it contributes to its evolution, among other things, by its inclusion of the conventions of romantic comedy in its western scenario and by the influence of Hawks's authorial vision. It would equally be reasonable to say that *Rio Bravo* is a romantic comedy because its treatment of the heterosexual relationship between Chance and Feathers invokes the conventions of this genre, and by locating this new version of the battle of the sexes in an unusual filmic setting, that of the western, it contributes to the evolution of romantic comedy in the 1950s. In other words, the film's use of generic conventions links it historically as much to *The Girl Can't Help It* (1957), *Pillow Talk* (1959), *Some Like It Hot* (1959), or indeed *I Was a Male War Bride* (1949), *Gentlemen Prefer Blondes* (1953), *Hatari!* or *Man's Favorite Sport?* (1964), as to *The Searchers* (1956), *Man of the West* (1958) or *From Hell to Texas* (1956).

Generic analysis should, therefore, concern itself less with issues of belonging and generic purity (or impurity) and more with the actual workings of generic elements in films. It should ask itself some of the questions proposed by Tom Ryall, for whom genres are also abstractions or 'overarching concepts', quite distinct conceptually from individual films: what genre or genres, or sets of generic conventions, constitute an appropriate context for reading a particular film?, what type of fictional world is invoked by each film in order to ensure the spectators' understanding and enjoyment? (1998: 329, 336). These fictional worlds provide the films with particular ways of seeing the world and are therefore relevant not only as specific articulations of generic form but also as reconstructions of social experience. They are, to use Medvedev's terminology, drive belts from the history of society to the history of film (in Morson and Emerson, 1990: 278), or, according to Opacki, the most appropriate 'language of translation' for socio-political phenomena (2000: 120). The history of genres, while dependent on the internal evolution of forms and industrial practices, is also closely linked to social and cultural history, with genres competing, at different moments of history, to become the most relevant ways of visualising given aspects of life (Morson and Emerson 1990: 299).

In the course of this metaphoric competition, genres interact with one another in various ways, a crucial factor in their individual evolution and in that of the genre system in general. The space in which these encounters are produced is the film text.

Filmic texts are meeting points in which various genres come into contact with one another, vie for dominance and are transformed. Whereas in many films one genre is clearly dominant over the rest, many others register the presence of more than one genre. Genre mixing is, therefore, not particularly specific to a tradition of films, nor to a period of the history of cinema, but something inherent to the workings of film genre. As Janet Staiger has argued, the alleged purity of classical or, in her terms, Fordian films, is a recent critical construction. Hollywood films were never pure (1997: 6 and *passim*). This does not mean to say, as both Altman and Neale admit, that postmodern generic combinations are not often more sophisticated than classical ones (Altman, 1999: 141) or that New Hollywood films are not more self-consciously parodic, hybrid (Neale, 2000: 250–1) or, in Staiger's terminology, 'inbred' (1997: 17). There may be different degrees of genre mixing but genre mixing *per se* is nothing to get nervous or ecstatic about. Asserting that a given film or group of films 'mixes' genres is not saying very much about the films: it is a premise of genre analysis, not a conclusion. Something similar can be surmised about other favourite critical terms connected with the study of genre like parody, transgression or subversion. Since genres are not fixed categories and constantly mutate into new forms, what critics call transgression or subversion is often nothing more than part of the evolution inherent to all film genres. There can only be transgression against a fixed norm. If the norm is flexible and it is part of its nature to constantly change, change is not particularly transgressive. Individual filmmakers may consciously attempt to parody or deconstruct what they consider to be the conventions of a particular genre, but the result of that conscious operation is simply to expand the genre or to take it in a different direction, to make it evolve, which is not very different from what most films do with genres anyway.

An introductory chapter is not the most appropriate place to carry out an in-depth analysis of a film, but, before concluding, I would like to suggest some ways in which the above theory of genre could be used for a generic reading of *Rio Bravo*. For most critics, a reasonable description of the film would be the one provided by Robin Wood: it is a Hawks western. However, because of the generally low cultural status of romantic comedy, especially among those who specialise in such male genres as the western, this genre's presence in the film has gone largely unnoticed. Critics generally prefer to assign the presence of such elements as might be found in romantic comedies in other genres to Hawks's particular perspective on heterosexual relationships, rather than to his use of generic conventions. Yet, since this director was perhaps more familiar with the conventions of romantic comedy than with those of any other genre, he may be seen as a conduit through which conventions travel from some films to others, from some genres to others. In this sense, a useful way of tackling this director's *oeuvre* and, more specifically, his use of romantic comedy, would be to analyse the different ways in which this genre becomes transformed depending on the various combinations with other genres that take place in each of his films. For the analysis of a film like *Rio Bravo* it is therefore useful to concentrate on how the combination of romantic comedy and western or, to be more accurate, the presence of romantic comedy in the midst of a western scenario, affects our understanding or our critical interpretation of the film, and, perhaps more ambitiously, to explore how the specific way in which Hawks (and the scriptwriters, Jules Furthman and Leigh Brackett) mixes the two genres contributes to the cinematic history of both.

As a western, *Rio Bravo* is a film about the role of violence in the consolidation of the new nation, with John Wayne's iconic figure representing the country's ambivalent cultural discourses about it. In this context, Chance's evolution as a character and his education will consist in learning how to behave properly, both socially and sexually, in front of a woman. This will happen through a process of apparent male humiliation at the hands of the woman, a process which in reality is making him a better person. This is a typical romantic comedy scenario, especially of the screwball comedy cycle to which Hawks contributed with such films as *Twentieth Century* (1934), *Bringing Up Baby* (1938), *His Girl Friday* (1940), *Ball of Fire* (1941) and later reformulations like *I Was a Male War Bride*, *Monkey Business* (1952) or *Man's Favorite Sport?* By placing this typically comic situation in the midst of a western, Hawks is underlining the importance of the process of feminisation of the western's tough hero, of the acquisition of a richer, more complete masculinity, for the securing of civilisation in the West. Society is not only constituted by defeating the outlaws and taming the wilderness but also by taming the excesses of violent masculinity. *Rio Bravo* suggests that the western, the quintessential male genre, with its narratives of violence and conquest, is dependent on the feminine, on the finding of a place for women and also a place for the feminine in men for this conquest and for the project of 'America' as a country to be truly successful, and for the genre's constitutive violence to be overcome and to be replaced by more positive, more productive values.

As many critics have pointed out, the western as a genre has traditionally relegated women to the background, to a position which is often not very relevant even as the love interest of a hero whose desire is generally directed rather towards homosocial forms of relations with other men, be those his buddies, the outlaws or even his dreaded Other, the Indian. In *Rio Bravo*, Hawks brings sexual tensions to the surface by suggesting that, in the hero's mind, women are initially more dangerous than the male antagonists because they bring about the emasculation of men and they are more unpredictable. The Wayne hero has no difficulty facing his enemies but cannot cope with the threat posed by women. Although in a more comic vein, his fear of women is comparable to the Wayne hero's fear of miscegenation in *The Searchers*. The text, however, sees this irrational fear of women as an impediment not only to the hero's humanity but to the future of the country. At this point romantic comedy, like the Seventh Cavalry, comes to the rescue, with its vindication of gender equality through desire, a discourse which is generally alien to the western. But Hawks, in *Rio Bravo*, places the western at a critical historical point at which untrammelled masculinity is no longer sufficient for the consolidation of the frontier. For a director who was particularly at home with Hollywood's generic conventions, his way of conveying this meaning is the significant mixture of the two genres, with John Wayne, the most forceful filmic icon of a self-sufficient and unassailable masculinity, at the centre of his experiment.

In conclusion, *Rio Bravo* is original in the particular way in which it combines its ingredients but not in the fact that it mixes genres. The Derridean substitution of participation for belonging, of open shelves for closed bags, in order to make better sense of the relationships, in our case, between genres and films allows us not only to question several critical commonplaces which do very little to explain either the history of genres or the specific workings of films but also to underline the importance of specific texts in the evolution of genres and of the interplay of generic conventions in textual analysis. In the remainder of this book I intend to propose a revised theory of romantic comedy and then test its validity through the analysis of texts, but these films must not be expected to fully embody the theory. Rather, the selected texts have seldom, if at all, been considered as belonging to the genre, combining as they do a historically specific use of romantic comedy conventions with those of other genres which, in most cases, tend to be dominant. Yet, it is my contention that the films do incorporate romantic comedy in their signifying structures and are all the more interesting and complex for it. And it is also the underlying assumption of this study that these films are not in a minority within the history of the genre with respect to such critically accepted cycles as the screwball comedy, sex comedies, nervous romances, new romances or post-romantic comedies. In fact, the history of the genre would probably not have been the same without those films that, by combining the conventions of romantic comedy with those of other genres, opened new directions which then became consolidated in more obvious instances of the textual workings of generic conventions.

1

The theory of romantic comedy

Romantic comedy has been described as a narrative of the hetero-sexual couple with a happy ending in which humour does not nec-essarily play an important part. In this book I would like to suggest the limitations of this conceptualisation and propose a change of approach in two different but closely linked directions: on the one hand, a comic perspective is a fundamental ingredient of what we understand by romantic comedy; on the other, the genre does not have a specific ideology – a single discourse which upholds the values of marriage and the stable heterosexual couple – but, more broadly, it deals with the themes of love and romance, intimacy and friendship, sexual choice and orientation. This shift from ideol-ogy to thematic specialisation is part of an attempt to move away from the Althusserian determinism that still pervades much con-temporary generic criticism and towards a view of genre as cultur-ally and historically mediated. In other words, romantic comedy articulates ideological discourses in the field of affective and sexual relationships but it does not, as a genre, tell us what to think or how to behave, even if some of the individual films may do. Rather, the genre uses humour and a comic perspective in order to convey ideas which are specific to each individual text and acquire sense within historical and cultural contexts, both those of the production and release of the movies and of their reception and consumption by different audiences.

The comic perspective is a crucial component of the definition of the genre not only because it generates a certain way of looking at human relationships but also because it constructs a space which transforms reality – like all genres do – by protecting the lovers from the strictures of social conventions and psychological inhibi-tions. This comic, protective, erotically-charged space is the space of romantic comedy.

Romantic comedy and laughter

Northrop Frye, one of the most important and influential theorists
of the genre in the twentieth century, distinguishes between two
basic types of comedy: 'There are two ways of developing the form
of comedy: one is to throw the main emphasis on the blocking
characters; the other is to throw it forward on the scenes of discovery and reconciliation. One is the general tendency of comic irony,
satire, realism, and studies of manners; the other is the tendency of
Shakespearean and other types of romantic comedy' (1957: 166–7).
This bifurcated account of the genre has been a constant feature
throughout the history of comic theory, from medieval reformulations of Aristotle and Cicero to film theory's much more recent
interventions. In a sixteenth-century response to one of the many
routine puritan attacks on the theatre, Thomas Lodge, author of
the source story for Shakespeare's *As You Like It*, starts his defence
by quoting from the late Roman grammarian Aelius Donatus on
the origins of both comedy and tragedy in ritual celebrations in
praise of the gods for a good harvest, and continues with the definition of the genre attributed to Cicero: '*imitatio vitae, speculum
consuetidinis, & imago veritatis*' (in Galbraith, 2002: 4). The beginning of his defence relates the genre, through its emphasis on fertility, regeneration and community, to Frye's romantic comedy; the
latter part refers to the Aristotelian, satirical tradition, with its
didactic and corrective goals, also famously summarised in Hamlet's
advice to the travelling players visiting Elsinore castle: 'to hold as
'twere the mirror up to nature; to show virtue her own feature,
scorn her own image' (*Hamlet* 3.2.18–19). Within the much shorter
history of film studies, Aristotelian comedy has received compara-
tively little attention, but a classification has emerged from accounts
of U.S. film comedy which can be considered parallel to that proposed by Frye outside cinema: the distinction between comedian
and romantic comedy (Seidman, 1981; Palmer, 1987; Neale and
Krutnik, 1990; Jenkins, 1992; and Karnick and Jenkins, 1995).
Although comedian comedy is not necessarily satirical in mode or
didactic in aim, it shares with satire a feature that differentiates it
from romantic comedy: the centrality of laughter.

Since traditional film criticism had always privileged the narrative tradition and romantic comedy, the authors mentioned
above have endeavoured to reassess the figure of the comedian in

Hollywood cinema and have convincingly argued that both types
of comedy derive from two different nineteenth-century theatrical
practices, with very few points in common: on the one hand, the
legitimate theatre of the well-made play and the great authors of
the past and, on the other, the popular theatre of the variety show,
the vaudeville and the music hall. In one of the key works of this
critical tendency, Steve Neale and Frank Krutnik distinguish between
comedy and the comic, suggesting that while in the first case the
emphasis is on the happy ending, in the second the crucial factor
is the generation of laughter, and they continue: '[a] happy ending
implies a narrative context; the generation of laughter does not'
(1990: 17). In a similar vein, Deborah Thomas differentiates
between the comic – that which makes us laugh – and the comedic
– a double fantasy of erotic desire and of a 'magical' and sheltering
place. She also downplays any possible interference between the
two when she argues that, although the two modes may overlap,
they are quite different things (1998: 58). Andrew Horton, for his
part, offers two definitions of film comedy: interlocking sequences
of jokes and gags which foreground narrative (and lean towards
the non-comic) *or* narrative as an excuse for holding together
moments of comic business (1991: 7). The first type would correspond roughly to romantic comedy, the second to comedian comedy.
Karnick and Jenkins insist on the same point when they affirm that
humour in Hollywood romantic comedy is something of a paradox,
since it implies a break in the narrative structure and a constant
threat to narrative logic and continuity. While the narrative strives
to contain comic moments within its structure, gags constitute a
danger for narrative balance and integrity (1995: 80–1). In the same
volume, Karnick affirms that humour is always opposed to narrative. Since the structure of romantic comedy is highly codified,
humour brings in an element of surprise and originality and com-
plicates a story which otherwise would be very similar to all the
rest (1995: 126–30).

As we can see, for Karnick, humour has no contribution to make
to narrative development. Rather, it is like the sugar coating that
helps us swallow the pill, or, in ideological terms, the bait used by
the texts to put forward an ideology based on monogamy, heterosexuality and social integration. In general, for Karnick and the
other critics, not only are laughter and the happy ending respectively the basic defining traits of comedian and romantic comedy

but also, when they do coincide in the same text, they remain separate, without impinging on one another. In other words, there are texts which happen to be romantic comedies, others that are comedian comedies and yet others which may contain both forms but always in isolation from one another. In short, in this formulation, romantic comedy and comedian comedy are largely incompatible.

The critical tendency to separate humour from narrative in accounts of comedy has always been very strong. Earlier mythical critics, for instance, aimed to minimise the importance of laughter in comic texts. Benjamin Lehman's opinion is typical of the comic theory of the 1950s and 1960s when he affirms that the main effect of comedy is 'a delight too deep for laughter, a joy too persuasive for laughter'. Such delight consists in 'a felt affirmation about life' and a 'deep human desire to be recreated by seeing true humanness prevail' (1981: 111). This emphasis on endurance, procreation and faith in humanity, related to the origins of the genre in ancient fertility rituals, is what caused the relegation of the comic to a subsidiary position, turning it into a by-product rather than an essential feature, even though a communal expression of generalised mirth was an important component of those ancient fertility rituals to which the genre had been traced back. The rise in the academic reputation of popular culture in the 1980s and 1990s, inspired in part by Bakhtin's theory of carnivalesque laughter and grotesque realism (1984), gave the study of the 'comic' aspects of comedy a new lease of life, but, as we have seen, the two dimensions of comedy remained disconnected.

However, for all the critics' efforts to keep humour and romantic narrative apart, this separation remains more theoretical than practical and the student of romantic comedy finds it difficult to match her/his experience with the available critical theory when it comes to analysing the films. Existing definitions of humour confirm the impossibility of such separation. Among them, Freud's short article is particularly illuminating. For him, humour entails a specific attitude towards de world: 'Look! Here is the world, which seems so dangerous! It is nothing but a game for children – just worth making a jest about!' (1985: 432–3). In an extension of this theory, Neale and Krutnik explain that the apparent distance provided by humour is only a form of disavowal of identification with the comic butt (1990: 77–8). Through humour, therefore, we indirectly acknowledge the humanity that is apparently being ridiculed as close to our own. In romantic comedy, this acknowledgement is crucial to understand our attitude towards the lovers' predicament but this predicament is precisely the subject of the narrative. Narrative and humour are, therefore, inextricably linked in the comic way chosen to present the vicissitudes of love and desire. It is true that most studies of romantic comedy, presumably still under the influence of Frye's structuralist model (1957), tend to focus on narrative structures, but this type of analysis always ignores an important part of our enjoyment and understanding of the films. This understanding is provided by a humour which, in most cases, far from subverting narrative development, contributes crucially to it by providing the perspective from which the narrative actually makes sense.

A closer look at the quotation that opened this chapter suggests, in fact, that Frye is not thinking so much of two different types of comedy as of one comic 'form' which is generally developed in two different ways. T. G. A. Nelson articulates this insight more explicitly when he argues that there are two ways of looking at the genre, depending on whether we focus on the narrative drive towards harmony or reconciliation or we pay more attention to laughter, hilarity, wit and subversion, all effects produced by the comic action and the dialogues. Yet these do not represent two different types of comedy but two points of view, two phases, two inspirations, even two ways of reading a comic text, which can and often *do* exist simultaneously in the same comic texts. In order to illustrate his theory, Nelson uses the example of marriage comedy, one of the oldest forms of narrative comedy, in which the spectator finds two types of pleasure: laughter at the frustrations and disasters of living together and, at the same time, pleasurable anticipation of the final reconciliation (1990: 1, 4, 183).

Although Nelson does not develop the links between the two types of pleasure, he points in a promising direction which has been all but abandoned by contemporary film comedy theory. Neale and Krutnik argue that laughter and the comic are not an indispensable element of romantic comedy and that some comedies, like *Going My Way* (1944), *It's a Wonderful Life* (1946) or *The Apartment* (1960) are 'only intermittently funny' (1990: 11), but the existence of some exceptions does not invalidate the general principle. Jeffers McDonald prefers to use the term 'light-hearted' to signal the important presence of tears in the genre as well (2007: 10), but tears and humour are not incompatible. As Edward Berry has argued, talking about comic drama, '[a]s a dramatic form, comedy can exist without laughter, but most of the plays that we consider comedies are engines of laughter, and one of the great pleasures of comic theatre is the feeling of exhilaration and release that laughter provides' (2002: 123). Likewise with the rest of comic texts, including those that are described as romantic comedies. Whereas in most of the theoretical formulations mentioned above laughter appears to subvert narrative and even question narrativity, cases in which it structures the narrative are just as frequent. Humour in romantic comedy is more often than not dependent on the narrative context and conversely, and even more crucially, the development of the narrative is always affected by the comic moments, particularly in the very important and generally neglected middle section of the film text. Gags, jokes and other comic business are not opposed to narrativity but integral parts of it. Humour and the comic must, therefore, be 're-admitted' into the theory of romantic comedy.

On the other hand, the constitution of two types of film comedy around the 'opposite' poles of laughter and the happy ending responds to the traditional approach to film genres criticised in the introduction of this book. When critics say that a film cannot be a romantic comedy if it does not have a happy ending or, conversely, that the fact that some romantic comedies do not make us laugh means that laughter is not an element of the genre, they are thinking of genres as groups of films and of films belonging to either one genre or another, in this case, comedian or romantic comedy. A film is a romantic comedy when it tells a love story with a happy ending, and a comedian comedy when it revolves around the comic antics of the central comic actor. Although the value of this powerful classification is that it has recuperated for academic analysis a very important comic tradition in the cinema, its downside, as we have seen, is that it has excluded humour from the theory of romantic comedy against the evidence of empirical research. If we stop thinking about genres as groups of films and consider them instead as a constantly shifting *langue*, abstract systems which are articulated in various ways in the actual texts, which do not belong but participate in various genres, an immediate consequence is that there are no specific conventions that a given film must have in order to participate in a genre, since membership is not necessary. A film may contain very few jokes or no jokes at all and still use romantic comedy as a genre. Or humour can be theorised as integral to the genre even if there are some films that do not provoke laughter in the spectator. What is important at this point is to recognise that humour and the comic constitute an essential ingredient of the way in which romantic comedy deals with discourses of love, sex, intimacy and gender.

Happy endings, forgotten middles and the ideology of romantic comedy

There can be little doubt that the happy ending is a recurrent convention of the genre, but excessive concentration on this feature has tended to obscure the importance of humour. Another consequence of this critical emphasis has been the relegation, often virtual disappearance, of the rest of the comic narrative from critical discussion, especially of the middle section. Attention to the middle section and, specifically, to the way in which the mechanisms of humour and the comic operate within the representation of the genre's discourses, will allow us to explore the flexibility of the genre and to abandon the ideological determinism mentioned above. This is not to say that in romantic comedy, as in all narratives, the ending is not important. As Peter Brooks has argued, the narrative plot moves the reader forward through the space of the text, in search of a totalising structure that will be perceived as such only retrospectively, from the vantage point of the ending. Therefore narratives only make sense once they have ended, allowing us to see the whole of what went before in relation to their final moment. But in order to reach the ending the narrative must go through what Brooks calls 'the vacillating play of the middle', or, elsewhere, 'the arabesque of plot' (1984: 107). It could also be said, therefore, that the ending only makes sense with respect to the middle, to what has happened before. There is an inexorable circularity in the dominant argument that condemns romantic comedy as the most mediocre and repetitive of genres because, since a romantic comedy is a love story with a happy ending, all romantic comedies end in the same way. If we accept that there are other dimensions to the genre apart from the happy ending then the recognition of much greater formal and ideological variety will immediately ensue. The ending of romantic comedy appears to be so highly conventionalised that it seems critically tendentious to draw so much attention to it, overlooking what makes the genre rich, varied and, in sum, culturally important.

This determinism is based on the inextricable link that is almost invariably established between the happy ending and a certain view of heterosexual relationships. Although the Aristotelian view that comedy and tragedy have different subject matters was generally abandoned by later genre theorists, it seems appropriate to argue that romantic comedy has indeed a very specific subject matter. Yet the Althusserian brand of ideological criticism that dominated film studies in the 1970s and 1980s and remains strong in genre criticism nowadays has combined this subject matter with a monolithic ideology: not only is romantic comedy about love and marriage but it always says the same thing about it, it invariably conveys the same conservative message: if the most important convention of the genre is the happy ending and this happy ending usually consists in the consolidation (or at least the more or less certain promise of consolidation) of a monogamous (and hence patriarchal) heterosexual couple, then it follows that the genre as a whole is conservative because it naturalises, celebrates and reinforces marriage, monogamy and heterosexuality, even against the hard evidence found in contemporary western societies where heterosexual monogamy is in permanent crisis and has become only one option among many others. This wholesale capitulation on the part of romantic comedy experts to fashionable critical trends tends to homogenise the genre and impoverish individual texts. For one thing, the link between the happy ending and heterosexual monogamy is not mandatory in the genre. Numerous contemporary films, including *Splash* (1984), *Big* (1988), *White Men Can't Jump* (1992), *My Best Friend's Wedding* (1997), *The Object of My Affection* (1997) and *Splendor* (1999), have proved that other options can be incorporated without drastically bending generic borders. In fact, such twenty-first-century mainstream movies as *In Good Company* (2004), *Prime* (2005) or *The Break-Up* (2006) suggest that the final separation of the lovers is becoming more and more usual as part of the happy ending. A recent romantic comedy scriptwriting manual admits as much when it argues that 'resolution no longer means that the featured couple will literally remain together' (Mernit, 2000: 116–17). Therefore, rather than all romantic comedies being the same, what we often find is a generalised critical blindness to that which differentiates the texts from one another, both narratively and ideologically, an insistence on imposing aprioristic meanings on the films.

Neither is this to say that the ideology of romantic comedy is irrelevant. On the contrary, even when the genre was born, in the European Renaissance, there was more ideological struggle, variety and contradiction than has generally been acknowledged. For some critics like Mary Beth Rose, romantic comedy flourished in the sixteenth century as a genre that celebrated erotic love and marriage in the context of a new sensibility which viewed marriage as the spiritual foundation of society and as the repository of personal happiness (1988: 28). For her, therefore, the origins of the genre are tied to a commitment to an ideological logic of heterosexuality and monogamy that feminist critics have openly critiqued as related to patriarchy. However, this view seems to suggest that romantic comedy was born more or less from one day to the next, out of the blue, as a propagandistic discourse of a certain sector of Elizabethan culture – the simple story of a new cultural attitude to love to be found in the works of John Lyly, Robert Greene and William Shakespeare. The reality was, in fact, much more complex.

As Louise George Clubb has explained, Lyly, Greene, Shakespeare and other English and non-English European writers found the inspiration and the sources for their stories in the Italian fiction and drama of the sixteenth century. The authors of these stories did not invent them either but constructed them according to the first premise of Renaissance dramaturgy: ransacking (2002: 32). In imitating the Italian authors, Shakespeare and the others were therefore ransacking the ransackers. Not only was the concept of *copy* (imitation of the right models) more artistically prestigious than the more recent, romantic celebration of originality but the Italian models themselves were as varied in their attitudes towards love and desire and as disparate in the concepts of love that they used as the sources from which their authors took their stories. The Italian dramatists imitated the classical comedies of Plautus and Terence and adapted some of their plots, but they also found inspiration for their stories in the classical tradition of Ovid's *Metamorphoses*, the literature of courtly love, the medieval romances and their later Italian manifestations in the works of Ariosto and Tasso, fictions from places as distant as Persia or India, and, very centrally, Boccaccio's *Decameron*. The resulting *commedia erudita* or *grave* developed into various dramatic forms, including tragicomedies, romantic courtship plays, satirical farces of adultery, pastoral plays and various combinations of them. Clubb singles out the female Sienese audience's preference for *Decameron* tales of resolute and loyal heroines as one of the strongest influences in the consolidation of romantic comedy (40). The concept of love that emerges from the new genre, therefore, is much more difficult to pin down than has later been argued, and its exclusive connection with the ideology of modern marriage, which can indeed be seen, for example, in Shakespeare's plays, is only part of the story, based on partial readings of the texts. In other words, Shakespeare's pastoral comedies, like those of some of his predecessors, include representations of various forms of sexual desire and various attitudes to gender relationships, among which must be mentioned a medieval perspective in which women were seen as evil temptresses, love was understood as a destructive passion and sexuality as a powerful, irrepressible and unpredictable human instinct. Shakespeare constantly acknowledges the magnitude of this passion, making the spectator marvel at its power, even as he puts marriage forward as a mechanism to tame and socialise it. At the same time, his plays, in order to be comprehensible to Elizabethan and Jacobean audiences, articulated views of love and desire that were part of the sexual and affective discourses of his age. Since then these concepts have undergone frequent and very important historical changes and, as a consequence, so have the artistic texts that have represented them.

Critics, however, have insisted on the unchanging nature of romantic comedy conventions and messages. In a recent study of contemporary Hollywood romantic comedy, Frank Krutnik, while admitting that the genre has always attempted a negotiation between the concept of heterosexual monogamy and a historically fluid intimate culture, still concludes that it routinely continues to celebrate love as an immutable, almost mystical force (2002: 130, 138). This view is extended among romantic comedy's contemporary critics and is, again, based on two problematic premises: 1) only those texts that appear to conform to the idea of love as an immutable force are considered romantic comedies, and 2) the happy ending is the only location of the films' ideology. I have very briefly broached the diversity of the attitudes towards love reflected in the Italian fiction and drama of the sixteenth century and referred to some of the conflicting ideologies of love and desire apparent in Shakespearean comedy, but this complexity extends to later periods. David Shumway, for example, has argued that, ever since medieval romances, Western stories of love tend to be triangular in structure with the reader or spectator often positioned to identify with the excluded character, and although in the nineteenth century romance became grafted onto marriage, the stories, while endorsing the social institution, continued to rely on the excitement and adventure of illicit love. From this it follows that the genre has always had difficulties to tell stories of marriage (2003: 14–15, 21). Catherine Bates concurs when she defines the genre as courtship stories because romantic comedies are never interested in marriage, only in what leads to it (2002: 104–5). This critical change of emphasis, away from marriage and monogamy, cannot be but welcome, even though it still leaves too much out. Shumway suggests that the discourse of romance, consolidated in the eighteenth and nineteenth centuries, coexists nowadays with the discourse of intimacy, one which is better equipped to deal with stories of love after marriage and with the new term – relationships – that emerged around the 1960s to cover new types of affective and sexual bonds between individuals (2003: 24–5). He finds, beginning in the 1970s, a new genre of films that reflect these changes, which he calls relationship stories (157). As these and many other examples suggest, the genre of romantic comedy has undergone as many transformations as the discourses of love, sexuality and intimacy in the course of the last five centuries.

Northrop Frye has argued that romantic comedy focuses on the creation of a more adult and complex identity, and the crucial factor in this is the discovery on the part of the protagonists of a more profound sexuality (1957). The celebration of marriage may have been, already in Shakespeare's times, an ideological aim of the genre but not the only one. What really characterised these narratives (and still does) was the artistic articulation of current discourses on love, sex and marriage, discourses which then, as now, were multiple and contradictory. The apparent universality of the happy ending and its obvious conventionality have led many to defend an homology between the genre's narrative structure and a stern defence of monogamy and heterosexuality, distorting what, in my view, is its main discursive space: the exploration of love and human sexuality and its complex and fluid relationships with the social context. Love may still be the answer to the exasperatingly complex questions the genre asks (Mernit, 2000: 250), but what 'love' means continues to change fast and, anyway, the questions are certainly as relevant and as essential to the genre as the answers. As I have pointed out above, some recent romantic comedies have proved that the happy ending need not be linked to the formation of the heterosexual couple but, even when it is, the genre's central theme is not so much that conventional union as the vicissitudes of the emotional and sexual relationships between the characters. This does not invalidate the importance of the happy ending, or indeed of any of the other conventions usually associated with the genre. Rather, it sets them within a more flexible framework and liberates them from ideological rigidity.

One way of handling the variety described above has been to ascribe different generic labels to different comic representations of these discourses: we do not need to say that romantic comedy deals with marriage, adultery or the discourse of intimacy if we decide to use other designations like marriage comedy, remarriage comedy, comedy of manners or relationship stories, thus restricting the term romantic comedy to only those cases which deal with courtship – or we can do away with the term altogether by introducing, as Bates does, the label courtship comedy. However, while the establishment of differences between different traditions, perspectives and histori-cal periods may indeed prove useful to understand the evolution of the genre, excessive labelling reveals an anxiety to classify, order and isolate that which in reality – the reality of the functioning of genres and of social intimate and sexual protocols – is by no means so systematic. Besides, excessive compartmentalisation will obscure the importance of the interrelations between the various types of stories. In my view, an overarching term is needed for all the comic texts that deal with love, desire, sexuality and their relation with discourses of identity, masculinity and femininity. Although the word 'romantic' has the conceptual drawback of applying only to one of the many love discourses that circulate through these texts, the substitution of a new umbrella term would only complicate matters. The cultural currency of the designation romantic comedy recommends its continuing usage as long as the variety of discourses, approaches and ideologies articulated by the texts is recognised. As Krutnik argues, the term romantic comedy has often been used to identify a particular type of love story which is told in a particular manner, but it also circulates to 'designate a bewildering array of possible combinations of sex and comedy' (2002: 133). Whether bewildering or not, it is this second meaning that I am most interested in. Romantic comedy could, therefore, be defined as the genre which uses humour, laughter and the comic to tell stories about interpersonal affective and erotic relationships. In a very simplified form, then, as the comic writer of the framing narrative in Woody Allen's *Melinda and Melinda* (2004) says, it tells stories that are funny and romantic. But humour and love are not enough to understand properly how the genre works. Through its comic perspective on cultural discourses of love and desire, romantic comedy proposes an artistic transformation of the everyday reality of human relationships by constructing a special space outside history (but very close to it): the space of romantic comedy.

The space of romantic comedy

In order to understand the nature of this comic space, it might be useful to return once again to the genre's origins in sixteenth-century Italian prose fiction and drama. In the favourite source of the Italian authors, Boccaccio's *Decameron*, the framing narrative presents a group of seven young women and three men who escape from the plague to a country villa near Naples where they spend ten days telling each other stories. Most of these are love stories which, according to the narrator in the introduction, seek to help people who, like the author in his youth, are affected by the pains inflicted by love, especially women, who have fewer means at their disposal to fight the passion. At the end of the ten days, the characters return to Florence, supposedly having become wiser from their experience outside society. While it cannot logically be said that Boccaccio's *opus* follows, as a whole, the conventions of a genre which did not exist yet, most of its hundred stories are comic and often explicitly erotic. More importantly, its structure coincides with that of the pastoral plays which, like the other flourishing genres related to comedy, derived their inspiration, at least partly, from the Neapolitan author. In this new genre, a change of location is generally used to represent the inner realities of emotion, psychological change and supernatural providence. In this pastoral setting the inexperienced lovers learn to know their own hearts and become more mature (Clubb, 2002: 37–8). By these early times in the history of the genre, a magic space of transformation, often associated with the countryside or nature, seems to be already firmly in place. This space becomes later on one of the best known features of Shakespearean comedy. According to C.L. Barber, the English playwright's recurrent use of festive elements responds to an attempt to create an atmosphere of liberation from unfriendly or abusive social institutions (1959: 8). The festive elements, on the other hand, relate the genre to comedy's general origins in village celebrations. Barber links this with a process of identity formation and maturation which is similar to that found in the theories of Northrop Frye and later critics like Leo Salingar (1974). For these critics, Shakespearean comedy traces a circular journey from the characters' society to the countryside or foreign city and back to society, in the course of which, through disguise, masquerade and mistakes of identity, including gender identity and sexual orientation, the characters learn something about themselves that they did not previously know and, armed with the strength conferred by this new identity, they return to take up their rightful positions in their social group.

We must not forget, however, that while some of Shakespeare's comedies clearly follow this circular structure, others, like *Much Ado about Nothing* or *Twelfth Night*, locate their action wholly within the foreign city, Messina in the former and Illyria in the latter. In these comedies, the social space and the magic space of transformation are superimposed on one another: the social space becomes symbolically charged with the meanings and functions of the magic space. In *Much Ado*, for example, Messina becomes a comic space for the soldiers who are returning from the war. As soon as the play starts, the time of war and male heroics, as well as tensions and homosocial bonding, has apparently come to an end and, as Richard Levin has explained, the characters must now realise that the time to marry has arrived in Messina (1985: 93). The city provides a benevolent context for the characters, especially the protagonist couple Beatrice and Benedick, to free themselves progressively of inhibitions and let their desire for each other reign supreme. At the end, they are still in Messina and it is only those who have not been able to adapt to the new erotic regime that must be exiled, like Don John and his friends, or remain on the margins, like the sexually ambivalent figure of Don Pedro.

Something similar happens in *Twelfth Night*: Viola and Sebastian are shipwrecked on the shores of Illyria at the beginning of the play but the rest of the characters are already there. For them, Illyria is both social and comic space. At the end the lovers will all stay on the charmed island, where they again, as in *Much Ado*, have found an ideal context for the expression of their sexual identities, however complex, and their erotic desires. Sebastian articulates the sense of wonder that accompanies the experience of the genre when, after noticing how, on their first meeting, Olivia behaves towards him as if they had been lovers for a long time, he says: 'This is the air, that is the glorious sun,/ This pearl she gave me, I do feel't, and see't,/ And though 'tis wonder that enwraps me thus,/ Yet 'tis not madness' (4.3.1–4). In this passage Shakespeare is aware of the duality of the play's space and of its centrality in the comic experience. By this time the other lovers have already been subjected to the influence of the comic atmosphere. Sebastian, on the other hand, is still new to its hypnotic power but immediately realises that in the same world in which he had been walking and breathing a few minutes ago, a world which is still perfectly recognisable and in which the transaction of a pearl from the hands of one character to those of another is still a physically ascertainable action, a new sense of wonder has suddenly set in. H.B. Charlton finds this sense of wonder a crucial element to understand Shakespearean comedy when he argues that 'its heroes [. . .] are voyagers in pursuit of a happiness not yet attained, a brave new world wherein man's [*sic*] life may be fuller, his sensations more exquisite and his joys more widespread, more lasting, and so more humane' (1966: 278). In this brave new world, the play, in this case *Twelfth Night*, allows its character, as it had done previously with the rest, to release his desire, as, more famously, had happened to the young Athenian characters after being 'treated' with Oberon and Puck's magic flower in *A Midsummer Night's Dream*.

Catherine Bates points out the absence of a journey in *Twelfth Night* and notices the presence, instead, of a new ingredient for our exploration of the genre's comic atmosphere. For her, the play places the spectator within the space and the time of carnival (2002: 120). Twelfth Night is the day of Epiphany, the last day of the Christmas celebrations but, as Bates reminds us, the play extends the festive mood indefinitely (although it simultaneously criticises this permanent holiday through the character of Sir Toby) and demands from the characters that they play by carnival's rules. This is not exactly the same concept of carnival as that theorised by

Mikhail Bakhtin but it comes close enough to it in so far as, according to the Russian critic, the world of carnival and its artistic generic manifestation – grotesque realism – exist in the real world, alongside the official institutions of Church and State which govern individuals, and have the power to bring about a radical change in our attitude towards the dominant order by breaking hierarchical impositions, privileges, rules and taboos. Carnivalesque comedy produces universal laughter, reverses the superiority of the mind over the body and releases repressed energies, in order to constitute an alternative space governed by a democratic principle of community and humanity in which high and low, heaven and earth, birth and resurrection share a common, non-hierarchical space (1984).

Bakhtin, like Barber later on, focuses on a type of comedy which evolves from folk festivals and street humour. This literary form is, like romantic comedy, easily traceable to traditional village celebrations and invocations to the gods. Its main objective is the subversion of the dominant order, whereas romantic comedy has been theorised as a conservative genre that seeks to perpetuate the status quo. This may be the reason why not many links have been found between the two outside Shakespeare. While romantic love as a historically specific formation has been the only ideological discourse to be recognised in the genre, the privileging of sex and the body in carnivalesque comedy has remained outside the boundaries of romantic comedy, but once we admit the presence of a multiplicity of discourses about sex within the genre, the links between the two theoretical formations start to become more visible. The space of romantic comedy, which the genre appears to inherit from its various sources, shares a similar potential for the release of repressed drives and the circumvention of social inhibitions to that of Bakhtinian carnival.

Medieval carnival, Boccaccio's erotic liberation and the pastoral green world constitute, therefore, the historical context of the magic space of romantic comedy, which becomes consolidated in Shakespeare's comedies and has since then remained a central feature of the genre. Whereas the happy ending affects only a relatively small section of the generic plot, the space of comedy pervades the whole text and is most often seen at work in the middle section, where the various discourses of the social space vie for domination and where the characters appear to be freer from social and psychological inhibitions. The comic space generally affords the characters a franker confrontation with their sexuality than society had previously allowed them. As a consequence of this, gender relationships, another discursive area central to a genre which has often been characterised as narrating the 'battle of the sexes', also become crucially affected by the deployment of the comic space. As in Boccaccio's stories, Shakespeare's plays and Bakhtin's theory, humour and the comic constitute the main source from which this magic atmosphere emanates. In other words, since humour is, as we have seen, one of the main ingredients of the genre, our experience of the space of romantic comedy is inseparable from our comic response to its fictional world. This space is not only benevolent but also funny. In most cases, it is benevolent because it is funny.

This is one of the main differences between the concept proposed here and Deborah Thomas's recent theory of melodrama, comedy and romance as the three general categories or ways in which films are experienced by viewers and which intersect with film genres in various ways. For Thomas there is a comedic space which in comedy articulates a fantasy of transformation that differentiates this category from the other two. The social space is influenced by a benevolent community which transforms it into something better. This, however, is a comedic and not a comic space. Although the status of the comic as a filmic category is not clear in Thomas's theory, she sees the comic and the comedic as two different modes, implicitly aligning herself with those critics who perceive a drastic difference between comedian and romantic comedy: the comic is what makes us laugh, whereas the comedic is a particular sort of transformation of the narrative world. For her laughter is neither a necessary nor a sufficient trait of the comedic (2000: 17–18).

In my view, on the other hand, the presence of humour is one of the main ingredients of this special atmosphere. In his study of Shakespearean comedy, Stephen Greenblatt quotes William Harvey as saying 'men and women are never more brave, sprightly, blithe, valiant, pleasant or beautiful than when about to celebrate the act'. According to Greenblatt, Shakespeare was a pioneer in generating comic plots that could appropriate and profit from the special beauty of sexual arousal. Since the direct representation of the sexual act was out of the question on the Elizabethan stage, the playwright learnt to replace it by verbal sparring: the erotically

charged battle of wits between the lovers (1988: 89). Comic dialogues, therefore, became part of the creation of that special atmosphere which, for Greenblatt, was simply a theatrical substitute
for sex. In more general terms, humour (which in the cinema is
not only verbal but also visual) became associated with the creation
of that erotic utopia which romantic comedy proposed, and is
still proposing, as an antidote against the sexual and affective
frustrations of everyday life. Sometimes, the happy ending may
not even be possible without the presence of humour, as in the
famous final words of Billy Wilder's *Some Like it Hot* – 'Nobody's
perfect' – which may be seen as a subversion of the traditional
happy ending of the genre but which also, I would suggest, underline the sexual utopia that the film is proposing through its
comic space. More often, however, the comic is most active in the
middle section of the narrative, where the comic space is generally
constructed.

Take, for example, one of the most important texts in the history
of the genre, Ernst Lubitsch's *Ninotchka* (1939), a film that exhibits
a keen awareness of the close cultural link between love and laughter. Count Leon D'Algout (Melvyn Douglas) has fallen in love with
Ninotchka (Greta Garbo) and is struggling to break the cultural
barrier between them and get her to admit that she is also in love
with him. Conscious of the power of laughter to break down inhibitions he tries several jokes while having lunch with her at a working-
class restaurant in Paris, but Ninotchka does not respond. In
confusion and despair he leans back on his chair and crashes on
the floor to the general hilarity of the café's patrons. The more
humiliated he feels, the louder everybody laughs. The class context
– workers laughing at a ridiculous aristocrat – turns the comic
moment into a self-conscious manifestation of the Bakhtinian and
Aristotelian power of comedy to upturn hierarchies, and this may
well be the reason why, when Leon (and the spectator) looks again
at Ninotchka, she has heartily joined in the infectious mirth. 'Garbo
laughs', announced the film's publicity, using this scene as the film's
slogan. Narratively, however, Leon's fall, and his almost immediate
readiness to join in and laugh at himself, works as a magic potion
of immediate effect and transforms the heroine into the willing
lover of the second half of the film. Garbo had, of course, loved
before on the screen but now she loves because she laughs. Whether
the spectator prefers the serious Ninotchka of the first half of the

film or the laughing lover of the second is a different matter, but the film has firmly inscribed itself within the genre's tradition by self-consciously creating its comic space around the characters' sense of humour. The comic is, therefore, not a by-product, a secondary ingredient of our experience of romantic comedy, but an integral element in the creation of the comic space and the particular lens used by the genre to comment on people's sexual and affective mores.

Garbo's presence in *Ninotchka* throws some light on the nature of the comic space precisely because the spectator may be used to seeing her in non-comic films also dealing with love and desire. For example, in the earlier *Flesh and the Devil* (1927), the film that turned her into a great star, she plays the part of Felicitas, the married woman who consecutively seduces two childhood friends and threatens to destroy their all-important relationship. The final duel between the two men is prevented in the nick of time when they both realise that Felicitas had been responsible for their estrangement all along, a realisation which coincides exactly with her death. To describe this movie even as a romantic melodrama would be problematic since the only romance that is promoted in it is that between the two friends. There is no comic space here but neither is there any heterosexual love or desire worth protecting. Love and desire constitute the external threat that must be destroyed since they bring about not happiness and freedom but hatred and oppression. In this film's melodramatic discourse there can only be happiness in a male friendship which excludes heterosexual desire.

I have been defining the comic space as a magic space of transformation but it must be pointed out that this transformation does not necessarily affect the characters in any permanent way but, rather, the fictional space in which they exist, a fictional space which represents the social space of cultural discourses on love, sexuality and intimacy. The comic space allows the spectator to glimpse a 'better world', a world which is not governed by inhibitions and repressions but is instead characterised by a freer, more optimistic expression of love and desire. In Billy Mernit's words, this is 'a realm, supposedly the world we live in, where true love is obtainable and overcomes every obstacle' (2000: 125). This 'better world' is, as I have mentioned above, an empty formal concept, not an ideologically charged one. Different texts, different cultural contexts, even different spectatorial perspectives may associate it with different discourses on love and desire. The genre simply provides the empty space for the individual text – as well as the individual spectator – to fill it with meaning.

Whether or not there is a transformation in the lovers is already part of the ideology of the individual text or of the spectator/critic's interpretation of it. Frye, Barber and Salingar, in their emphasis on progression and maturation, betray a teleological bias which may be more dependent on the critical tradition in which they write than constitutive of the genre. The view of classical narrative as based on a journey towards a physical/psychological destination would seem to favour such a transformation and this may indeed be the case in many comic texts. Shakespeare's green world comedies, for example, seek to transform their characters into better, wiser versions of themselves, at least as far as love and desire are concerned. The comic space, however, does not guarantee such a transformation. If the dominant ideology in the individual film includes this transformation as part of what it has to say about relationships, then it will probably take place. If, on the contrary, the film favours a more contingent view of love and desire, as is the case of many contemporary texts, including multi-protagonist comedies, the characters may well end up exactly as they were at the beginning (Azcona 2007: 275–7). What counts is the generic transformation of the social space and what this transformation has to say about the discourses which constitute the social space.

For Thomas, the romantic couple of comedy 'can aspire to a state of mutuality and playful improvisation, and, rather than ending up embattled or under siege, may find a benevolent and sheltering community to welcome them in its midst' (2000: 14). Whereas in the dominant critical paradigm romantic comedy is always conservative, for this author it appears to be more liberating, coming closer to Bakhtin's subversive potential of carnival or the ideological effect posited for comedian comedy by critics like Palmer, Jenkins, Krutnik (1995) and others. From my perspective, however, the genre is neither one nor the other (nor anything in between). The way to escape from the determinism of current theories of the genre is not to replace it by another form of determinism, even if it is one of a different sign. The relationship between form and content, in art in general and in romantic comedy in particular, is always fluid and contingent on the historical context and the specific circumstances in which the text is created and received. The conventions of a given genre do not predetermine the ideological discourses deployed in the individual text. Romantic comedy as a genre deploys discourses on love, sexuality, gender and identity. Its special atmosphere allows the intimate, sexual, social and gender relationships between the characters in each individual text to be expressed in a less inhibited way; it protects them from social pressure and repression and it may allow them to change their identity and mature. However, the nature of these changes is specific to each text, although obviously affected by cultural and historical determinations. The humour deployed by the genre both shores up the magic space and channels the ideological discourses of the text, but it does not homogenise or predetermine them. In sum, romantic comedy (like any other genre) is neither conservative nor radical, although the films that deploy its conventions may be one or the other, or, very often, both at the same time. The next section briefly illustrates how a film generally taken as a romantic comedy (although not only) might be analysed taking into account what I have described as the main characteristics of the genre.

The Sydney issue

In *The American President* (1995), the 'Sydney issue' is initially not, as U.S. president Andrew Shepherd (Michael Douglas) hopes when he hears one of his advisors utter the phrase, some conflict that his country is having with Australia, but a euphemistic expression employed by his entourage to refer to his relationship with political strategist Sydney Wade (Annette Bening) and the problems it may cause for his presidency and, especially, for his re-election. This mid-1990s mainstream Hollywood film mixes two genres which had acquired, for different reasons, a high level of visibility at the time of its release. Starting with Woody Allen's nervous romances of the late 1970s and continuing with the new romances of the mid-1980s, romantic comedy had become one of the most popular Hollywood genres – a position that it continues to occupy at the beginning of the twenty-first century – resulting by the mid-1990s in a remarkable 'state of grace' noticeable, among other things, in its rising flexibility to blend with other genres. The figure of the president of the United States, on the other hand, had always exerted a powerful attraction in U.S. culture, including the cinema, but Bill Clinton's term of office brought about a renewed interest in Hollywood through films like, among others, *Dave* (1993), *The American President*, *Mars Attacks!* (1996), *Independence Day* (1996), *Absolute Power* (1997), *Wag the Dog* (1997), *Air Force One* (1997), *Primary Colors* (1998) or *Bulworth* (1998). While comedy is not a generic ingredient in all of these films and the type of comedy activated in them varies from one to the other, it may be argued that both *Dave* and *The American President* tap into the optimism of the first years of a president who was at the time seen as more human and approachable than his predecessors. Later films like *Primary Colors* and *Bulworth*, released after the Monica Lewinsky scandal, also use comedy, albeit of a different kind, to explore the darker mood that beset the country as a consequence of the media appropriation of what could perhaps be described as the excesses of Clinton's humanity.

Specific internal and external historical circumstances, therefore, make the combination of romantic comedy and U.S.-president movie possible but, at the same time, this combination produces in the texts certain results which must also be interpreted individually within their historical context. From the perspective of the political movie, the presence of romantic comedy facilitates the articulation of the film's liberal message: a president who, in his own words, has been 'so busy keeping his job that he forgot to do his job', is brought back to the reality of his own political ideas through the beneficial influence of his romantic attachment with Sydney. In the film's climax, in view of the danger of a break-up in the relationship, he announces an aggressive bill calling for a twenty percent reduction in the emission of fossil fuels, something that, from the perspective of a decade later, could only happen within the magic fictional space of romantic comedy. The film mixes the conventions of the two genres so hopelessly that it stops making sense when, in the final reunion immediately after the president's speech, Sydney assures him that she has not come back to him because of his change of mind regarding national policy. The spectator knows that this is precisely why she has come back to him and that the fear of her leaving him is what has shaken him out of his political inertia. However, this may not even be counted as a weakness on the film's part since from the perspective of romantic comedy the political plot has become both comic space and metaphor for the representation of the central relationship. As I shall argue later, it is perhaps through this relationship that the film is making its most important political statement.

Authors like Babington and Evans (1989), Neale (1992), Krutnik (1990; 2002) and Shumway (2003) have related the rise of romantic comedy at the end of the last century to changes in social and intimate relationships in contemporary society and have mentioned the aftermath of the sexual revolution, the new discourses on sexuality and intimacy and the impact of feminism on gender relationships as important factors in the renewed commercial clout of the genre, whether, as Neale suggests, because it has functioned as a nostalgic evocation of a safer past in which gender equality was not even dreamt of, or, as I have argued, because the genre has proved itself particularly adroit at adapting itself to contemporary intimate discourses (Evans and Deleyto, 1998). *The American President* offers arguments for both interpretive tendencies but grounds its construction of the central affective relationship on the activation of a comic space, here distinctively related to the 'real' space of the White House, and on the deployment of humour in order to convey certain ideological discourses.

After one of her visits to the White House, Sydney returns to her sister's apartment, where she is temporarily staying, and explains that she has kissed the president on the mouth in the china room. Beth (Nina Siemaszko) asks her: 'And then what happened?', to which Sydney replies, 'He had to go attack Libya.' 'There's always something', her sister concludes. The humour of this exchange lies in the incongruence between what is taken to be a regular conversation between two sisters or two friends about their love life and what is seen as the everyday routine of an exceptional person, the president of the United States, or in the film's annoying words, 'the leader of the free world'. *The American President* activates its liberal credentials, U.S. cultural conventions and the conventions of the U.S. presidency genre to suggest that in the most perfect democracy in the world the president is both a unique person because of the position he occupies and a 'regular guy' with the same personal hopes, dreams and anxieties as anybody else. The joke employs this almost mythical continuity between the normal and the exceptional to achieve its effect and argues both that a man can passionately kiss a woman and then give the order to attack Libya without missing a beat and that this sequence of events is funny because of the unlikelihood of it happening to most of us.

Moreover, here as in the rest of the film, Andrew's position as president and Sydney's as professional political campaigner work as metaphors for the contemporary scenarios in which intimate relationships take place. Beth's deadpan reaction – 'There's always something' – is funny because bombing Tripoli is not just 'something' and because it refers, indirectly, to the difficulties and fears of commitment between modern men and women. The jobs of the two lovers are exceptional and the obstacles that these jobs pose to the relationship only too obvious, but the film, as a romantic comedy of the 1990s, suggests that these obstacles are not so different from those experienced by many professional men and women trying to make their personal and professional lives compatible in an increasingly tough capitalist culture. Given the amount of time and energy demanded by many people's professions, one does not need to be the president of the United States nowadays to become involved in various ways with another person at work and to wish to pursue a relationship of whatever kind in spite of the pressures and incompatibilities found on the way. The romantic comedy strives to find a space in which neither the relationship nor the job will suffer, and one in which, in fact, the two will blend successfully.

The humour of this moment, and of much of *The American President*, highlights a contemporary intimate setting which is not

2 'There's always something': love in the workplace. Michael
Douglas and Annette Bening in *The American President*
(dir. Rob Reiner, 1995, Columbia, Universal)

only attributed to modern working conditions but also to the growing visibility of women in professional positions. Romantic comedy had always featured working women as its protagonists but films of the same period like *Broadcast News* (1987), *Working Girl* (1988), *Green Card* (1990), *Accidental Hero* (1992), *Sleepless in Seattle, Groundhog Day* (1993), *The Truth about Cats and Dogs* (1996), *One Fine Day* (1996), *My Best Friend's Wedding* or *You've Got Mail* (1998) consistently explore the conflicts and also the romantic and sexual possibilities of mostly middle-class white women's presence in the workplace, offering different perspectives and ideological discourses. One of the consequences for many women of the relative success of second-wave feminism was the unequal demands placed on them by a contemporary society that may have grudgingly accepted their social and sexual equality but still expected them to continue doing what they were doing before. This development was denounced by feminists like Susan Faludi as part of the culture of patriarchal backlash (1992) and, within mainstream Hollywood, memorably summarised by the Julianne Moore character in *The Hand that Rocks the Cradle* (1992): 'These days a woman can feel like a failure if she doesn't bring in fifty grand a year and still make time for blow jobs and homemade lasagne.'

Sydney feels some of these pressures and the film suggests that in the past it is her job that has taken precedence, creating an emotional void which is unacceptable for romantic comedy. Her brilliance as a political operative has left her increasingly powerless to pursue affective relationships or has turned her half-hearted attempts into a long chain of failures. Yet, *The American President* does not suggest that, in order for the protagonist to regain her ability to engage with another person intimately, she should surrender her gains within the social sphere. Rather, it proposes a scenario in which the two can coexist and feed off each other. As her romance with Andrew develops, Sydney continues to be as tough and relentless in her job as she had been in the past and, moreover, uses her influence to bring back to life the president's dormant liberal ideas. Conversely, awareness of their difficult professional relationship makes their desire for each other more urgent and even helps their sexual imagination along, as when, after their first meeting, Andrew summarises their rapport to his friend and Chief of Staff, A.J. (Martin Sheen): 'We had a nice couple of minutes together.

She threatened me. I patronised her. We didn't have anything to eat but I thought there was a connection.' In general, Sydney becomes an icon of both female social independence and hetero-sexual desire. In other words, Reiner's film presents itself as an instance of the blend of second-wave feminism and femininity that Jacinda Read, in her analysis of rape-revenge movies, has found as characteristic of 1990s popular culture (2000: 249–51 and *passim*). Sydney's political sway on the president and her simultaneous engagement in an affective-sexual relationship with him turn her into an embodiment of what Read has called 'common-sense under-standings of feminism' (103), in which femininity and feminism are not opposites but compatible. This lived compatibility probably underscores the more obvious meanings of the comic phrase 'the Sydney issue'.

Before starring in *The American President*, Michael Douglas had consolidated a very specific persona of more or less affluent white masculinity in crisis through a series of films including *Fatal Attrac-tion* (1987), *The War of the Roses* (1989), *Basic Instinct* (1992), *Falling Down* (1993) and *Disclosure* (1994). Reiner's film uses this persona in various ways in order to enrich the verisimilitude of its sexual scenario. Following the trend set by the protagonists of those films, Andrew is attracted to Sydney because she is a strong woman, who has triumphed in a world of men and who, as he discovers later on, earns more than the White House could afford to pay her. When a character tells Sydney that 'men like being insulted by women; it makes them feel loved; don't ask me why', the statement is easier to understand if we visualise Douglas in, say, *Basic Instinct* as the object of that description. The president of the United States is a very powerful man but, because of Douglas's performance, Andrew Shepherd is immediately read by the spectator as far less imposing than his position portends. The film reverses the story of male anxiety and failure in front of the powerful woman that the spectator had become familiar with, but the romantic comedy recu-perates his masculine weakness to make the equality between the two protagonists more credible. While the contemporaneous thriller or the black comedy castigate outmoded male attempts at sexual supremacy, the romantic comedy can only use a masculinity that is prepared to accept comic humiliation as part of the sexual game.

This becomes most obvious in the scene in which his lecturing of Sydney on the reasons why she does not want to pursue their relationship is suddenly interrupted by her appearing half naked before him, ready for their first sexual encounter, and he immediately turns his condescending attitude into a string of excuses comically revealing his anxiety about sexual performance. That the sex is apparently satisfactory on both sides is not so much surprising given his initial misgivings as a logical consequence of the relative positions of power mandated by the genre: for the relationship to work, sexually as much as romantically, not only is some degree of equality necessary but also an understanding that a successful heterosexual relationship at the end of the twentieth century must be based on a number of requisites, including male acknowledgement of the unfairness of patriarchal privilege, female refusal to give up the social and sexual gains of feminism and a mutual ability to turn pre-given power positions into a *mise en scène* of desire.

Much of the humour of the film, including some of the instances briefly analysed here, is directly related to the way in which the White House is presented as both the centre of important political action – bills against global warming and the free use of personal guns, swift responses to threats to U.S. supremacy, even the improvement of state education – and a warm and homely environment for the expression of sexual desire. The film opens with a montage sequence of detail shots of various objects supposedly housed in the building which make up a celebratory, brief history of the country, while Marc Shaiman's swelling score underlines the symbolic dimension of the place. The scene culminates with a long shot of the exterior of the site as the name of the producer and director concludes the opening credits, suggesting that this space is going to play a crucial role in the story. The vividly portrayed hectic everyday activity of the place starts immediately but there is a relaxed mood in all its inhabitants which, in the film's romantic utopia, underscores the importance of interpersonal relationships in the president's circle for a smooth operation of the country as a whole.

At the same time, the president's initial attitude – which manifests itself in the casualness with which he is ready to compromise his ideals in order to get re-elected – conventionally suggests that he is in urgent need of a change. The atmosphere constructed by the film in the first few minutes, through the friendliness, good humour and tolerance of all the characters and the exhilarating realistic detail employed to shore up the basic decency of all concerned, anticipates to the genre-experienced spectator that this change is going to be brought about by love and desire, precisely because it has already been made clear that love and desire will flourish easily in this benevolent and liberal space. As I have argued above, Andrew's position as president works, from the perspective of the genre, as a metaphor for the contemporary reality of men and women pursuing affective and sexual relationships in their workplaces and the difficulties that such a situation entails, both in terms of work pressures and power struggles. The mixture of genres confirms this contemporary reality as a central part of the film's construction of a national identity, beyond more familiar and less palatable descriptions of what the country has become. This could only happen in a social context in which affective relationships are considered of the greatest cultural importance and in an industrial context in which the genre of romantic comedy reigns as one of Hollywood's most proficient ways of talking to audiences around the world.

What romantic comedy does in a film like *The American President* is to select culturally relevant intimate situations, such as, in this case, the predicament of the professional woman, the evolution of 1990s popular feminism, the visibility of the masculinity crisis or, more centrally, the unstoppable presence of love and sexual desire in the workplace, and cast over them the benevolent mantle of the comic space. While the erotic thriller, for example, visits similar scenarios and highlights the fears and anxieties that they may produce in the spectator, romantic comedy takes a more optimistic perspective and suggests that where love and desire are concerned everything is possible, including that a president of the United States will take active steps towards stopping global warming. In the meantime, however, the genre keeps on recording similar anxieties to those found in other genres and looking for ways of turning them into an opportunity for fun and sexual excitement.

Genres and films

The genre of romantic comedy can, therefore, be described as the intersection of three, closely interrelated elements: a narrative that articulates historically and culturally specific views of love, desire, sexuality and gender relationships; a space of transformation and fantasy which influences the narrative articulation of those discourses; and humour as the specific perspective from which the fictional characters, their relationships and the spectator's response to them are constructed as embodiments of those discourses. Given the pervasiveness of stories of love and desire in the cinema, especially in Hollywood, the constant presence of humour in many filmic narratives, and that films always transform reality in one way or another, it could be argued that this definition is so inclusive that most Hollywood films could be seen as romantic comedies. This would invalidate the value of the term as an analytical tool. My argument, however, is not that films that incorporate these features are romantic comedies. Rather, the genre of romantic comedy has operated and continues to operate in a great variety of filmic texts, including many that cannot be defined as romantic comedies. It is the recurrence of these features in films that are routinely described by other generic labels that makes the genre culturally relevant. Genres are categories used by the industry, the filmmakers, critics and spectators to communicate with one another and, consequently, they are also sets of expectations brought to the films by the spectators. From a textual perspective, these expectations are turned into abstract systems of conventions. Films are individual articulations of those conventions and each film carries out its own selection of conventions from one or several genres. This means that films as texts are not romantic comedies but, rather, use the conventions of romantic comedy in specific ways, and also that the absence from a text which we may consider as representative of the genre of one or several of these conventions does not invalidate its participation in the genre as such.

Besides, films are not obliged to deploy genres in homogeneous or easily predictable ways. While the three characteristics discussed here would seem to constitute the conceptual core of romantic comedy, the genre's presence in a text does not immediately signify the sustained visibility of these characteristics. The comic space may be virtually absent from a film like *Husbands and Wives* (1992) (a film in which humour also appears in very small doses) in order to suggest desolation and despair in the realm of intimate relationships. This does not mean that romantic comedy is not important for the analysis of a film which constructs its precariousness precisely around the absence of such a space. If we were not aware of the existence of this space in the genre, we would not be able to notice its absence from Allen's film so acutely. Another example:

the celebration of friendship as opposed to love and desire with which romantic comedy associated itself in numerous films of the 1990s constitutes a comment on the profound crisis of the heterosexual relationships that the genre 'should' be dealing with. Perhaps love and desire hold a thematic exclusivity over the genre but what better way to articulate a pessimistic view of their effects on people than by subordinating them to friendship (see Deleyto, 2003). Nevertheless, as a general rule, the simultaneous presence, however fragmentary or intermittent, of these three characteristics in a given text would suggest the centrality of romantic comedy in its generic makeup.

On the other hand, since genres, like other cultural formations and like all complex systems, are never static but are in constant and often unpredictable evolution, none of the characteristics discussed here are fixed or permanent. Although when the critic tries to describe a genre of such longevity as romantic comedy, s/he often looks for theoretical articulations that can encompass as many of its historical manifestations as possible, there is no way in which we can aspire to fix it forever. We cannot predict the directions in which it will evolve in the future, the mutations that it will undergo, or the specific ways in which it will continue to be culturally relevant (or not).

If films are the specific manifestations of generic conventions at work, it is also in the films that genres constantly intersect with one another and it is, therefore, partly through the films that genres evolve. But genres are also systems of communication, which involve industrial decisions and audience reception, and are also, crucially, cultural discourses. The history of a specific genre is, therefore, also related to extrinsic factors: in the case of romantic comedy, the evolution of ideological struggles and the historical realities of love, sex and intimate relations. These factors, however, stop being wholly extrinsic when, as in our case, the artistic genre has become very influential in the way people think about love and sex, and perform the social protocols related to these affects. If it can safely be said that romantic comedy has changed drastically in the twentieth century because sexual and affective protocols have evolved in very rapid and sometimes radical ways, it can also be argued that the popularity of romantic comedy has affected the way people have behaved and continue to behave with respect to love and sex.

Within the boundaries of Hollywood film history – the immediate concern of this book – cultural, industrial and formal changes
have crystallised in various periods, tendencies or subgenres.
Babington and Evans divide their account of the Hollywood comedy
of the sexes in five chapters, each of which discusses one such tendency or period: the 'screwball comedy' of the 1930s, which they
identify as the golden age of Hollywood comedy, the Lubistschean
romantic comedy of the same decade, the sex comedies of the 1950s
and what they call, writing in the late 1980s, 'romantic comedy
today', to which they interestingly add a chapter which deals with
the films of three 'comedians', Bob Hope, Mae West and Woody
Allen (1989). Frank Krutnik follows a similar pattern and distinguishes three main periods: the screwball comedy of the 1930s, the
sex comedies of the 1950s and the nervous romances of the late
1970s (1990). To these, Steve Neale adds the 'new romances' of
the 1980s (1992) and Charles Musser, using Stanley Cavell's term
'comedies of remarriage', argues that these start not in the 1930s
but much earlier, in the immediate post-World War I era, with Cecil
B. de Mille's cycle of divorce comedies (1995: 282–5). When authors
write about a specific decade, more subgenres or traditions are
usually found. For example, James Harvey, writing about the 1930s
and 1940s, finds not only the screwball comedy and the Lubitsch
comedy, but, after further distinguishing within Lubitsch's comic
films between 'the naughty operetta' and 'comedies without music',
goes on to discuss various other categories, like the classy comedy,
the tough comedy, the Astaire and Rogers musicals and the Preston
Sturges comedies, among others (1998).

Historical categorisations such as these fulfil their main objective, which is to offer the spectator a much needed general panorama of the evolution of the genre, but they seldom tend to do
justice to the individual texts. More specifically, they have the dis-
advantage of grouping together, for the sake of clarity, films which
might be better understood within not one but several parameters,
and of leaving out texts which, because of their specific characteristics or their historical placement, cannot be included in any of the
categories. Take, for example, Preston Sturges's comedies. While
The Lady Eve (1941) and *The Palm Beach Story* (1942) can profit-
ably be seen as screwball comedies, where exactly do we place
Sullivan's Travels (1941), a film that is clearly indebted to the
screwball tradition but incorporates other traditions as well?, and

what about *Christmas in July* (1940), less controversially a romantic comedy, but one which perhaps is not as close to the conventions of screwball as the previous ones? Other films directed by Sturges in the same period are more clearly not romantic comedies, like *The Great McGinty* (1940), *Hail the Conquering Hero* (1944) and *The Miracle of Morgan's Creek* (1944), but, given the apparent coherence of Sturges's *oeuvre* and the many similarities among all his films, is it accurate or convenient to separate them in various traditions? And where can *Unfaithfully Yours* (1948) be placed, a film made when a new era of romantic comedy was beginning but which seems to have as little to do with Sturges's earlier comic work as with the comedies of George Cukor or Howard Hawks which were, among others, ushering in the new period? *Auteur*-minded critics might conclude that the obvious solution is to analyse the films of the director as a whole, leaving aside generic traditions, but this choice underplays the objective importance of such traditions for the understanding of the individual films.

The main drawback of generic groupings such as those mentioned above is that they still envision genres, and different generic traditions, as groups of films, and therefore need to decide which group each film best fits in. Within their parameters it is still possible to include a single film in several groups but this cannot be done too frequently because it would defeat the purpose of the groupings. In the case of romantic comedy, this has also meant that only those films that can unequivocally be considered as romantic comedies are likely to appear at all within any of the traditions. As a consequence of this, only a very limited number of texts have generally been considered romantic comedies. Harvey's approach to classical romantic comedy is more flexible, as he manages to incorporate in his study groups like the tough newspaper comedies or even the Fred Astaire and Ginger Rogers RKO musicals, which are not often considered within the canon of the genre, yet this is done at the expense of a gradual waning of the genre from a book which seems to end up as an account of the author's favourite films and directors of the period, but has relatively little to say about romantic comedy as a genre. Nevertheless, his book provides numerous examples of films which *are not* romantic comedies while remaining essential to understand the history of the genre in those crucial decades.

Therefore, in order to understand the evolution of romantic comedy in U.S. cinema following the perspective proposed in this chapter, we need to take into account not only films like *Bringing Up Baby*, *Pillow Talk* or *Pretty Woman*, but also many other films which would not be immediately recognisable as romantic comedies and yet both use the conventions of the genre and contribute to its historical change. Films like *Out of Sight*, *Before Sunset* or *Rio Bravo*, mentioned in the introduction, would be examples of this, as would *Sullivan's Travels*, a film that combines several types of comedy, along with other non-comic genres. Since Sturges's film is not clearly a romantic comedy, critical analyses tend to ignore the genre's contribution to its overall meanings even though it is easy to perceive that it is partly the film's generic impurity that makes it what it is. In terms of the history of the genre, romantic comedy may not have changed significantly after Sturges's film. Yet the ways in which the genre's conventions interacted within its textual structure with other generic conventions announced the end of screwball comedy and anticipated that a different kind of generic combinations would characterise the history of the genre in the following years. Or, by looking at the immediate past of the country, the movie reflected an awareness of the historical changes that were about to take place. Of course, this was a phenomenon that could be perceived in *Sullivan's Travels* and also in other films of the same period.

In general, the history of U.S. cinema, like that of other national cinemas, abounds in such examples. The ideologically and formally rigid conceptualisations that have been described here are both cause and consequence of the critical tendency to overlook these films. To look only at the contemporary situation, the last two decades have witnessed a rebirth of the genre which was not only brought about by the films of Julia Roberts, Tom Hanks, Meg Ryan, Sandra Bullock, Jennifer Lopez or Nora Ephron. Films like *Big*, *Pretty Woman*, *Sleepless in Seattle*, *You've Got Mail* or *Maid in Manhattan* are important to understand the genre's evolution. Such labels as 'the new romance' or 'romantic fabrication' (Krutnik 1998: 15) accurately describe some of these films' incorporation of cultural changes in the realm of love, romance and desire into the conventions of the genre. Yet romantic comedy has appeared in many other places and in very different forms. It is significant that independent cinema is never included in studies of romantic comedy, and yet it could be argued that it was in that field that the evolution of the genre became more invigorating, as the final chapter of this book will try to prove. The films of Woody Allen were instrumental in bringing about the rebirth of the genre in the late 1970s and yet, since then, even though the New York director continued to make (and still does) one film every year, his movies have virtually disappeared from discussions of 1980s and 1990s romantic comedy. The action-adventure film and the buddy movie have dominated New Hollywood production, particularly through the preference of contemporary blockbusters for this generic configuration. However, the cultural confrontation between homosocial and heterosexual desire (Sedgwick, 1985) and its complex re-emergence as a consequence of the second wave of feminism would suggest that textual combinations of romantic comedy and action-adventure would be frequent. Yet, the presence of romantic comedy in films like *Speed* (1994), *Out of Sight* or *Entrapment* (1999) has gone unnoticed, even though it appears to be fundamental to an understanding of the social/sexual dynamics of the plot.

The ostensible reason for this neglect is that 'independent' comedies, Woody Allen's films or action-adventure spectacles cannot be made to fit the formally constraining and ideologically deterministic definitions of the genre that have dominated generic theory and analysis. Scriptwriter and studio analyst Billy Mernit's contention that the most successful contemporary romantic comedies are often cross-breeds (2000: xi) seems to have gone largely unheeded by the critical institution. This situation is by no means specific to the last two decades but appears time and again wherever we look in the history of U.S. cinema and, although it falls outside the scope of this book, in other national cinemas. Romantic comedy has had a rich secret life underneath the canonical texts and the traditional classifications. Satirical comedy, marriage comedy, comedian comedy, metacinematic comedy, parody, gross-out comedy, slapstick and comedy of regression have repeatedly combined with romantic comedy in individual films, often producing permutations that have sent the genre in new directions. Outside comedy, the genre has appeared in combination with many other genres, on equal footing or in subsidiary form, and many of these films have cast new light on romantic comedy's conventions. Romantic comedy has appeared in mainstream Hollywood cinema but also in the independent sector or on the periphery of the big studios. And this is only in the United States. The array may be bewildering but the variety and complexity of the combinations of love, sex and comedy

and the multiplicity of ideological uses to which the genre's transformative space has been put, make it imperative that we begin to
come to terms with the secret life of romantic comedy. Following
Derrida's generic law, Wittgenstein's and Lakoff's views of categories, Rick Altman's critique of traditional film genre theory and the
chaos theory concept of the fractal, I visualise the genre of romantic
comedy as a huge pan-historical virtual multi-protagonist film. In
this macro-text culturally specific discourses on love and sexuality
are narrativised from a comic perspective and within a benevolent
comic space. Actual individual films repeatedly 'plagiarise' or
'exploit' the genre for ideas and, in so doing, contribute to its permanent transformation.

Although, as has become clear from the above discussion, film genre
always exists in history, my approach in this book is more generic
than historical, more textual than contextual. At the current point
in the development of Film Studies as an academic discipline, there
is no arguing against the importance of the industrial, cultural and
historical context for the accurate understanding of film texts and
film history, but it is often the case that, in the midst of contextual
arguments, the texts have tended to disappear, as if there was only
the outside and the inside was empty, or not worth looking at any
more, or as if everything that could be said about the texts had
already been said. For this reason, this book proposes a return to
textual analysis, and an acknowledgement of the complexity of
texts, even though the context will necessarily be present. No
textual analysis can be blind to the text's existence in history and
society, nor can it ignore its evolution from the time of its release.
And, while textual analysis may carry its own ideology, the aprioristic ideological overgeneralisations of classical ideological generic
criticism can, as has already been argued, often be easily countered
with the 'realities' of the texts themselves. My main focus of analysis is not historical but generic, that is, I concentrate on the ways
in which the selected films employ the genre of romantic comedy
in order to produce meaning and, crucially, on the ways in which
that meaning is also produced through the intersection with the
conventions of other genres.

Therefore, the book is not primarily concerned with the changing
shape of the virtual multi-protagonist movie mentioned above
but with the specific narrative and cultural mechanisms used by a

selection of individual films to actualise some of its multiple stories and discourses. My aim is not to offer a new history of romantic comedy but, less ambitiously, to ascertain whether such a project is at all feasible and to suggest some of the possible directions that such a history might take. For this reason, the films analysed here have never been considered as part of the genre's canon before. On the other hand, all of the chosen films, with the partial exception of *Before Sunset*, are more or less canonical texts directed by established *auteurs*. This does not mean that only 'great works of art' are amenable to this type of generic analysis, or that only important artists can transcend generic purity in interesting ways. Impurity is consubstantial to generic working and does not depend on the individual filmmaker. The specificities of the various directors' work with romantic comedy are necessarily taken into account here but my approach is by no means *auteurist*. Rather, I have chosen relatively well-known texts in order to underline the visibility and the crucial role played by romantic comedy outside the very restricted dominant canon.

Chapter 2 is devoted to two films directed by two of the most prestigious figures in the history of Hollywood comedy: Ernst Lubitsch and Billy Wilder. Neither *To Be or Not to Be* (1942) nor *Kiss Me, Stupid* (1964), however, have been previously thought of within the context of romantic comedy. Because both movies combine different comic traditions or conventions from different comic subgenres, their romantic comedy allegiances have often been overlooked. And yet, I would argue, their study from the point of view of romantic comedy would help to change dominant views of what the genre has been or should be, and of the ideological discourses that it has allowed within its boundaries. This chapter is, therefore, devoted to cases of texts in which romantic comedy interacts with other comic subgenres, such as marriage comedy, satire, comedian comedy, parody or metacomedy.

Chapter 3 attempts to move beyond the borders of comedy and examine what happens when romantic comedy is combined with a non-comic genre such as the thriller. The aim here is to give an idea of the intricate paths along which the secret life of the genre has developed and to suggest ways in which the analysis of the proximity between apparently incompatible genres can alter our perception of films and our interpretation of the cultural discourses which they articulate. Although Ed Sikov has insightfully included Alfred

Hitchcock within his study of 1950s U.S. comedy (1994), the British director is certainly not one that springs to mind when we think of romantic comedy, and *Rear Window* (1954) has never, to my knowledge, been analysed as a romantic comedy although it is one of the texts most often discussed in the history of cinema. Not that I will be arguing that the film is indeed a romantic comedy – no film is strictly a romantic comedy from the perspective proposed here – but our understanding of its meanings, especially its sexual and affective discourses, changes significantly when we take on board the crucial presence of this genre in its narrative structure. Whereas Hitchcock has never been seen as a romantic comedy director, Woody Allen has oddly disappeared from discussions of the genre in contemporary cinema. *Crimes and Misdemeanors* (1989) is perhaps not the most comic text in his *oeuvre* but its position on the margins of the genre, or even beyond its borders, can powerfully explain generic mechanisms, as well as provide useful insights into a specific cultural moment in the evolution of the genre. Allen's career illustrates in itself the variety of meanings and discourses, together with the formal experimentation, that contemporary romantic comedy encompasses, against dominant views of the genre's recent history. The final chapter suggests some of the possible directions that the genre's secret life might take in the twenty-first century and focuses on a film, *Before Sunset*, which, again, makes abundant use of the genre's conventions but has not been primarily seen, perhaps surprisingly, as a romantic comedy, probably in this case because of its allegiance to the aesthetic forms and conventions of independent cinema.

2

Comic negotiations

I. Laughter, love and World War II: *To Be or Not to Be*

There can be little doubt about the importance of history for a proper understanding of *To Be or Not to Be*. When the film started production on 6 November 1941, the United States was a neutral nation in the war that was raging in Europe and was rapidly extending to other parts of the world. Before production ended, on 23 December, Pearl Harbor had been bombed and the country had entered World War II. In 1940 Charles Chaplin had forcefully put forward the anti-isolationist perspective in his war comedy *The Great Dictator* (1940), and a year later Howard Hawks had marked the path for his country's inevitable involvement with *Sergeant York* (1941). Now events begin to develop very fast. Famous Hollywood names, connected in the 1930s with the genre of comedy, are joining the armed forces left, right and centre. Frank Capra, who had just finished his post-Depression comedy *Meet John Doe* (1941) – the last of his social-problem comedies –, becomes now Major Frank Capra, on active duty in the Army Signal Corps, while Corporal James Stewart is promoted to Second Lieutenant, a rank in which he is joined by Ronald Reagan. Clark Gable shaves off his moustache and enters the army, soon to become also a Second Lieutenant, while Henry Fonda and Tyrone Power enlist in the Navy and the Marines, respectively, and even Cary Grant becomes a U.S. citizen. In 1942 patriotism is running high: Bob Hope completes his first tour of army camps in June, the movies are declared an essential activity in the war effort and the new Hollywood Office of the Office of War Information Motion Picture Bureau proclaims its famous slogan: 'Will this picture help win the war?' One of the most popular films released that year, James Cagney's *Yankee Doodle Dandy*, donates the $6 million worth of admission tickets of its New York premiere to the war effort. Two months before the release of *To Be or Not to Be*, on 6 March 1942, its female star Carole Lombard is killed in a plane crash near Las Vegas when returning to her home in California from a war bond rally in Indianapolis. In the meantime, the extermination of the Jews as the Final Solution is being discussed by Nazi high-rank officers and, even as the film is being released, Jews are being deported to Auschwitz. As Peter Barnes emphatically puts it, 'everything is Poland' (2002: 7). The time is rife for war rhetoric, heroism and grand gestures. The time is wrong for laughter and comedy.

In this extremely charged atmosphere, a film that treats the invasion of Poland as a farce is bound to be controversial. The great Academy Award winner of the year is William Wyler's *Mrs. Miniver*, a war-time hybrid of marriage comedy and melodrama with its heart in the right place which never takes its theme lightly. A few months later, in November of the same year, the most popular World War II film, *Casablanca*, is also released to general acclaim. As complex a generic hybrid as *To Be or Not to Be* – romantic melodrama, exotic adventure, war movie, antifascist and anti-isolationist propaganda film – Curtiz's film, like *Mrs. Miniver*, strikes the right note by tracing through the character of Rick Blaine (Humphrey Bogart) the progress of the U.S. attitude towards the War in Europe and ending with his reluctant compromise with the Allied cause. Like Lubitsch's film, it also features at its core a love triangle. Yet, while the triangle in *Casablanca* transcended its immediate context and went on to become paradigmatic of contemporary Western discourses on love, desire and marriage, that of *To Be or Not to Be* remained almost invisible next to the prominence of the film's more 'serious' concerns and the controversial nature of its comic perspective – oddly, if we consider that *Casablanca* gave people the kind of patriotic discourse they wanted to hear at the time, which should have made the love plot secondary, while Lubitsch's movie wore its tongue impertinently in its cheek, which could have driven spectators to ignore its Nazi plot and concentrate on its love story.

Yet, right or wrong, politically correct or not, the film was a comedy and as such it became part of film history. If the historical context and the war-time industrial rearrangements that Hollywood was undergoing during the film's production and first run are relevant, equally relevant is its pivotal position, simultaneously central and marginal, in the history of Hollywood comedy. Although Lubitsch would still make two more comedies – *Heaven Can Wait* (1943) and *Cluny Brown* (1946) –, *To Be or Not to Be* represents one of the closing stages of a brand of comedy of love and desire which, running for over twenty years, constitutes a unique phenomenon: a one-director comic tradition. Although 'a Lubitschean comedy' is a label generally used to refer to a specific type of comedy, it is also almost invariably a comedy directed by Lubitsch. He is not just the central figure of the cycle – he *is* the whole cycle. Connected at its outset with Cecil B. de Mille's silent marriage comedies and with Chaplin's *A Woman of Paris* (1923), and, in the early 1930s, vaguely reminiscent of what James Harvey has called 'the classy comedy' (1998: 61), the films' closest relatives must otherwise be found in other comic love narratives: the German director's musicals of the same period and the turn-of-the-century European tradition of plays and operettas on which the movies were often based. This film's inclusion of a love plot seems to many an almost unnecessary and frivolous distraction from its central theme but this generalised opinion says more about the inferior cultural status of intimate matters in both Lubitsch's times and our own than about the structure of the film itself. The secondary position that these matters occupy in the critical discourse on the film represents a repeatedly missed chance to contextualise it within the Lubitschean comedy of the sexes and to explore both its links with the main body of his films and its marginality with respect to them.

Traditional accounts of the history of romantic comedy tend to agree that the war puts a sudden end to the strong comic output of Hollywood in the 1930s, and nowhere is this more visible than in the abrupt disappearance of its most brilliant cycle, screwball comedy. 1942 is for many already too late a date for screwball, but a closer look suggests the inaccuracy of this assessment. This is, for example, the time of greatest effervescence in Preston Sturges's short career as a director. Although his movies are often felt to be too idiosyncratic to be safely lodged within a generic label, considerations of this type are based on the traditional attitude to genres as *corpora* questioned in this book. If a genre is seen as an abstract system that evolves historically rather than as a group of texts, then the importance of Sturges's contribution to screwball becomes immediately obvious. Both *The Lady Eve* and *Sullivan's Travels* had been released in 1941 and *The Palm Beach Story* would appear in 1942.

Apart from Sturges's films, there were also screwball ingredients in *Meet John Doe* and certainly in Howard Hawks's *Ball of Fire*, which, also released in 1941, evokes in retrospect, both in its story and *mise en scène*, the impending onset of *film noir* (*The Maltese Falcon* also appears in 1941, *This Gun for Hire* in 1942). 1942 is also the year of *Take a Letter, Darling*, a 'minor' screwball generally overlooked because of its late date, which, directed by Mitchell Leisen, does suggest the end of a road in the genre's sexual politics: the strong, powerful, fully screwball heroine played by Rosalind Russell happily but incongruously submits to the unearned and inexplicable supremacy of her mediocre employee-lover, played by Fred McMurray. The film's disappointing ending, perhaps not so drastically different from those of earlier, more famous screwball texts (think of another late example, *The Philadelphia Story* (1940)), does suggest an uneasiness with the New Woman discourses that had found its Hollywood home in the cycle in the second half of the 1930s, and looks forward to later cultural debates on the place of women with respect to the home/labour force dichotomy. *To Be or Not to Be*, on the other hand, uses the Lubitschean love triangle and the screwball persona of Carole Lombard to a drastically different effect, and its gender politics are revealed, as will be discussed later on, as an ideal combination of egalitarian ideological discourses stemming from the two comic traditions of the 1930s.

Lubitsch's film, then, stands, together with *The Palm Beach Story*, at the end of an era of comedy, but, unlike Sturges's movie, its hybrid use of comic genres places it on the margins of both the screwball and the Lubitsch mainstream, underscoring perhaps the impossibility of a future for both cycles. *Film Noir* is not the only new genre that is being gestated while *To Be or Not to Be* is produced and released. Hitchcock, who in 1941 had unexpectedly made his one contribution to screwball, *Mr. and Mrs. Smith*, specialises now in contemporary spy thrillers like *Foreign Correspondent* or *Saboteur* (both released in 1942) and also inaugurates what feminist critics would later label the paranoid woman's film with *Rebecca* (1940) and *Suspicion* (1941), while Val Lewton and Jacques Tourneur release their influential 'B' horror *Cat People* (1942).

In spite of the growing visibility of these new genres, which undoubtedly reflected a changing mood in the country, comedy was far from dead. 1942 was the year of *The Woman of the Year*, the first of the nine Katherine Hepburn/Spencer Tracy popular romantic comedies which would span the 1940s and early 1950s, and it was also the year of *The Road to Morocco*, the third instalment of a series which would continue to turn out new instalments in the following years. Its two male stars, Bing Crosby and, especially, Bob Hope represent the prominence of comedian comedy in the 1940s. At the same time, the relevant narrative roles played by female stars like Dorothy Lamour in the *Road to* series, Virginia Mayo in Hope's *The Princess and the Pirate* (1944), or Jane Russell in *The Paleface* (1948) and *Son of Paleface* (1952) guarantee the importance of sexual discourses in the comedian comedies of the decade, even if these discourses are different from those of the 1930s comedies and from the sexual politics of the Hepburn and Tracy vehicles. In this respect, *To Be or Not to Be* also occupies a historical middle-of-the-road position between the comic actor-based screwball of the 1930s and the comedian comedy of the 1940s: while Carole Lombard was the most glamorous screwball star, Jack Benny, who did not make many films, was a comedian and, perhaps for reasons not unrelated to Bob Hope's popularity, he brings into the film conventions, meanings and structures related to this type of comedy. As we shall see later on, this combination is also crucial to understand the movie's comic meanings.

In sum, *To Be or Not to Be* may not be as central to the Lubitsch comedy as *Trouble in Paradise* (1932) or *Design for Living* (1933) or to such screwball comedy as *It Happened One Night* (1934), *The Awful Truth* (1937) or *Bringing Up Baby* (1938), but its historical location as a kind of epitaph to both cycles, its almost unique generic combination of the two, its position as a meeting point between the romantic comedy of the 1930s and that of the 1940s and its intersection with other comic traditions grant it an interest which 'purer' films within their respective traditions, like *Trouble in Paradise*, *Bringing Up Baby* or *The Paleface*, lack.

Love and the invasion of Poland

Lubitsch's film is as good an example as any in the history of cinema of the critics' self-appointed role as the guardians of generic purity. Although, as William Paul reminds us, not all contemporary reactions were equally negative (1983: 281), the movie's blend of the dramatic and the comic offended many of the reviewers. While the British critical establishment congratulated itself on the certainty that Britain could not possibly produce such nasty little films (Barnes 2002: 46–8), Bosley Crowther led U.S. attacks on the German director for engendering a cinematic monster, a 'shocking confusion of realism and romance' (in Eyman 1993: 301). The general view was that the director had struck a hopelessly false note in mixing the real, contemporary suffering of Polish people under the Nazi invasion with a frivolous comic perspective, that he was laughing at things that should not be approached comically. *The Great Dictator* had done something superficially similar but Chaplin's more sentimental brand of comedy had been felt to be more acceptable and the film had achieved redemption by taking itself seriously in its final reel. Lubitsch was less accommodating and, as a consequence, broke the Derridean law of genre. In the French philosopher's terms, he played the dangerous game of mixing genres and dramatically failed to obtain the certificate of guarantee. Or, in the phrase of another egregious genre mixer, Charles Dickens, echoed in Peter Barnes's recent appreciation of the film, he produced a piece of 'streaky bacon', a smooth mix of melodrama, documentary, slapstick, farce and high comedy (2002: 55).

There are two types of intergeneric encounters in the movie. On the one hand, there is the intersection between what could be termed adventure drama or spy thriller, and comedy. On the other, at least two types of comedy, corresponding to the two interwoven plots, are joined together by the narrative: satire or black comedy, and romantic comedy. Notice that the quotation from Crowther refers to realism and romance as two incommensurable genres. If we take the famous U.S. critic as representative of a more generalised opinion, what offended was not only that he mixed the serious and the comic, or the dramatic and the comic, but, more specifically, realism and romance, implying, therefore, that romance is not realistic or that reality, in times of war, does not include romance. There was not only the accusation of bad taste in tackling such a delicate and pressing issue as the invasion of Poland but also that of inserting a frivolous topic like the love triangle in the middle of a serious plot about the defeat of Nazi rule. Small wonder, then, that when the film was elevated to the status of masterpiece, the love triangle practically disappeared from critical discussion.

Among scholarly accounts of the film, William Paul most usefully engages with what he calls the genre conflict between the two plots. Placing himself on the camp of the defenders of comedy as a subversive genre, he explains the negative reactions in a predictable way: 'the anarchic side of comedy might always seem an affront to good taste, an attempt through laughter to purge bad taste' (1983: 230). Paul brilliantly relates comedy, theatricality (the favourite subject of most criticism of the film) and politics, but seems to tread on much shakier ground when he tackles the romantic side of the film's comedy: because of the casting of Jack Benny as the protagonist Josef Tura, he argues, 'love has been displaced from the center of this film so that any romantic feeling between these two characters functions simply as a given of the narrative' (232). Benny could never be fully at home in romantic comedy. There is romantic comedy in the film but not as far as the comic star is concerned. Later on he affirms that due to the age discrepancy between Maria Tura (Carole Lombard) and her admirer, Lieutenant Sobinski (Robert Stack), the love scenes between these two are more comic than romantic, and therefore there is no romantic comedy here, either. Where, then, is the romantic comedy? Paul does not seem able to find it anywhere and, as a consequence, ends up dismissing the love plot and concentrating on the deception scenario.

Here I would like to continue the generic analysis initiated by Paul by concentrating on the interaction between the two comic plots and on the relationship between the use of romantic comedy and black comedy, between the comic treatment of love – through the intersection of the Lubitschean love triangle narrative and screwball comedy – and the comic treatment of the Nazis. Satire and romance may be seen to exist in very distant worlds from one another but within the generic space of comedy they can and often do intersect. As has been seen, satirical or Aristotelian comedy exposes and ridicules vices and human folly with a corrective aim. As Jonathan Swift says about his own poetry, 'His satire points at no defect, / But what all mortals may correct.' Since the folly related to love, desire and marriage is one of the most frequent types of folly to be satirised in literature, theatre and film, especially in such generic configurations as farce, comedy of manners and marital or divorce comedy, satire often coexists with romantic comedy, which is also centrally concerned with love, desire and marriage even if its comic atmosphere may, in principle, exclude satire. In the same way as authors like Neale and Krutnik (1990: 13–14, 23–5), Rowe (1995: 110–14) or Thomas (2000: 21–2 and *passim*) affirm that melodrama is often very close to romantic comedy, the other side of the same coin, or constantly knocking at the door and demanding to be admitted inside, it could be argued that satire is similarly near, its ridiculing impulse often struggling with the protecting vocation of the beneficent comic space of romantic comedy.

There are, therefore, two types of intersections that demand our attention in the generic analysis of *To Be or Not to Be*: on the one hand, the consequences of the simultaneity of the love plot and the Nazi plot and of the interferences existing between them; on the other, the mixture of satire and romantic comedy in the articulation of the love plot and, more specifically, of the love triangle. What does the love plot contribute to our understanding of the Nazi plot, and, conversely, how does the Nazi plot affect the representation of intimate relationships? What does the interaction between satire and romantic comedy say about the film's representation of love and desire, sexuality and identity? Finally, in more historical terms, what is love doing in the middle of the invasion of Poland, and what discourses on love and desire can be articulated in such a historical context?

A table for three: the love triangle

The film's title, through its reference to Hamlet's monologue, used as a central event in the love plot, links identity and sexuality: Josef Tura's theatrical rendering of the Shakespearean character's internal journey becomes the repeated excuse for Sobinski's clandestine visits to Maria Tura's dressing room. Maria and Sobinski's relationship, based on his adolescent admiration and growing love for her and on her undisguised lustful attraction towards him, soon becomes part of the film's erotic landscape and remains in place while Maria flirts with the various German officers and Tura impersonates them to save their country. At the same time, whatever her feelings for the young Lieutenant are, these prove to be compatible with her love for her husband. As Paul says, 'there is a mutuality of character that binds [Maria and Josef] together and [cannot] be threatened by Stanislav's foolishly serious intentions' (1983: 237). Benny plays a variation on the classical *senex*, the cuckolded husband who, at least in Maria's terms, is never really betrayed. His jealousy grows from scene to scene, climaxing in his discovery of his rival in his bed, but then it seems to subside somewhat when he allows the aviator to say goodbye to his wife under his close supervision before they leave on their final theatrical mission. The last scene finds Sobinski as a permanent fixture, a kind of accompanying fan, of the theatrical troupe during their stay in Britain. He finally joins Tura in his angered shock when a younger Navy officer leaves the second row as the actor again intones the *Hamlet* monologue. Although his role in the new scenario is not spelled out, it seems clear that Sobinski has become part of a family which, by the look of it, seems elastic enough to admit more members in the future.

The brilliant contrivance of the Nazi deception plot, which has just reached its *dénouement*, may prevent some spectators from considering the consequences of this final intimate/erotic arrangement seriously, and yet, from the perspective of romantic comedy, this is a crucial moment. Historically, the narrativisation of the love triangle in *To Be or Not to Be* comes at the end of a long and memorable series of explorations of marriage and desire in Lubitsch's film career. Although the love triangle was his favourite narrative configuration, that in intimate matters he did not particularly fetishise the number three is proved by his silent masterpiece, *The Marriage Circle* (1924), a continuation of the marital farces he had directed in Germany, in which marriage and desire link not just three but four or even five characters. This exploration continued in his adaptation of Oscar Wilde's *Lady Windermere's Fan* (1925), *Trouble in Paradise*, *Design for Living* and *Angel* (1937), among others. Of these, only *Design for Living* ends, like *To Be or Not to Be*, with a triangle still in place, the three characters striving to work out an arrangement outside the established social order which can accommodate their emotional situation (although without sex). *Design for Living* concentrates intensely on the relationships between the three lovers and minutely spells out the terms of and the reasons for their pact.

To Be or Not to Be, on the other hand, does not go into such detailed explanations and simply suggests that the status quo reached at the end of the film is feasible. Similarly, the split between affection and comradeship on the one hand and romance and desire on the other is not very different here from the situation in which Angel/Lady Maria Barker finds herself in *Angel* and is therefore also familiar to Lubitsch-knowledgeable spectators. In 1942, therefore, these emotional patterns can be seen as a continuation of those already displayed in earlier Lubitsch films. In a sense, the film does not need to explain any more because the plots of the earlier films provide enough explanation. Since those films do not just constitute the *oeuvre* of a director, but can be seen as an important tradition of the genre, *To Be or Not to Be* ought to be considered within that tradition, and failure to do so brings as a consequence the omission from critical discourse of an important part of its plot. This is not so much a return to *auteur* criticism as an understanding of filmic texts within the history of genre, in this case, the history of romantic comedy.

Eve Sedgwick has suggested that the typical form of the love triangle, with two men and a woman as their common object of desire, reflects the cultural superiority of male homosocial desire over heterosexual desire in Western patriarchal society, the woman being the silent object of exchange between the two men (1985: 21–7). This theory has become a potent ideological template to explain many Western narratives, including many movies, but it feels rather inaccurate in the case of Lubitsch's films in general and of *To Be or Not to Be* in particular. Lubitsch is centrally concerned with the exploration of heterosexual desire and in his films homosocial bonding clearly recedes into the background: men are not really all that interested in one another. This is not to say that society, with its rules and conventions, its repressions and its limitations, does not play a crucial part in Lubitsch's erotic scenarios in other respects, as both Paul and Babington and Evans, in their book on the Hollywood comedy of the sexes, have pointed out. In terms of the representation of desire, society is a crucial factor and not necessarily a negative or repressive one. Babington and Evans assert, referring to the famous 'no sex' clause of the *ménage à trois* with which *Design for Living* ends, that 'the ending preserves a realism about the power of sexual ideologies and even, it may be, from the anthropological perspective, the power of pairing as the basis of all known social life, while wondering if some other kind of arrangement is possible' (1989: 72). For these authors, Lubitsch separates himself from screwball comedy by preferring mature love over the youthful innocence and energy of first love.

Love after marriage is also at the core of the cycle of screwball comedies labelled by Stanley Cavell as 'comedies of remarriage' (1981). Yet, with their emphasis on fun and games and their unrepentant optimism, these films project a sense of the erotic as untainted by the sufferings, disappointments and precariousness of experience, and are thus closer to screwball than to the typical Lubitschean comedy. Marriage in Lubitsch is, on the other hand, 'the object of romantic desire (perfect union), its regulator (since, having found the perfect object, desire should cease, except for that object) and, inevitably, its ironiser (desire, sadly, fades, the overestimation of the love-object [. . .] lessens as the object is possessed, and desire for a different object springs to life)' (Babington and Evans 1989: 60). From this perspective, marriage immediately and inevitably calls forth its logical complement, the third element, and therefore the triangle appears both as a catalyst for the renewal of a dead marriage and as an expression of the hope in the existence of better modes of organising sexuality, while still emphasising conflict and fragility (61–2). The triangle, therefore, is not used, or at least not used primarily, to negotiate different types of relationships between men, but, rather, to suggest the unstoppable power and simultaneous volatility of desire, the fragility of love and the repressive yet occasionally also productive role played by society in the expression and fulfilment of desire.

The Marriage Circle, without using the triangle, encapsulates the Lubitschean perspective on love and desire. In this film, the four married people are shown to truly love their spouses at least at some point, while three of them – the fourth one, Professor Josef Stock (Adolphe Menjou), is an early, grimmer version of Josef Tura who is more jealous than desiring – feel attracted to somebody else. Extramarital desire is never fulfilled but neither is it denied or rejected. Within the boundaries posed by social conventions, marital love and extramarital desire appear to be compatible. However, as in later films, there is no true happy ending for these lovers: one married couple remains married but their desire for others has not been placated and their future together seems at best uncertain; the man who wanted a divorce from the beginning gets what he wanted but he is none the happier for it; his wife may find some temporary consolation in her best friend's rejected lover but her excessive desire seems to have led her to an emotional dead end. As Harvey argues, what for others may be a tragedy for Lubitsch is the richest joke. In his films, 'to feel strongly and passionately about anything, even in love, is to be alone' (1998: 43). However, the Lubitschean response to this is not despair but, rather, quiet acceptance and simultaneous amusement at human frailty.

In *To Be or Not to Be* similar affective structures are repeated although the film nurses, paradoxically, a stronger Utopian vision, closer in its optimism to films like *Ninotchka* or *The Shop around the Corner* (1940). If we had been given time to plumb the psychological depths of desire maybe the conclusion would have been analogous to earlier films, but the characters, while never rejecting the dictates of their passions and affects, also have other things in mind, i.e. the defeat of the Nazis, and do not have much time for ruminating. Rather than the psychology of desire, Lubitsch's concerns here appear to be more social, even more political: the overcoming of peace-time morality in exceptional moments and the carving out of a space for a different morality in Western society as a consequence of the profound social changes that are beginning to take place. Earlier films by Lubitsch, as well as the whole tradition of the erotic triangle, had seen this geometrical figure as the correlative of obsession, frustration and ultimate loneliness. Here, by bringing it into contact with the Nazis, Lubitsch is airing it, breathing some new energy into it and turning it into the liberating representative of a new Utopian order in which the all-important link between love and desire can be articulated in new inventive ways. Paul has noticed that, since *Ninotchka*, Lubitsch's films had become more openly political and had moved from the individual to the social (1983: 331). This is because, he argues, the historical and industrial contexts forced him to move away from his hitherto almost exclusive focus on love and sex. Yet, the mixture of comic modes in *To Be or Not to Be* (as in all the rest of his last films) points in a different direction: it is not so much that individual desire gives way to social concerns; rather, the perspective on desire is made to shift – from psychology to social Utopia. That this Utopia should be located in a historically tragic moment, in the midst of social anxiety and massive personal suffering, may have been partly to blame for the negative reception of the film in some quarters. That the liberal sexual discourse was conveniently 'hidden' behind a satire of Nazi totalitarianism and tyranny may explain why the outrage was not greater.

Lubitsch meets screwball royalty

Jack Benny brings comedian comedy into *To Be or Not to Be* and his star clout contributes an important variation on the *senex* tradition and on the Lubitsch brand of comedy by bringing the jealous

husband to the fore and turning him into the romantic protagonist.
This generic shift humanises the stereotype: Josef is still a laughable,
gullible fool but he is also a hero and Benny's presence ensures that,
even at his most ridiculous, the spectator is never too far from
sympathising with him. Carole Lombard is a different matter. While
films like *Design for Living* or *Bluebeard's Eighth Wife* (1938) may
occasionally come close to the conventions and ideological concerns
of screwball comedy, Lubitsch's *oeuvre*, as has been argued before,
remained clearly distinct from the more native U.S. tradition
while running parallel to it throughout the 1930s and early 1940s.
Claudette Colbert, who had featured in one of the first instances
of screwball, *It Happened One Night*, proved to be adaptable
enough and became an almost completely Lubitschean heroine in
Bluebeard's Eighth Wife. Perhaps, in spite of her iconic presence in
the Capra film, Colbert never was as characteristic of screwball as
Katherine Hepburn, Cary Grant or Irene Dunne, Myrna Loy or
William Powell. Although it is always risky to associate film stars
with specific genres, it seems difficult in retrospect to imagine any
of these performers in a Lubitsch film. I am even doubtful that
Edward Everett Horton and Ralph Bellamy would be interchangeable as the wrong partners of both traditions. Without *To Be or
Not to Be* the same would have been true of Carole Lombard. She,
more than Benny, crucially contributes to the film's uniqueness.
Apart from other generic considerations, therefore, Lubitsch's
direction and Lombard's star performance manage to achieve a
fusion between the two main 1930s romantic comedy traditions.

It could almost be said that Lombard invented screwball comedy.
Screwball was a publicist's term, originally taken from baseball
slang and first applied to her performance in *My Man Godfrey*
(1936) to convey the blend of madcap dizziness, liberation and
romantic exaltation that the genre came to represent (Harvey 1998:
xi). Although, apart from that film, she only appeared in another
three which are regularly associated with the genre, *Hands across
the Table* (1935), *Nothing Sacred* (1937) and *Mr. and Mrs. Smith*
(a film that is just as often ignored in accounts of romantic comedy
because of the unlikeliness of a 'marriage' between Hitchcock and
this particular genre), Lombard is justly regarded as the 'queen of
screwball' (Harvey 1998: 201). At the risk of overgeneralising, it
could be argued that while Lubitsch's comedy is centrally concerned
with the vicissitudes of desire and can therefore be related to the

growing centrality of sexuality in Western cultural discourses, screwball deals with desire in famously more indirect ways (the walls of Jericho in *It Happened One Night*, the protagonists marching out of the Ritz restaurant 'stuck' to each other in *Bringing Up Baby*, the sudden change in the direction of the walk of the male doll in the cuckoo clock at the end of *The Awful Truth*, the snake in *The Lady Eve*) and appears to be more interested in social exchanges between men and women.

As Tina Olsin Lent has shown, screwball was instrumental in adapting the cultural visibility of the 'New Woman' of the 1920s to the cinema. For Lent the films appear as a result of the reconceptualisation of gender relationships brought about by the first wave of feminism, consequent changes in people's attitudes towards the institution of marriage and the ensuing increase in divorce rates (1995: 314–17). Although many instances of the genre still end up with women being subjected, often after very unlikely plot turns, to their male counterparts for the sake of love, the general impression left by these films is one of strong women who either take the leading role in their heterosexual relationships or who, at least, struggle bravely to achieve equality, as in the case of *His Girl Friday* or *The Philadelphia Story*, in a relationship which is not only about fun and games but also very clearly about power. Conversely, many of the heroes played by Cary Grant, William Powell, Joel McCrea or Henry Fonda become attractive to women and to spectators in general for their capacity to accept a certain degree of well-deserved humiliation at the hands of women and to engage happily in scenarios of social and (indirectly) sexual subjection.

In this sense, Maria Tura is a perfect blend of Lubitsch and screwball: as driven by desire as the heroines of *The Marriage Circle, Trouble in Paradise, Design for Living* or *Angel*, she brings to the Lubitschean paradigm the strength of character, the giddy capacity for manipulation, and the degrees of mastery and control of the screwball heroine. These are all features which openly separate her from the characters played by Margaret Sullavan in *The Shop around the Corner*, Jennifer Jones in *Cluny Brown* or even Greta Garbo in *Ninotchka*, at least after the protagonist of the latter falls in love with Leon. Thus Maria becomes the powerful, openly sexualised woman who is very rare in romantic comedy but easier to find in *film noir*, and can be seen, therefore, as a link with a genre which was then about to irrupt in the Hollywood scene. She can in fact be seen as part of a transition between two genres with several cultural and historical links which can also be appreciated in such contemporary Howard Hawks films as *Ball of Fire* and *The Big Sleep* (1946). It may be argued that the almost humiliating superiority she shows with respect to all the men around her and her sexual forwardness can only be culturally readable in the state of uncertainty provoked by the war and representable through an unlikely blend of, on the one hand, romantic comedy and satire and, on the other, Lubitsch and screwball. Through this generic complexity the film anticipates the temporary liberation and rise in social visibility of women in countries like the U.S. or Great Britain during World War II. Maria is, therefore, a fantastic filmic construction which, through a very specific blend of comic genres, becomes a powerful representation if not of the realities at least of some of the aspirations of her female contemporaries.

Maria's first appearance in the film, wearing her spectacular evening dress for a concentration camp scene of the Gestapo play, sets the standard of her part and becomes the first indelible instance of her performance. Lombard's usual self in her mixture of star glamour and ironic distance, the character uses the star's beauty to express her disregard of conventions, in this case theatrical conventions, in order to assert her right to be herself, no matter what the demands of the context may be. She starts off as an amusing mixture of conventional femininity, diva vanity and aloofness. The moment, however, is not only important in itself but as an introduction to her first dialogue with her husband, in the course of which she accuses him of always putting himself in front of her. His jealousy and his insecurity as an actor are introduced and his total dependence on his wife revealed. We soon learn that she uses this dependence of his as a weapon to assert her right to be a desiring subject even outside marriage. In this dialogue with Tura, Maria expresses her wish to be treated on equal terms and her right to be as vain and as powerful professionally as her husband, since she is at least as good as him as an actor.

The dialogue is also the preamble to her first encounter with her young admirer. The interval between her husband's exit from her dressing room (once she has reassured him that she loves only him in spite of the flowers she keeps receiving) and the aviator's arrival takes the form of a dialogue with Anna (Maude Eburne) which

3 Love between prima donnas: performing marriage in
To Be or Not to Be, starring Carole Lombard and Jack Benny
(dir. Ernst Lubitsch, 1942, United Artists)

works as a confession. In this scene the spectator has unmediated
access to the character's 'true self', or, rather, our access is mediated
by the comments and facial expressions of the maid, clearly a
deadpan realistic representative of the text's ideology in her amusing
blend of sexual tolerance and awareness of social conventions.
Maria rejoices here in both her power over men and her right to
be a desiring subject, and Anna's guarded approval becomes the
spectator's own. When the lieutenant comes in, Maria shows how
smoothly she can extend the power she exerts over her husband to
other men. Ever since Shakespeare, romantic comedy has expressed
both sexual friction and the war of the sexes through verbal sparring – as Stephen Greenblatt has pointed out, the greater the friction, the more powerful the sexual charge (1988: 89–90). There is
not as much friction here as in the scenes with her husband because
these two partners are so unequal, but Maria's suffocating superiority is also expressed through her verbal brilliance. When she engages
in a sexual innuendo of which Sobinski is not even remotely aware,
evoking now the Restoration comedies of Etherege and Wycherley,
the film confirms the result of the combination of Lubitschean
comedy, screwball and satire: Maria is both the strong contemporary woman of screwball and the desiring subject in whose
hands young men become mere sexual toys, reversing patriarchal
conventions and expectations, and reasserting the film's utopian
dimension.

These initial scenes, in which the scenarios of power and desire are played out within the space of a marital comedy which focuses not so much on the husband's inferiority as on the woman's right to have it both ways, display the importance of humour in romantic comedy. The first verbal exchange between husband and wife introduces the excessive mixture of vanity and jealousy that defines Tura as a character through a joke in which Maria accuses him of always grabbing attention: 'Whenever I start to tell a story you finish it, if I go on a diet you lose the weight, if I have a cold you cough, and if we should ever have a baby I'm not so sure I would be the mother', to which he replies: 'I'm satisfied to be the father.' Later, Anna encourages Maria through such gnomic observations as 'what a husband doesn't know won't hurt his wife', recommending a combination of sexual freedom and caution. In the next scene, Maria shows her overawed excitement at Sobinski's strength as a bomber. The comic perspective of this section culminates in the brief dialogue that takes place when, just after the lieutenant has left the dressing room, Josef comes in distraught because somebody (Sobinski) has just walked out on him during the soliloquy. The protagonist is unwittingly right to ask his wife: 'Tell me, Maria, am I losing my grip?', the implication being that the grip he is losing is not as an actor but as a husband and, more specifically, as a sexual partner – Sobinski walked out not because he disliked Josef's performance but because he had been given a *rendez-vous* by an apparently unsatisfied (but not complaining) Maria. The blindness of his limitless vanity overpowers jealousy and certainly love, which makes it not only easier but also reasonable for his wife to be unfaithful. Comically, Maria replies that he is not losing his grip and that she is really sorry, both admitting and hiding her part in her husband's humiliation. She offers her consolation genuinely and heartily because, as she will soon tell an impetuous Sobinski, she loves only her husband but prefers to look elsewhere for sex: Tura's implied impotence is not something his wife is overly worried about, as will be proven later on when the young lieutenant ends up occupying Tura's place in his bed.

The utopia of desire that the optimistic future of the triangle portends is linked to the female utopia, where the 'queen of screwball' reigns supreme in a fantasy world in which women not only come into their own in terms of gender politics, as they had done intermittently in screwball, but also sexually. Lombard's screwball pedigree allows her to join the gallery of Lubitschean desiring women but with a superior intelligence and flair for domination to overcome their anxieties and fear of loneliness. That the exceptional circumstances provided by the war have a lot to do with this Utopia is proved by the fact that when Maria begins to have difficulties to explain to Sobinski that she is not planning to divorce her husband but that he is, more or less, welcome to the family, the war breaks out, the lieutenant has to leave immediately and she can freely and, again, genuinely, embrace him and give him something to come back home to. Just when, following the logic of romantic conventions, she was beginning to feel the pressure of having to choose, the film arrests that logic and substitutes a provisional scenario in which a different logic applies, one in which the female character will not be forced to choose.

We will return to this scene in connection with the issue of performance but, in generic terms, it looks as if Lubitsch had been waiting to meet screwball comedy, which had been his neighbour and rival for almost a decade, until an exceptional event took place, an event which, sadly, would bring both comic traditions to an end. When the situation is finally favourable, he metaphorically invites screwball to his house in the form of its most iconic representative, and the visit not only changes both his house and the visitor but also produces an exceptional comic text which can be seen as a culmination of sorts of both traditions without fully belonging to either of them.

That great, great Polish actor

Sobinsnki's repeated walks out of the stalls take a heavy toll on both Tura and Shakespeare. The famous soliloquy passes as one of the English dramatist's profoundest explorations of human identity, a philosophical debate on the nature of true living as opposed to a life of self-betrayal, with death as a corollary for both, probably a forerunner of twentieth-century existentialism and certainly one of many reasons why the bard has remained the most relevant literary figure through the centuries. For Josef Tura, the soliloquy is also a marker of his identity as an actor and the sublimity of the lines just an excuse for the really important sublimity – that of his performance every evening in front of an enraptured audience. Maria, with her apparently innocent (and, in Anna's words, safe) decision to ask the lieutenant to visit her at this point, is deriding her husband's elevated sense of self-importance and, by extension, also Shakespeare, by suggesting that from a female perspective there are more important things in life than Hamlet's tragic and desperate search for identity. Paradoxically, she is doing something that Shakespeare's comic characters would also have done: for the playwright human identity was to be found not only in the tragic confrontation between life and death but also in the scenarios of love and desire for another (or for several others) of his comedies, and to him, in spite of the tenor of most traditional criticism, both types of exploration were equally significant. So, perhaps, in getting Sobinski to disrupt the famous soliloquy, Maria, and Lubitsch through her, is also asking the spectator to look at Shakespeare differently, to look at *Hamlet* comically – as Hamlet himself occasionally does, too, as when he tells her uncle that the dead Polonius is at dinner –, not so much bringing the playwright down as demanding, like the secondary actors of the troupe, that his plays be seen also as an occasion for laughter and/or joy.

Shakespeare can then take the repeated spite better than Tura. When the aviator leaves his seat for the second time, Tura calls it a foul conspiracy, which makes the other actors think that he is referring to the outbreak of war. The film cuts to another scene before we have the chance to ascertain which of the two crimes – the interruption of his performance or the Nazi invasion of Poland – is more important to him but, given his record, we are entitled to entertain doubts. In any case, as with the budding affair between Maria and Sobinski, the war puts Tura's acting crisis on hold, and yet, as with the love affair, the war situation which takes over the rest of the film does not make it disappear but, rather, manages to present it more obliquely. We have seen that the film links the protagonist's growing doubts about his own acting abilities with his sexual impotence. He is losing his grip in more than one sense, and more than one type of performance is being questioned. In the rest of the narrative, Tura will be called upon to perform a part several times and on every occasion there is a moment when his brilliant and convincing performance turns into overacting and threatens to expose him for the ham he really is. On these occasions, his anxiety about theatrical performance recalls his marital anxieties, which the Nazi invasion has temporarily shelved. His humiliation is most comically articulated through the repeated gag that has the Germans keep failing to recognise his name as that of a famous actor.

This is the context in which the joke that the film was widely criticised for, even among those closest to Lubitsch (see Eyman 1993: 289–305), takes place. Josef, disguised as Professor Siletsky, asks Colonel Ehrhardt (Sig Ruman) whether he has heard of that great, great Polish actor, Josef Tura. Ehrhardt, unlike those who have preceded him, unexpectedly replies that he has seen him once on the stage and gives his famous opinion of Tura's performance: 'what he did to Shakespeare we are now doing to Poland.' At the beginning of the twenty-first century, comedy continues to be taboo for certain social groups and it is consequently at least understandable that many people could be offended by this joke in 1942. What is perhaps more surprising is that it was this particular line that was considered offensive, instead of being perceived as the bold attack on Nazism that it really was. In any case, the joke does not only envisage Hitler's dreams of grandeur as a poor performance but it also contributes to the escalation in the humiliation of the protagonist as an actor, his 'devastation' of Shakespeare being as tragic as the German destruction of Poland. More interesting, however, is Maria's part in the effect of this joke on the spectator.

As we have seen, the film has already prepared the spectator to link Tura's limitations at both types of performance: theatrical performance and sexual performance. It is inevitable that we link the two again in Ehrhardt's reply, especially since the sexual connotations of the destructive power of dynamite as released from a plane over an enemy city, something comparable to the German military campaign in Poland, had already been highlighted in Maria's first interview with Sobinski. The devastating power of Sobinski's dynamite is totally opposed to that of Tura's performance, which makes both curiously compatible: in sexual terms, the lieutenant's excess of sexual potency (in Maria's fantasy) contrasts with the actor's overblown sense of himself and consequent inability to give himself sexually to his wife. In other words, through the Nazi colonel's words, the film is, without apparently alluding to it, confirming Tura's sexual impotence. In his analysis of the joke, William Paul argues that the complexity of the laughter at this point stems from the fact that it is directed against both the speaker and the listener (1983: 230), that is, against Nazi horror and, in the reading proposed here, Tura's serious limitations as a lover. These limitations are behind Maria's sexual voracity (in intention if not in fact) and facilitate the power she holds over her husband. In a sense, therefore, Ehrhardt's reply is equating Hitler's military mastery over Europe both with the husband's poor acting and with the wife's sexual power. Acting works not only as a metaphor for the horrors of military invasion but also as a mediator between war and sex. It may not be too far-fetched to affirm that the joke offended not only because it treated acute suffering frivolously but also because it indirectly equated two types of performance (another black comedy about war, *Dr. Strangelove* [1963], would do it more openly twenty-one years later) and unconsciously evoked the ghost of a sexual regime dominated by women.

Performing love, performing war

The extremely mixed comedy of *To Be or Not to Be* places its characters in a comic space which protects them from the dangers and threats of the social space. In a movie like this, the social space is clearly framed by the Nazi domination of Europe and conquering plans over the rest of the world, including the United States, but it is also the more habitual social space of romantic comedy in which characters are inhibited in their intimate protocols by social and psychological pressures. In the case of the spy plot, this comic space is secured by the presence of performance: the actors get out of danger and, in their small way, defeat the Nazis through a series of inventive and successful theatrical tricks. Because of the film's comic perspective, the spectator understands that their play scripting and playacting will save them from all harm. On the other hand, its generic instability, the vividness of danger and destruction, suggest that, at a time like this, the protection given by comedy can only be precarious and can disappear at any moment. This is why we laugh with the characters' antics but are never completely sure that they are going to be safe. The generic mixture works both ways: it constructs an unlikely safe haven in the midst of the spy thriller or the wartime melodrama, and it gives a dangerous edge to the comedy by making the spectator aware of the presence of death outside the theatre door.

Performance, theatricality, even metacinema have been the preferred topics of most academic criticism of the movie. Marc Gauchée argues that the film teaches that the theatre always precedes reality (2004: 4). William Paul reads the film's politics, or rather, its take on Nazi politics, through its theatricality. Theatrical behaviour is transformed into distinct political behaviour and, as a consequence, politics is revealed to be inherently theatrical and Hitler is exposed as the ultimate ham actor (1983: 248–9). Leland Poague contrasts two types of theatricality, that of the professional actors and that of the Nazis, and concludes that 'extreme theatricality, outside of its proper context, becomes a genuine threat to human existence' (1978: 92). Hassan Melehy summarises the general consensus when he argues that the film's use of a theatrical context calls into question the authenticity and authority of Nazism (2001/02: 36). However, performance also dominates, as we have seen, the relationships between the three main characters in the love plot. Sheila Whitaker, who is mainly concerned with the film's 'fundamental questioning of representation', also relates, if only briefly, the film's general use of theatricality to the members of the triangle's acting abilities and establishes a hierarchy between them: while Maria and Tura can act with each other, Sobinski, the more straight player, is at a loss (1976/77: 13). Our understanding and enjoyment of the romantic comedy conventions deployed by Lubitsch is also dependent on our awareness that at least husband and wife are always performing in their interactions with each other and with the young aviator. Further, we need to understand that, within the film's parameters, this sense of performance is not a signifier of deceit or falseness. Rather, in the same way as the actors' playacting protects them from the Nazis, performance also constitutes the comic space which protects the three principals from inhibitions and allows them to interact with one another. In other words, it is also performance that guarantees the film's deployment of its sexual and intimate discourses against the weight of reality and it is through the concept of performance that the two parts of the plot and the various generic configurations are linked and brought to bear on one another.

If Josef and Maria play the parts of the vain theatre star/jealous husband and the flighty wife/professional rival to perfection in their scenes together, Maria's amusing combination of untrammelled sexual desire and easy domination in her scenes with Sobinski is also based on her faultless rendering of her part and on the spectator's understanding that she is indeed playing a part. Both the war of the sexes represented in the exchanges between husband and wife and the representation of female desire in Maria's secret dates with her young lover appear to the viewer as contrived as her later attempt at Mata Hari and as Tura's impersonations of various Nazi officers and spies. But contrivance does not stand here as opposed to reality. In *To Be or Not to Be*'s brand of romantic comedy there is no reality, no truth beyond performance. The multiplicity of ontological levels produced by the actors' easy slippage into theatrical performances as real people (within the fictional world of the film) provokes the feeling that there is no drastic difference between the parts played by Josef and Maria Tura and those played by Jack Benny and Carole Lombard. There is no reason why a realistic representation (on the part of the fictional characters and on the part of the actors) should tell deeper truths about love and sexuality. In fact, in the world of the film, reality consists not only of the ugliness and horror of the Nazis but also of the repressions and contradictions of real social institutions that frustrate desire. It is only at the level of performance that the characters can be truly themselves in sexual and affective matters.

Maria finds herself in several situations of real danger in the course of the film, especially when she visits the Nazi spy in his room at the Gestapo headquarters, but there is only one moment in which she appears to momentarily lose her cool and is at a loss as to what to do, and that is, as has already been mentioned, when Sobinski, after ascertaining that she loves him, announces his plans to talk immediately and openly to her husband so that he gives her a divorce and they can live happily ever after. She looks surprised and starts to explain that she loves Tura and has no intention of divorcing him. In other words, she had assumed that the lieutenant understood the terms of her performance and did not expect him, always the straight player, to misjudge it. Fortunately, she is saved by the bell in the shape of the news of the Nazi invasion. She would have had to explain to him that the loving poses that she had struck and the clichés that she had conjured up were to be taken as a sexual game, as an appropriation of convention for the expression and enactment of desire. He might not have understood then, yet when we next see them together, after Tura has found him in his bed, Sobinski seems to begin to be adept at the game, a game in which the parts are fluid, as proved by the ease with which the lieutenant amusingly slips from the part of young lover into that of jealous husband in the final scene of the film.

In spite of the constant presence of similar scenarios in earlier Lubitsch films, some contemporary audiences may not have been prepared to fully appreciate the 'seriousness' of the sexual and power games proposed by the text, and their apparent frivolity may have worked to worsen their incensed attitude to the director's incongruous genre mixing. For one thing, the sexual discourses produced as a consequence of the historical combination of the so-called sexual revolution of the sixties, the second wave of feminism and the gay and lesbian liberation movements were not available to audiences then. The shift from the idea of sex as representing the deepest truth of ourselves and love as an essential, universal feeling to that of both as cultural constructs and scripted protocols, together with the notion of sexual and gender identity as the product of a series of social performances, allows early twenty-first-century spectators to understand the 'truth' of sex and love in a different way and, therefore, to appreciate the series of performances proposed in *To Be or Not to Be* as perfectly valid expressions of intimate matters. With this film, Lubitsch not only brought 1930s romantic comedy to a brilliant end by combining his own brand of sophisticated comedy with screwball but also, with his emphasis on performance, anticipated future emergent discourses on love and sex.

Performance is, then, central in the text, not only for its construction of the spy adventure plot and the discourses on Nazism, politics and even the nature of cinematic art, but also for its contribution to the articulation of an ideology of love and desire. The links between both types of discourses also revolve around the various performing scenarios activated by the film: if both politics and desire can be explained as performance, then there is no drastic separation between them, no reason to be offended at the combination of both in a single text. Ehrhardt's controversial line relates, negatively, Nazi horror with male impotence, and inventively contrasts its destruction with the devastation of Lieutenant Sobinski's dynamite, but there are more positive meanings attached to the trope: the theatrical troupe's brilliant series of semi-improvised scripts and impersonations, including Maria's flirtation with Siletsky, also evoke the married couple's attitude to love and sex as a series of performances, the parallelism suggesting a deeper similarity between the Polish actors' (and the film's) love of freedom and the freedom of love promoted by the film's sexual discourses.

The importance of performance to the construction of Maria as a desiring subject can best be seen in her first dialogue with

Sobinski. Her undisguised flirtation here follows what appear to be well-rehearsed patterns but, unlike later on with Siletsky, there is no goal in the flirtation beyond the activation and enactment of desire. She does not pretend to be attracted to him: she is attracted to him and shows it by apparently pretending. The view of sexuality as a discursively constructed and highly regulated network of pleasures and sensations, and the conclusion that sex is subordinated to sexuality, rather than the other way round, and as such equally regulated, was first proposed by Michel Foucault. Foucault was a sexual pessimist and fantasised about an asocial regime in which a multiplicity of bodies and pleasures replaced the inevitably regulated notions of sex and desire (1981: 157), a fantasy that has been criticised by Judith Butler as an essentialist move (1990: 97–9). Post-Foucauldian critics like Butler or William Simon have theorised the constructedness of sex with greater equanimity. Simon, for example, in his conceptualisation of sexuality as a script, argues that desire follows rather than precedes behaviour: 'not only do individuals often "fake" their sexual responsiveness, often they must simulate sexual interest in order to invoke authentic sexual excitement' (1996: 47). In the scene from *To Be or Not to Be*, the aviator's mention of his abilities at dropping tons of dynamite command Maria's 'faked' admiration but this pretence immediately becomes an expression of her desire for him, of her excitement about his comically fantasised infinite potency (infinite, especially,

4 'Quite a bomber': Maria Tura takes the lead in the performance
of desire. Carole Lombard in *To Be or Not to Be*
(dir. Ernst Lubitsch, 1942, United Artists)

if compared to her husband's). The sexual scenario, then, is not only facilitated by her performance but predicated upon it: no desire without performance. The fact that it is the woman that takes the lead in the performance of desire, and that she is celebrated for it, makes the film's sexual discourse a relatively extreme form of the sexual liberation sought by early feminist discourses, because, as Simon argues, the very idea of female commitment to sexual pleasure was then, and still is now, threatening to many men and women (48).

This fear of female sexuality and of female sexual agency may be partly soothed by the fact that Maria is, like Carole Lombard, a star and, as such, larger than life, or else the anxious spectator can take shelter in the idea that comedy is not serious. Narrative development, however, should alert the spectator to the real intentions of the text: once the small crisis provoked by Sobinski's plan to marry her has been overcome, Maria is never punished, not even comically, for her 'excess'. Rather, she is supported by the text when, after the bed episode, both her husband and her lover seem more or less content with the arrangement. Her wish to have both a husband to love and a lover to desire is finally granted by the story's *dénouement*. Whether marginal or dominant, the presence of this ideology of female agency and liberation from the sexual and psychological norm in a mainstream film attests to its readability, to the fact that in 1942 women's claims for sexual equality were seen as a possible, if only minority, option. Lubitsch's activation of screwball conventions, through his use of Carole Lombard, also suggests the potential of the genre to convey such egalitarian meanings, even if that potential was not often realised because of the screwball's often excessively oblique approach to sexual matters. It is screwball's encounter with the much more openly sexualised intimate scenarios of the Lubitsch comedy that facilitates such activation.

Judith Butler, in her influential theory of identity, takes issue with the Western metaphysics of substance according to which gender identity is constructed but sex is natural. She accordingly rejects the opposition sex/gender and argues that sex was constructed by specific discourses on gender. The production of sex as a natural, unchangeable fact is the consequence of a social act of regulation which requires the existence of two genders, two sexes, two differentiated desires. She rejects psychoanalysis' interest in gender normality but appropriates the psychoanalytic perspective that suggests the coexistence of multiple identifications which produce conflicts with the fixity of normative concepts of masculinity and femininity. The construction of sex and gender is for Butler, as it is for Foucault, part of the dynamics of power but, for her, this construction is based on a series of performances. She concludes that 'gender reality is created through sustained social performances' and that the notions of masculinity and femininity are part of a strategy that conceals the performative character of gender and therefore the possibility of proliferating gender configurations (1990: 141). *To Be or Not to Be*, a mainstream Hollywood film of the 1940s, cannot possibly explore the multiplicity of configurations of sex and desire that Butler finds, for example, in the drag performer. Its sexual scenarios may be much tamer by modern standards but they share with both Foucault and Butler the awareness of sex as a strategy of power and of sexuality as a matter of performance. Both Josef and Maria (notice the iconicity of their names) play according to well-known masculine and feminine stereotypes, but their constant awareness that they are playing reveals their view of sex and gender as acts of performance and their interest in appropriating them for their power games. What is at stake in their employment of the cultural constructions of the jealous husband, the betraying wife, the vain actor, the nurturing woman, and so on, is a struggle for power in the couple and, more positively, a search for a workable script that can be used as the basis for a relationship which exists in society but which uses social norms as part of the script rather than as laws by which to abide. That Maria is the more accomplished player of the two is beyond doubt, even though Josef displays an unexpected degree of adaptability to his wife's wishes which, ultimately, saves the relationship and the social and sexual configuration that the film's comic space protects. This configuration sees Maria as the centre of the family, and is formed by an affectionate relationship with her husband which is based on a series of well-rehearsed but flexible performances, and an understanding that her desire must not be impaired.

II. Romantic comedy in no man's land: *Kiss Me, Stupid*

To Be or Not to Be is important from the perspective of romantic comedy because of the liminal position it occupies between two moments of the genre's Hollywood history. *Kiss Me, Stupid*, a movie that was as controversial on its release as Lubitsch's but, unlike it, subsequently failed to achieve the status of masterpiece, may also represent the end of an era but hardly the beginning of a new one.

Romantic comedy in the 1950s

What was the situation of the genre in the 1950s? If the 1940s remain underrepresented in film comedy criticism, there is no short-age of excellent accounts of the following decade. Both Neale and Krutnik (Neale and Krutnik, 1990: 169–71; Krutnik, 1990: 58–62) and Jeffers McDonald (2005: 38–58) choose the so-called sex com-edies as most representative of the period, accurately establishing a contrast with the 1930s. Babington and Evans's study, on the other hand, reflects some of the complexity of the period by refer-ring not only to the Doris Day cycle of the end of the decade but also to the Tracy–Hepburn series (as much part of the 1940s as of the 1950s), the Billy Wilder farces, the 'B' family comedies directed by Douglas Sirk at Universal in the early 1950s and, less interest-ingly for these authors, the lush romantic comedies characterised by glamorous European locations and high production values (1989: 179–266). Ed Sikov, from his auteurist perspective, adds to the list important films by Howard Hawks, Frank Tashlin and Alfred Hitchcock that had been overlooked by the earlier critics (1994).

As in the case of the 1930s, many of these cycles went on after the end of the decade (the Doris Day sex comedies do not get under way until the end of the 1950s and continue uninterruptedly during the first half of the 1960s) but by the mid 1960s it was obvious that all the comic trends that had developed in the last two decades had virtually ground to a halt and there was nothing to replace them. In this sense, the box-office and critical failure of *Kiss Me, Stupid* may have been due less to the controversy that surrounded its opening and to the boycott it suffered, as the received critical opinion goes (see Sikov, 1998: 478–96), than to the fact that the genre was moving fast into the dearth which would years later lead Brian Henderson to announce its death (1978). Not that *Kiss Me, Stupid* can be said to be out of touch with its time or to be a back-ward looking film, but the future that it envisaged, rather like the sexual utopia represented in *To Be or Not to Be*, was a future that would never find a place in mainstream Hollywood cinema. The film's apparent message – that a marriage can be revitalised through the partners' infidelities, that the roles of wife and prostitute can also be sites of wish-fulfilment fantasy for women, and that women's sexual desire can be stronger and narratively more interesting than men's – was not only ahead of its time but, to a very great extent, also ahead of our own time. We may now recognise that the film's sexual discourses look forward to the future but by the time that future re-emerged within the genre, it looked very unlike the one this movie had predicted or fantasised about fifteen years before. In this sense, it can be surmised that *Kiss Me, Stupid* is a film without a proper place in history.

The crisis of romantic comedy was probably difficult to predict in 1964. Doris Day and Rock Hudson had been the darlings of the box office since the beginning of the sixties and films like *That Touch of Mink* (1962), *Lover Come Back* (1962), *The Thrill of It All* (1963), *Move Over Darling* (1963), *Man's Favorite Sport?*, *Under the Yum Yum Tree* (1963), *Sex and the Single Girl* (1964) or *Send Me No Flowers* (1964) seemed to suggest, on the surface, that the genre was alive and well. In a more openly satirical vein, Billy Wilder had enjoyed uninterrupted success with *Some Like It Hot, The Apartment, One, Two, Three* (1961) and even the love story between a prostitute and a cop-turned-pimp, *Irma La Douce* (1963). Wilder's positioning of sex at the centre of most of his comedies of the time, and its only slightly less overt importance in the rest of the films mentioned above, is a logical consequence of the cultural saliency of sex and sexuality in the 1950s, a saliency that has been sufficiently documented by sociologists, film scholars, and romantic comedy specialists (Seidman, 1991 and 1992; Dyer, 1986; Babington and Evans, 1989; Krutnik, 1990). This interest in sex increased at the beginning of the 1960s and would eventually lead to the so-called sexual revolution.

For the time being, however, the revolution had not yet arrived although institutional and cultural norms – including cinematic ones – with respect to sex were increasingly felt to be badly out-dated. For example, demands for the relaxation of censorship regarding female nudity were becoming more and more pressing: while Rudi Gernreich is making a furore with his topless bathing suits for women, producer Martin Ransohoff of MGM calls for an end of the ban on nudity in the cinema following the removal of some topless scenes from *The Americanisation of Emily* (1964), but shortly afterwards *The Pawnbroker* (1965) displays some naked female breasts for the first time in mainstream Hollywood films. The central female character of the third James Bond film, *Goldfinger* (1963), is called Pussy Galore (Honor Blackman) and Hollywood stars like Elizabeth Taylor, Kim Novak, Carol Lynley or Stella Stevens begin to appear naked in the pages of *Playboy* to the dismay, among others, of the newly renamed National Catholic Office of Motion Pictures (formerly the Legion of Decency). Billy Wilder may have misfired spectacularly by planning his film as a 1964 Christmas release, but his open and sympathetic treatment of sex, prostitution and adultery in *Kiss Me, Stupid* was, at least in theory, very much in tune with the *Zeitgeist*.

The film's resonant failure, on the other hand, may be proof that, while the cultural consideration of sex was changing very fast, romantic comedy as a genre was still not ready to incorporate such changes to its conventions. Jeffers McDonald explains the end of the sex-comedy cycle as a consequence of the ready availability of the contraceptive pill, which made the withholding of sex until marriage suddenly obsolete. Romantic comedy was, according to her, not yet willing to incorporate 'young women successfully shedding [their] virginity' (2007: 43). The *innuendo* and *double entendre* that the genre had revelled and excelled in from the beginning of its history now seemed inappropriate to a franker treatment of, especially female, sexuality. Henderson, writing about the decade that followed Wilder's film, suggests precisely the linguistic openness towards sex that can be found in a film like *Semi-Tough* (1972) as one of the reasons for the decadence of the genre in that period (1978: 22). The constant sexual references in *Kiss Me, Stupid* stand somewhere on the borderline between *double entendre* and explicitness, what Krutnik calls 'aggressive innuendo' (1990: 61). Thus they satisfy neither the taste for subtlety of traditional Aristotelian comedy nor the need for sexual openness that the sexual revolution would demand, and leave the film in a kind of no man's land, too offensive for some, too tame for others. Or it could be said that Wilder and I.A.L. Diamond use a traditional comic form in order to convey what they consider a contemporary attitude. The genre as an institution – that is, as a phenomenon which includes not only texts and changing conventions but also an industrial and cultural context, the audience and the critics – cannot contain their experiment, demanding either a less problematic continuity with the comic tradition or a more drastic rupture which in the mid-1960s it was still too early to bring about. The critical and audience failure of the film represents, in sum, an important moment in the history of the relationship between Hollywood romantic comedy and the cultural discourses it addresses.

Satire and comedy

The low cultural and academic status of comedy has already been noted here. Satire has often managed to escape this generalised attitude because of its seriousness of purpose, and the anger and aggressiveness that it sometimes conveys. This characteristic stern-ness allows it to dissociate itself from comedy even though, since Aristophanes, the vast majority of satire has remained within comic boundaries. Sikov, without explicitly describing *Kiss Me, Stupid* as a satire, performs a similar operation when, in order to 'save' the film from the ferocious attacks it has received, he argues that 'its tone is so consistently depressing, its vision so assiduously dispir-ited, and its jokes so relentlessly bad, that the malaise it engenders in its audience becomes a kind of triumph' (1998: 479). Unlike this critic, I would like to argue that an appeal to seriousness, sadness and a depressing and dispirited vision is not necessary to appreciate a text artistically and culturally, and that, in the case of *Kiss Me, Stupid*, the satirical impulse exists wholly within the realm of comedy, *along with* the seriousness of purpose. More centrally for the main argument of this book, satire proves to be, as in *To Be or Not to Be*, not only compatible with romantic comedy but also crucial for the creation of its comic space. In other words, satire is not only often a close neighbour of romantic comedy, as has already been discussed, but can be used in combination with it in comic texts in order to enhance their romantic potential. In *Kiss Me, Stupid* romantic comedy articulates the utopian vision that the satire finds missing in the movie's social world, while satire proves to be an integral component in the construction of that vision. By highlighting the compatibility between both genres, this film sug-gests that there is always a potential satire lurking behind the sexual fantasies of romantic comedy.

In his theoretical account of film satire, Geoff King betrays a similar bias to that present in Sikov's analysis of Wilder's film. For him, satire is 'comedy with an edge and a target'. Yet when won-dering why use comedy in order to attack social vices or corruption, he argues that satire has an unstable quality, ranging from 'safer' comic forms to darker realms beyond the comic. Really cutting satire is relatively rare in mainstream cinema because comedy tends to 'pull the punches' (2002: 93–4). That is, the truly interesting satire, the dark, cutting edge one, is rarely comic. Comic satire tends to be 'safer', not completely honest, not genuine, not radical – not angry or not depressing – enough. King takes his inspiration from Northrop Frye, who finds in the mythos of winter (as in the other three) six different phases, three of which are closer to comedy and another three nearer tragedy. Yet Frye reminds us elsewhere that there are two basic elements in satire: an object of attack, on the one hand, and wit or humour founded on fantasy or a sense of the grotesque and the absurd, on the other (1957: 224). That is, although as his phases come closer to tragedy they become more serious, the first three phases are for Frye, precisely because of their use of humour, truly representative of the mythos, the other three being more marginal, less satirical. Satire's favourite procedure for the attack of its target is ridicule – of a person, a social class or a cultural norm – in order to make it laughable, and if in classical authors like Ben Jonson, Swift or Dryden satire may become stern and even violent, its comic tone is hardly ever absent from view.

Frye also defines satire as 'militant irony' (223) and this is related to his notion that the genre always has a standard of correct morality or social normality against which to measure deviations, vices and corruptions. While the moral standard in irony may often be ambivalent, satire's moral norms are always relatively clear, yet the two forms often work together in texts, confirming once and again satire's comic tendencies. Take, for example, one of the most popular satirical novels of the nineteenth century, William Thackeray's *Vanity Fair*. The narrator often uses his licence to separate himself from the characters and discuss them as fictional characters in direct address to the reader, but, in his extremely and even fiercely ironic stance, we often doubt whether we should trust his words and take them at face value. Consider the following passage:

> And, as we bring our characters forward, I will ask leave, as a man and a brother, not only to introduce them, but occasionally to step down from the platform, and talk about them [. . .]. Otherwise you might fancy it was I who was sneering at the practice of devotion,

which Miss Sharp finds so ridiculous; that it was I who laughed
good-humouredly at the reeling old Silenus of a baronet – whereas
the laughter comes from one who has no reverence except for pros-
perity, and no eye for anything beyond success. (1968: 117)

There is no need for much narrative context to realise that this
narrator, in spite of his words, is indeed laughing *with* his protagonist, Becky Sharp, both at the hypocrisy of the aristocrat's family
and at the baronet himself, and including them within his satire.
The customs of the country gentry, as well as those of several other
strata of nineteenth-century English society, are the constant target
of the novel's satire, and an ironic narrator, who conveys the exact
opposite meaning from what he states, as well as an ironic protagonist, are consistently used to ridicule the author's multiple social
targets. This does not mean that the narrative prompts the reader
to identify with the protagonist, either. Becky is consistently, one
would say even obsessively, attacked in her behaviour, as a character with no moral scruples and a woman with no feelings, in what
we might today read as the author's desperate and useless attempt
to prevent the almost certain sympathy of future generations of
readers. Her intelligence, resourcefulness and relentless ironic stance
do not save her from severe criticism and narrative punishment, her
meek counterpart Amelia Sedley coming much closer, in her silent
suffering and forbearance, to being a point of identification and
moral model for the reader. Yet, Becky's character and actions
constitute the main channel for the satire of the novel, a satire in
which irony becomes one of its main tools.

Vanity Fair represents an obvious template for *Kiss Me, Stupid*
(as well as for much twentieth-century satire) in its use of comic
forms and in it, as in Wilder's film, irony and satire function closely
together. This is most obvious in the development of the character
of Orville J. Spooner (Ray Walston). Initially the traditional *senex*,
the pathologically jealous old husband, Orville is the easy butt of
ridicule or *alazon*, but the spectator's attitude towards him may
change as the target of the film's satire becomes more complex and
far-reaching. We will come back to Orville later on but in order to
understand his narrative function and that of the other main characters we must start by ascertaining what exactly is the butt of the
film's satirical impulse.

Unlike in many illustrious precedents in European theatre and
narrative, old jealous husbands are not the main object of attack

here. Orville is never really criticised for having married Zelda (Felicia Farr), a much younger woman. In fact, by the standards of the Hollywood cinema of the time, the age difference between them is practically average (above average would be, for example, the thirty-year gap between the Humphrey Bogart and Audrey Hepburn romantic lovers in Wilder's *Sabrina* [1954], or the twenty-eight-year gap between Gary Cooper and, again, Hepburn in *Love in the Afternoon* [1957]) and the film never insists on this point. Marriage as an institution is not an obvious target, either, since the text does not suggest that it brings about the death of love or that it has become the representative of a repressive, hypocritical or corrupt society – if we exclude, that is, the scene with Zelda's parents. But theirs is a very traditional, excessively socialised union. As in *To Be or Not to Be*, the type of marriage that the film envisages as its moral norm is not incompatible with sexual experimentation and fantasy, and occasional infidelity is presented as a healthy way of solving a marriage crisis. It is, therefore, dominant moral standards regarding marriage and patriarchal gender politics that come under attack.

Capitalist ambition, in its readiness to prostitute even marriage, is perhaps a clearer object of ridicule, but even here those who are guilty of it are never really punished. While Orville is always half-hearted about the plot to trick Dino (Dean Martin) into buying his songs, Barney (Cliff Osmond), a more openly venal character, finally achieves the success he yearned for. Not only is there no hint of a comeuppance for him but, in a narrative move which has perplexed the critics, he becomes in fact Zelda's ally in her chastisement of her husband in the final part of the movie. It is not so much that his and Orville's behaviour are condoned as that capitalism is this time not the text's main target. The 'honour' of being the main object of the film's invective is left to the type of sexuality that was quickly becoming contested in the surrounding culture but which still fared strongly in dominant discourses: late Victorian middle-class small-town sexual discourses, which defended the exclusivity of marriage, the sanctity of female sexuality and wholesale repression, a discourse scathingly represented in the film by the well-meaning grapefruit-loving vicar and the committee of comically repressed married women who go around asking for signatures to close down the Belly Button. More specifically, the sexual double standard comes under heavy fire in a text whose radical defence of gender equality in sexual matters did not do it any favours, either, in a sexist society which the impending sexual revolution never fought to reverse as clearly as this film did. It is primarily in this social space constituted by competing sexual discourses that *Kiss Me, Stupid* displays its complex satire.

Moral standards and character identification

Polly (Kim Novak) and Zelda always command the spectator's sympathy, although not necessarily for the same reasons. Like Irma la Douce (Shirley MacLaine) before her, Polly the Pistol is the prostitute with a good heart and the text soon engages in a full-length account of the road that led her to her present state to ensure the spectator's understanding of her 'essential purity'. In Novak's performance, she constitutes the most unambiguous point of identification for the spectator and, in the long central scene at the Spooner household, she 'rescues' Orville from satirical attack and farcical ridicule, humanising him and facilitating spectatorial identification with him. Her dream of leaving Climax and becoming a wife may seem suspect from the point of view of gender equality but it is partly offset by the text's espousing of Zelda's infidelity. The temporary exchange of roles between the two women turns the characters into elements of a formal pattern with ideological connotations: the fact that the wife becomes a prostitute for one night while the prostitute becomes a wife suggests that there are no moral hierarchies between them and that the roles of prostitute and wife are interchangeable, not so much, as second-wave feminists would argue, because marriage is a form of prostitution for women but rather because they are both social roles with their own attached sexual fantasies. Neither of them is final or irreversible, neither is more morally reprehensible than the other and both are equally celebrated by the text. *Kiss Me, Stupid* does not only satirise the social repression of (particularly female) sexuality but, from the perspective of romantic comedy, it liberates sex from its institutional dimension and places it in the space of fantasy.

Zelda is a more complex case than Polly: while initially appearing to be just a narrative function of her husband's jealousy and inadequacy, and therefore the secondary and colourless female counterpart of traditional marriage comedy, she gradually comes into her own through her unremitting resistance to Orville's inexplicable behaviour and, particularly, in the final-reel fulfilment of her fantasy of spending the night with Dino, the idol of her high-school years. Her centrality after the trailer scene suggests that her tryst with Dino is not just a punishment of Orville's jealousy and, especially, of his agreement to 'sell his wife', but a positive stand-point from which to measure her society's sexual habits and norms. From this position she becomes the clearest mouthpiece of the satirical text, the moral standard to be followed – a standard which was perhaps too difficult to accept in 1964, especially because Zelda never gives an explanation for her actions. The text demands that we see her behaviour not as a deviation, certainly not as a vice, but as a viable alternative to dominant discourses on women's sexual habits.

The complication in terms of identification with the character comes because her night with Dino occurs as a consequence of her husband's reprehensible behaviour and, especially, of the singer's unadulterated machismo. In the scene of their sexual encounter the spectator is expected to close off her/his awareness of the identity of the man and concentrate solely on the woman's position, or, to put it differently, to celebrate Zelda's defeat of her inhibitions while continuing to abhor Dino's treatment of women. It is a delicate narrative balance which demands a simultaneity of apparently con-tradictory subject positions on the part of the spectator, not dis-similar from how Thackeray's narrator expects the reader to respond to Becky's 'sneering' at her surrounding society: against the dominant morality of its time (and, to a large extent, that of the early twenty-first century also), we are asked to not only under-stand but also celebrate and enjoy Zelda's extramarital fling while at the same time condemning Dino as a sexist predator. Ultimately, Dean Martin's character is, like, say, Horner in Wycherley's *Country Wife*, more a fallen angel sent by the narrative to expose the vices of the Climax society than a convincing 'autonomous' character. This is the reason why he is never punished by the film, in spite of his abominable behaviour. In any case, by the time his encounter with Zelda is over, *Kiss Me, Stupid* has already sufficiently estab-lished its satirical standpoint and has shifted gear, using, as will be shown below, its attack on the sexual mores of its social space as the solid foundation of the magic space of romantic comedy.

Orville, for his part, embodies better than no other character the film's ironic ambivalence and its extreme demands on the audience. After the first few minutes, in which he comically accuses the milkman, his teenage piano pupil and even Barney of having an affair with his wife, we soon realise, as he reluctantly puts into practice his partner's plan to sell their songs to Dino, that, like the text and like the spectator, he is at all times aware of the immorality of his behaviour and feels guilty about it. When he finally decides to behave like a human being and throw the famous singer out of his house, thus apparently jeopardising his last chance to sell his songs, the spectators realise that we have been gradually coming closer to him and recognising ourselves in him, not only in his weaknesses but also in his growing courage and sensibility. His moral and personal growth, achieved during the central set piece of the evening meal with Dino and Polly, in the course of which he comes to realise the impossibility of accepting Dino's and his own behaviour and to respect women, definitely turns him, with the help of Polly, into a strong figure of identification. But then, after getting rid of the singer, he invites his pretend wife to go to bed with him, thus contravening received moral standards. At first it may be hard for the spectator to accept that this moment represents the alternative proposed by the text to the venality, hypocrisy and sexism that it has previously exposed. It is a moment in which the spectator radically hesitates about the extent of her/his distance from the character. As he opens the door to his bedroom and lets Polly/ 'Zelda' in we wonder whether we should stay outside the door criticising his infidelity, or go all the way with him and accept his behaviour, thus placing ourselves on the wrong side of dominant views of marriage. Our decision, however hard, is facilitated by Zelda's parallel behaviour but by this time we have already come to realise that in order to appreciate this film's satire we need to be ready to occupy a position which most films would not dare offer the spectator. We may also have realised that satire in *Kiss Me, Stupid* is not an end in itself but, rather, the scaffolding for the construction of a powerful comic romantic narrative.

Climaxing in Climax

Ginette Vincendeau has argued that comedy as a genre is both mimetic of social reality and distanced from it through exaggeration and performance (2001: 24). By performance she means the actor's rendering of a fictional character but we have already seen that a related type of performance, that of social or sexual roles, is also central to romantic comedy, as is proven not only by the plot of

5 'Coming Mrs. Spooner?': marriage as fantasy in *Kiss Me, Stupid*,
starring Kim Novak and Ray Walston (dir. Billy Wilder, 1964,
Lopert, MGM)

To Be or Not to Be but by the conventions of role reversal and
mistakes of identity familiar to the genre since Shakespeare and
before. In romantic comedy, the distance from reality is provided
by the creation of the comic space, a space in which sexual and
affective scenarios are more or less freely played out by the characters, but, as Thomas argues, this space is superimposed on the
social space and transforms it (2000: 14, 21). Yet, it might be added
that the transformation is never so thorough that the spectator
forgets the presence of the social space. In romantic comedy both
the social and the comic space, cultural discourses and fantasy,
remain separate but very close to one another. It is the recognition
of this simultaneity of duality and proximity that attracts the spectator to the genre's specificity. This simultaneity is particularly
striking in *Kiss Me, Stupid*. The character of Dino and his remarkable similarities to the actor that plays him, his journey from Las
Vegas – where he has just finished a professional engagement – to
Hollywood, his drinking and womanising, the references to the Rat
Pack and the Beatles among others, place the not so fictional
Climax (there may be no Climax in Nevada but, according to *The
Britannica Atlas* there are four Climaxes in the U.S. plus one in
Canada) as close to a recognisable U.S. location as is possible in
fiction, a place as remote from the well-trodden track between the
two great centres of entertainment as the Bates Motel had been

from the main road a few years before. At the same time, however, the characters' increasingly unexpected attitudes towards received sexual discourses and their ability to embody alternative discourses without any negative consequences soon alert the spectator to the fantastic overtones of the place. This persuasively constructed double ontology turns Climax into the ideal physical and meta-phorical space of a romantic comedy directly concerned with sex and sexual discourses.

The film is based on the Italian play *L'ora della fantasia* (2001), written by Anna Bonacci in 1944 and previously adapted to the screen by Mario Camerini with the title *Moglie per una notte* (1952). The original's title already underlines the importance of fantasy both in the play and in the two films, yet it is in Wilder's movie that sexual fantasy occupies a most central position. *Moglie per una notte* engagingly transfers the action of Bonacci's play from Victorian England to nineteenth-century Parma but it is otherwise very close to the original in its deployment of sexual discourses: Enrico (Armando Francioli), the young musician, lusts after Geraldine (Nadia Gray), the experienced courtesan, from the moment he sees her. His desire is seen by the film as no more than evidence of his immaturity, while Geraldine yearns after the simple life that Enrico and his petit-bourgeois household represent, but remains too detached throughout to succumb to any wish-fulfilment fantasy. Enrico's wife, Ottavia (Gina Lollobrigida), for her part, is the faithful wife whose disappointment at her husband's adolescent behaviour never even tempts her to indulge in extra-marital sexual fantasy. Instead, with the help of Geraldine, she uses her husband's jealousy to win him back. Camerini's film, while stressing the female perspective, works as a more conventional mar-riage farce in which sexual fantasy is only represented indirectly by the potentialities of the various sexual scenarios and never directly through the characters' actions. The romantic comedy of the film lies in the final triumph of love over jealousy and professional ambi-tion, and the comic space provided by the reconstruction of a fairy-tale past protects a love that remains opposed to unbridled sexual desire.

Apart from the easy transformation of Lollobrigida's Ottavia from ugly duckling to beautiful swan and her husband's subsequent surprise and rekindled desire for her (and the female star's very presence in the cast, representing a new, explosive type of post-war

female sexuality), there is little in Camerini's film that evokes the
healthy connotations of sex that were then beginning to constitute
an emergent discourse in both U.S. and some European societies.
Twelve years later, Wilder's movie turns that emergent discourse
into its central ideology and represents it through a very different
comic space, the space of romantic comedy. The geographical isolation of Climax facilitates the transformation that the story under-
goes when Dino takes a detour from the highway and precipitates
unexpected developments in the little town's sexual scenarios. As
his presence among the locals confirms his larger-than-life rakish
behaviour and brings to the open their miseries and hypocrisies, the
spectator may not be prepared for the generic shift that the town's
name, if nothing else, had already anticipated with the film's usual
'aggressive innuendo'. Indeed, this generic shift remained invisible
for most critics who were not able to see beyond the film's satirical
content: 'A stop-and-start sex farce that is sometimes funny and
sometimes isn't' (Powers 1964: 3); 'a comedy of pimpmanship
[which] cuts to the moral quick of American ambition' (Durgnat,
1965: 27). Later authors, in monographic books on Wilder, have
not been able to redress the balance: 'at the dawn of the sexual
revolution, Wilder set out to make sex seem filthy again' (Sikov,
1998: 479); 'less morally outrageous than aesthetically crude'
(Armstrong, 2000: 109); 'a bawdy comedy, in the manner of the
Restoration theater, which would satirize some American preoccu-
pations with sex' (Lemon, 2001: 40). Only Richard Lippe, in an
early reappraisal of the film, called attention to its blend of satire
and fantasy and wondered why earlier critics could only see morally
repulsive, sordid realism where there was, more importantly, 'a
strong romantic spirit [. . .] which carries [the film] beyond day-to-
day reality and casts a suspended enchantment over the action'
(1971/72: 34).

Without theorising it, Lippe assumes a very similar theory of
comedy to that put forward in this book. The drab day-to-day
reality of Climax and of the entertainment industry represented by
Dino is the object of the film's satire, but as the action develops,
the 'spirit' or romantic comedy transforms the story, recasting the
sexual and affective discourses it defends under the benevolent
atmosphere of the genre. This transformation takes place very
gradually during the central scene of the film – the evening for three
at the Spooner household, in which, following the advice of his

song-writing partner Barney, Orville hires hooker Polly to replace his wife Zelda so that he can offer her sexually to Dino as a way to get him interested in their songs. The description of the set-up suggests almost endless possibilities for satire in a film which has already spent its first hour relentlessly attacking both the society of Climax and the Vegas and Hollywood star, particularly in the objectification of women by men and the prostitution of moral principles for the sake of social success and material wealth. This is the warped version of the American Dream which the spectator of Wilder's comedies had already been familiar with for over a decade. As the scene develops, the film's focus on the roles played by the two men – the reckless womaniser and the obliging husband – guarantees generic consistency with what had gone before, while the growing concentration on the substitute wife announces melo-dramatic interpolations of the type already featured a few years before in *The Apartment*.

Yet, Novak's performance and the film's general take on prosti-tution, not as a fall from grace but as a socially significant but morally neutral profession, ensure that pathos and pity are not among the options offered the spectator. Rather, both the script and the star's performance enhance a more comic potential of the scenario: the role playing and mistakes of identity of romantic comedy. As Viola becomes Cesario and Rosalind becomes Ganymede in the Shakespearean stories, Polly, the prostitute, becomes Zelda, the married woman, for a night. From a satirical perspective this enforced performance would have allowed the film to continue its denunciation of moral squalor, but the film now chooses a romantic comic perspective, in which the character is given the chance to play out a sexual and social fantasy. Through the satire of the first half, the film has established its ideological position with respect to sexual desire and the role it plays (and should play) in society. Now that position is used as a starting point from which the same discourses will be positively presented through the conventional deployment of the comic space. Polly's enthusiasm is such that, once Dino has been thrown out of the family house, she drags Orville into joining her in her fantasy. Now they are not playing parts for a third party anymore but only for themselves and each other. Now the film is not satirising society any longer but allowing the two characters to drop their inhibitions and play out a sexual scenario characteristic of the genre.

Bang, bang

The scene fades out on Orville inviting the substitute Mrs. Spooner
to go to bed with him, and the spectator remains outside, wondering, as has been pointed out before, whether, given the male character's recent record, to criticise him for taking advantage of the
situation or forget our moral scruples and join in the fantasy. The
critics predictably took the former option, a path that led them
nowhere in moral terms. Yet the film clearly prefers the latter, if
we take into account what happens next: while Orville and Polly
spend the night as husband and wife, Zelda impersonates Polly the
Pistol in her caravan when Dino lands there on the rebound still
looking for action – not the filmic action enjoyed by Polly's Western-
obsessed parrot but nevertheless one that can be summarised by the
same words: 'Bang, bang'. A greater transgression by the patriarchal moral standards of the mid-1960s, the singer's seduction of
the wife cannot be explained by his consistently abominable behaviour with women or by her drunkenness as much as by the woman's
willingness to indulge her teenage fantasy when the opportunity
unexpectedly presents itself. Since it would be inconsistent with
what had gone before to understand this climactic (in more ways
than one) episode within the generic boundaries of satire, the scene
confirms that the film has definitively abandoned this mode and
replaced it by a romantic comedy that does not celebrate, as in the
case of Camerini's earlier version, received versions of romantic
and/or married love but rather the importance of sexual fantasy in
stable relationships.

'How can there be romance in a world of bodily functions?',
wonders Sikov, adding that the comedy has an unpleasant aroma
(1998: 489–90). Yet, as has been seen, Western cultural discourses
on love and marriage had been moving relentlessly towards a more
sexualised form of love in which not only was sexual pleasure
an essential component of happy marriages but sex was being
seen increasingly as a healthy pursuit in itself, a discourse which
would eventually incorporate the concept of 'recreational sex'
(Seidman, 1991). *Kiss Me, Stupid*, in its articulation of sexual
fantasy as an important ingredient of a healthy marriage, may have
been ahead of its time as far as filmic representations of the genre
were concerned but it does, nevertheless, narrativise perfectly recognisable and growingly prestigious emergent discourses of its time.
Hollywood romantic comedy had been gradually moving towards

a franker acknowledgement of sexuality in heterosexual relationships and the growing complexity of its links with the concept of
romantic love, yet it did not seem ready to incorporate the positive
representation of sex that can be found, for example, in some
Ingmar Bergman comedies of the 1950s, especially his Shakespeare-
inspired *Smiles of a Summer Night* (*Sommarnattens leende*, 1955).
The so-called 'sex comedies' used the uprightness of stars like
Doris Day to label male sexual desire as reckless womanising
and to repress female desire under social respectability, and Wilder
had previously joined the ranks by ridiculing the married man's
sexual fantasy in *The Seven-Year Itch* (1955) and by offering
a relentlessly grim view of sex as commerce in *The Apartment*.
Even *Some Like It Hot*, a film in which an openly sexual scenario
– the night Sugar Kane (Marilyn Monroe) and Joe (Tony Curtis)
spend on the yacht – becomes the starting point of what might
turn into a stable relationship, seems ambiguous and leaves too
many questions unanswered about its attitude to sex with its
famous open ending. Perhaps Howard Hawks, by adapting his
screwball origins to modern cultural changes, succeeds best at
incorporating sexual desire into notions of heterosexual romance
and marriage in such films as *I Was a Male War Bride*, *Monkey
Business* (1952), *Gentlemen Prefer Blondes* or *Man's Favorite
Sport?*

Sex had, of course, been the subject of comedy for centuries but,
after Shakespeare, it had been gradually displaced away from
romantic comedy and had found its natural space in satire. Meanwhile, sex had been gaining cultural visibility and prominence
ever since the end of the nineteenth century and had become, after
the end of World War II, an important concern in U.S. society
and, therefore, as Richard Dyer has cogently argued, also in
Hollywood films (1986: 23–42). 1950s romantic comedy had
acknowledged this centrality and had brought the discourses of
sexuality and the concept of romance as close as they had ever been,
but it was still reluctant to openly welcome sexual desire under the
protection of its comic space. Steven Seidman argues that, while the
sexualisation of love had been a long process and was not restricted
to the 'sexual revolution' of the 1960s, what this decade brought
about in sexual matters was the defence of sexual choice, variation
and pleasure, greater challenges to the heterosexual, romantic and
marital norms, and the legitimation of the body as a site of sensual

pleasure (1992: 45). Satire's traditional link of sexual desire with deception, hypocrisy, the crisis of marriage and the double standard, and its usual deployment of these sexual discourses in marriage comedy, was not the most appropriate way to tackle this emergent discourse, but there was, of course, still much to satirise in traditional attitudes to sex. Yet *Kiss Me, Stupid*, instead of adopting a satirical approach to sexual desire and presenting it as sordid, dirty and exclusively masculine, offers a more positive view, in tune with contemporaneous cultural discourses, and, consequently, abandons satire as a way of representing sex. Romantic comedy provides the logical alternative and, within its comic space, the critique of the double standard and of women's repression becomes the starting point of a celebration of sex as healthy, socially acceptable and conducive, in unexpected ways, to conjugal happiness. In generic terms, satire is not simply replaced by romantic comedy, but, rather, the latter succeeds the former and can only be articulated on the basis of the satirical structure it eventually overcomes.

Alexandre Trauner's sets contribute significantly to this generic hybridity, the realism of the representation of the social background of Climax subtly shoring up the magic spaces that the Spooners' home, Polly's caravan and, finally, the street outside the television shop gradually become. However, it is more spectacularly the filmic construction of Zelda's face that underlines the possibility of transcendence conjured up by the genre. Two tracking shots to a close-up of Felicia Farr's face in the film's final moments mark the transition to a world of sexual fantasy that is protected by the space of comedy. The first one takes place when Zelda realises that her visitor in Polly's trailer is no other than Dino, the idol of her teenage years, and her initial shock at the possibility of one of Polly's customers treating her as a prostitute is replaced first by a curiosity mixed with wonder and then by a growing willingness to bring her fantasy to fruition. The combination of the actress's performance and the frame movement confirm the film's intention: to protect and fulfil female sexual desire and turn it into an object of celebration rather than repression. This is a characteristic moment of the genre in which the comic space becomes visible.

The second time this stylistic option is taken comes in the film's penultimate shot. As Dino's live performance of 'Sophia' on the television continues to be heard in the background, a two-shot of

6 'Kiss me, stupid': Zelda's face and the comic space. Felicia Farr in *Kiss Me, Stupid* (dir. Billy Wilder, 1964, Lopert, MGM)

Zelda and Orville frames their reconciliation even though the husband still does not know what is going on. As in Shakespeare's comedies, the character not only comes to accept but also embraces the wonder and mystery of human relationships and this marks the culmination of the transformation of his identity into a more tolerant, mature and – hopefully – sexually confident human being. An earlier moment, when he is alone in the house after his wife has left him, finds Orville longingly looking at Zelda's dummy, in a not dissimilar way from Dino's earlier look, suggesting that, after his night with Polly, Orville is finally ready to learn to see his wife as a sexual being. Now Zelda, who had already undergone a similar process, but one which included a specifically feminine liberation of her hitherto repressed sexuality, has stayed silent, waiting for her husband to finish, while the widescreen format has kept the two characters onscreen in virtual close-up. Once Orville runs out of unanswered questions – 'how would you?, when did she?, why would he?' –, Zelda utters the film's famous final line: 'Kiss me, stupid.' Repeating the previous tracking shot, the frame moves now to an extreme close-up of the woman's smiling face, the night time lighting and the crooning music in the background contributing to the articulation of a space as thoroughly transformed as ever in the genre.

That this is practically the film's final shot suggests that it is in the space signified by Zelda's expression that the characters are to stay, the return to society traditionally predicated by the genre only acceptable if the fantasy scenario so spectacularly represented remains forever in place. With Dino safe and sound in his preferred Hollywood environment, Barney unpunished for his mendacity cheerfully signing autographs just offscreen, Polly finally driving away, having managed to purchase a car with the money Dino paid her replacement for one night, and the married couple happily reconciled in spite of their infidelities, this is as far as can be from the satirical mode in which the film started. It is precisely the length of this journey from satire to romantic comedy that makes the film significant from a generic point of view. The particular combination of the two genres described here provides an important insight into the changing role of sex in romantic discourses, a changing role that in Hollywood terms proved too drastic for critics and audiences in 1964.

Comic combinations

The analyses of *To Be or Not to Be* and *Kiss Me, Stupid* have explored the presence in specific texts of romantic comedy in combination with other comic genres, particularly satire. The two selected films are very useful for this type of analysis because of their historically significant position, closing in both cases what historians have seen as the two most productive periods of Hollywood romantic comedy. Perhaps the kind of precarious historical position occupied by the two texts lends itself to departures from the norm and rejections of generic purity more readily than when the films are more 'safely' located at the peak of the popularity of a given genre. At the same time, it is, as has been seen, this generic instability that allows them to articulate more forcefully the conventions of the genre and to explore its meanings and discourses, by placing them side by side with other conventions. It is not that these films are representative in their extreme hybridity of how romantic comedy generally works. There is little doubt that many other films use the conventions of the genre in 'purer' but equally interesting ways. Rather, the theoretical perspective proposed here allows us to account for *all* texts in a more consistent way, to acknowledge the frequency of the presence of conventions belonging to different genres in a great many individual texts, and to treat such cases not as exceptional, radical or transgressive but, rather, as historically significant.

In the case of romantic comedy, the ideological uniformity generally found by critics is, as I have argued before, more a consequence of a narrowing in critical definitions and conceptualisations than of empirical observation. As these two texts show, the combination of its central tenets with other comic conventions almost immediately contradicts the determinism ascribed to the genre previously. Additionally, the study of filmic texts as blends of various comic genres solves oft-rehearsed taxonomical problems: a text does not have to be, for example, a romantic comedy, a marriage comedy, a satire or a farce – it can be all of them at the same time. While the term comedy may ultimately prove too large and unwieldy for the study of film genre, the constant crisscrossing and overlapping of other generic terms proves to be nothing but a logical consequence of the fact that all genres crisscross and overlap in the texts, as well as a corollary of the relentless historical fluctuation of all generic configurations.

To Be or Not to Be and *Kiss Me, Stupid* are not romantic comedies but use the conventions of the genre in significant ways. As I have argued here, in Wilder's film romantic comedy eventually becomes the dominant genre, satire remaining an essential generic ingredient precisely in so far as it is finally superseded, whereas in Lubitsch's film there is a greater balance between the various comic genres. In both cases, the different genres feed off each other and contribute a degree of textual complexity to which conceptualisations of genres as groups of films and of films as belonging to specific genres do not have access. Both films additionally illustrate the low cultural and academic status of romantic comedy. *To Be or Not to Be* became part of the canon as one of the most brilliant comedies in the history of Hollywood in so far as its romantic comedy elements remained invisible. *Kiss Me, Stupid* was almost universally rejected because its satire was too base, too obscene, too vulgar, or because its satirical view of love, sex and marriage was too hard to take. Romantic comedy had no share in the success of the former or in the resonant failure of the latter. It may be the critical fate of the genre that, in combination with other genres, it becomes invisible, and it is only when the happy ending coincides with or can be interpreted as a defence of a conservative view of heterosexual romance that romantic comedy is allowed to shine forth . . . if only to be immediately chastised for its conservativeness. If this is the situation when romantic comedy appears in combination with other comic genres, it is even more pronounced on those occasions – again much more frequent than has been acknowledged – in which it is seen in the company of more serious genres, such as the thriller or melodrama. It is to these instances that I would now like to turn.

3

Romantic comedy on the dark side

I. The other thrills of *Rear Window*

Alfred Hitchcock, more than any other director, has been identified with a single genre, the suspense thriller. While it took several decades and the joint effort of various *auteurist* critics and scholars such as Eric Rohmer, Claude Chabrol, François Truffaut, Donald Spoto or Robin Wood to rescue his films from the sphere of popular entertainment and usher them into the Olympus of high cinematic art, they have remained there by virtue, not only of their cinematic purity, as the director and Truffaut agreed about *Rear Window* (Truffaut 1986: 319–21), but also of their generic purity. Hitchcock's revitalisation of the format and conventions of the suspense thriller, and his enormous influence on the genre's subsequent history, allowed critics virtually to identify the director with this genre and, consequently, to take the films' genericity more or less for granted in order to concentrate on auteurist, psychoanalytic, feminist or philosophical issues which made the artist truly great or, at least, interesting from a cultural standpoint.

More recently, however, considerations of a greater generic variety have gradually begun to emerge in writings on Hitchcock, and the presence of comedy and romance in his films has become more noticeable. Lesley Brill started by highlighting the importance of the romance genre in his *oeuvre* and went on to compare his films to those of Preston Sturges (1988, 1999), while Dana Polan (1991), Susan Smith (2000) and James Naremore (2004), among others, have focused, from different perspectives, on Hitchcock's use of humour. Stanley Cavell, most centrally for my argument here, approached *North by Northwest* (1959) as a 'late' screwball comedy, as a continuation of the 'comedies of remarriage' that he himself had labelled and explored some years before (1986), fully contextualising the film within the generic field of romantic comedy. *North by Northwest* is also a central text in Brill's theory of the Hitchcockian romance, a film which he considers a modern version of the medieval romance of adventure, good and evil, quests, lucky coincidences, animism and psychological transparency (1988: 6), a film in which, for example, 'Eve retains hints of Persephone, the goddess of flowers and vegetative fertility kidnapped by the king of Hades and finally rescued through the agency of Demeter and Zeus' (12–13). Romantic comedy and romance, therefore, have joined the suspense thriller and the adventure movie – itself a modern version of the romance story (Taves 1993) – as part of the generic context of this particular film, producing an instance of Hitchcockian impurity in a film which paradoxically remains thoroughly Hitchcockian. Thus, *North by Northwest* appears as an example of the genre mixture that characterises the workings of most films, or, to use the words of Robert Stam and Roberta Pearson in their analysis of *Rear Window*, of 'the generic intertext in which fiction films operate' (1986: 195).

Naremore, like Smith before him, notes Hitchcock's tendency to play variations of tone between different scenes of a film, and even within the same scene, and this is facilitated by what he calls the 'classic Hollywood's all-purpose plot'. He goes on to mention as examples of such variations *The Thirty-Nine Steps* (1935), *The Birds* (1963) and *Rear Window* (harrowing violence plus a New-Comic plot) (2004: 25). Comedy and romance are important ingredients in these films, as they are in others like *The Farmer's Wife* (1928), *Rich and Strange* (1932), *To Catch a Thief* (1955), *The Trouble with Harry* (1956) and certainly *Mr. and Mrs. Smith*. Since the exploration of love and sexuality in Hitchcock's work had already been a central critical concern since the heyday of feminism and psychoanalysis, the space is now open for a consideration of his films as generic intertexts. Yet, with the exceptions of *North by Northwest* in the analyses of Cavell and Brill, and *Mr. and Mrs. Smith*, as a more or less standard screwball comedy, no work has been done so far on the presence of romantic comedy in the director's canon. Additionally, neither Cavell's philosophical approach nor Brill's treatment of the romance as an eminently 'serious' genre do justice to the comic dimension of Hitchcock's use of romantic comedy.

In this chapter, I look at *Rear Window*, again not as a romantic comedy, but as a text in which this genre interacts with another one, in this case the non-comic suspense thriller, producing, as a result of this cross-fertilisation, relevant consequences for our understanding of the film. For this purpose, *The Birds*, which like *Romeo and Juliet* may be described as a romantic comedy gone wrong, could also have been chosen because of the way in which the horror of the main section brings to the surface the unconscious drives and anxieties of the romantic comedy structure of the beginning. However, I have decided on *Rear Window* partly because, with three full books and hundreds of academic and journalistic articles to its name, the references to the presence of romantic comedy in it are surprisingly almost non-existent.

Look at me

Throughout the film, Jeff (James Stewart) insists on looking through his window at the other side of the courtyard and ignores what is going on inside his own apartment. When Hitchcock describes the film to Truffaut he shares this blindness: 'You have an immobilized man looking out. That's one part of the film. The second part shows what he sees and the third part shows how he reacts. This is actually the purest expression of a cinematic idea' (1986: 319–21). For the director, the 'two parts' of the film are Jeff looking and the courtyard outside. His apartment remains invisible. With some important exceptions, the majority of critics, starting with Jean Douchet, Robin Wood and Laura Mulvey, follow the lead of the character and the director and keep looking out of the window. Douchet inaugurates the discussion of the film as metaphor for the cinema, equating Jeff's look with that of the spectator and the window with the screen: the protagonist is chair-bound like ourselves and, like ourselves, projects his guilty desires onto the other characters and situations (1960: 10). Since then, as with *To Be or Not to Be*, the metacinematic perspective has been dominant. Mulvey argues that Jeff does not find Lisa (Grace Kelly) interesting until she crosses over to the block opposite and becomes the exhibitionistic object of his gaze. In a move not unlike that performed by much feminist criticism, this critic replicates the male protagonist's attitude and finds Lisa as boring as he does while she remains in his apartment (1989: 23–4). Wood partly departs from Douchet from the beginning by calling our attention to the relationship between the two protagonists but immediately introduces the link between this relationship and the various stories across the yard. He then goes along with Jeff's preference for these stories when he sees the film rather as a therapeutic cure of Jeff's and, by extension, modern society's alienation than as a condemnation of prying and voyeurism (1989: 100–1).

Tania Modleski's departure from Mulvey's view of Lisa as solely passive and exhibitionistic object of male desire and positing of her, instead, as a powerful presence and a strong, active woman (1988) starts a trend of recuperation of the female protagonist which culminates with Sarah Street's analysis of fashion in the movie (2000) and John Fawell's later monograph on the film (2001). For this critic, the text is an 'ode to feminine wisdom and style, an appreciation of women that avoids the condescension or paternalism that Hitchcock often displayed in his interviews' (2001: 6). Yet, this has not necessarily meant greater attention to the dynamics inside Jeff's apartment. For example, one of the main points made by Modleski is that in *Rear Window* the woman also looks, that Lisa is a representative of the female spectator at the cinema (a spectator that had been erased by Mulvey's theory) in that, rather than interested in spying on her neighbours, she relates to them through empathy and identification. This leads her to conclude that both spectatorship and narrativity may be more feminine than Mulvey had thought since they place the spectator in a passive and submissive relation to the film (1988: 80–3). Although the film's final look is Lisa's at Jeff in the last scene, the text remains for this critic first and foremost a metacinematic commentary on the relationship between spectator and screen. What has changed from Douchet to Mulvey is that Mulvey's is a gendered spectator, and from Mulvey to Modleski that for the latter the spectator is not just male.

The scarcity of analyses of the Jeff–Lisa relationship, outside indirect reflections of it in the other stories, has gone hand in hand with the virtual erasure of the film's genericity from critical commentary. Although *Rear Window* has occasionally been mentioned in connection with Hitchcock's use of humour and comedy, and even though John Michael Hayes's script is acknowledged to have contributed a lighter touch, breezy dialogue and witty double entendre (Fawell, 2001: 3), the film's use of the suspense thriller format for the murder story that Jeff discovers from his window has tended to override any other generic considerations. One exception is Stam and Pearson's article, which follows the dominant trend in dealing mostly with voyeurism, the cinematic apparatus and reflexivity, but they see the apartment complex across the yard not only as an artistic and filmic microcosm but also as a combination of several classic Hollywood genres: in Miss Lonelyhearts' apartment is played out a 1950s social realist film, in Thorwald's a murder mystery, in Miss Torso's an MGM musical or even a 1950s soft-core porn film, the dog couple echo a domestic comedy and the songwriter a musical biopic, with Jeff as the substitute director coordinating all of these 'framed genre pantomimes' (1986: 195).

Although Stam and Pearson only mention these cases as instances of the 'generic intertext' of popular films, and do not aspire to give an exhaustive account of all the genres present in the different apartments (for example, they do not mention the newlyweds), it is noteworthy that they fail to refer to Jeff's apartment as also containing another 'genre pantomime', even though this is the most important space of the film. This absence is almost as remarkable as that of the movie from Lesley Brill's list of Hitchcockian texts which relate, more or less directly, to the genre of romance. Brill analyses some twenty films but sees no connection between *Rear Window* and romance, maybe for similar reasons to those that made Wood revise his view of the film in the course of the 1980s and 1990s: from such general interpretations of the text as representing the 'chaos world that underlies the superficial order' (1989: 107), he moved first to 'the impossibility of successful human relations' (1989: 378) and then to the 'seemingly hopeless incompatibility of male and female viewpoints within our socially constructed arrangements of gender and sexuality' (1999: 81–2). That is, rather than a romance narrative, *Rear Window* is, for Wood, about the impossibility of romance and, beyond that, about the hopelessness of any kind of communication between men and women.

However, the film is much more ambiguous about men and women's incompatibility, especially if we consider not only the stories developing in the other apartments but also what actually happens between Jeff and Lisa. To start with, those other stories are decisively coloured by Jeff's perception: they reflect his more or less unconscious fantasies and anxieties about heterosexuality (and maybe homoerotic desire, too). As much a film about the spectatorial process of interpreting clues and 'the full complexity of the viewing activity' as about the look (Bordwell 1985: 40), the text constantly emphasises Jeff's construction of his own narratives on the basis of the very vague snippets of other people's lives that he sees. Those constructed stories reflect not just his own experience with Lisa, but, more importantly, the fears that this experience raises and that he projects onto the people across the yard. The spectator follows Jeff's initiative and generally accepts his interpretations and articulations of desire, frustration, loneliness and hatred, largely on the basis of the character's reactions to what he sees. Even when Jeff is asleep, as happens at the beginning and at the end of the narrative and a few more times in the middle, what we see in the various panning shots becomes coloured by Jeff's interpretation, perhaps not so much by what he sees, since he is asleep, as by what he is imagining in his dreams or nightmares. As a consequence, the other stories necessarily reflect Jeff's attitude – they could be said to constitute assorted projections of his identity – and so they only tell one part of the story. In other words, it is not the text but Jeff that thinks that men and women are incompatible. What is missing is Lisa's part of the story, her perspective on relationships, her opinion on whether men and women are compatible or not.

Romantic comedy gives us access to this perspective or, to put it in slightly different words, we cannot have access to Lisa's perspective unless we focus on the film's engagement with the conventions of this genre. Since romantic comedy defends, as we have seen, romantic, affective and/or sexual compatibility between people (generally, although not necessarily, between men and women), it goes without saying that Jeff is an unlikely candidate for the genre, given not only his reluctance to even consider a future for his relationship with Lisa but also the extreme aggressiveness of his opinions and attitudes towards Lisa in particular and women in general. Additionally, the cast which immobilises him in his wheel-chair and that covers the whole lower part of his body is, as many critics have pointed out, an all-too-obvious metaphor for sexual impotence. Yet, although the presence of the cast is prolonged beyond the end of the film by the fracture of his other leg as a consequence of his fall from the window, Jeff does change his attitude in the course of the action and is finally converted, however ambiguously, to the pleasures of heterosexuality, as his contented smile suggests in the film's final shot. Like other romantic comedy heroes before him, he has been changed by the experience provided by the comic space, the genre consisting, as Steve Neale has pointed out, of, among other conventions, a learning process (1992: 292–4). Like *North by Northwest*, according to Cavell's analysis, *Rear Window* is about the process whereby the male character becomes a worthy candidate for marriage (1986: 263 and *passim*). Accordingly, in the final stages of the story, Jeff's attitude shows several signs of softening: his reaction when Lisa comes back to his apartment after slipping the anonymous note under Thorwald's door; his surrender to her love when she holds him in her arms after his fall; and his smile as he sleeps with his two legs in casts with Lisa sitting next to him in the last scene.

In any case, it must be admitted that Jeff never makes it easy for the comic space to take hold of his apartment. Lisa is a different matter. For much of the film she is only half-heartedly interested in the various people she can see from the window, but when she comments, jokingly or in earnest, on what she sees, her views are pointedly different from Jeff's: Miss Torso, for example, rather than the Queen Bee surrounded and pampered by all the drones among which she chooses the wealthiest men, as Jeff's sexist interpretation of her life goes, is, for Lisa, forever 'juggling wolves' because she is not interested in any of these men. From her first appearance, Lisa consistently carries with her the comic space of the genre, not only personifying its firm belief in compatibility but also relentlessly seeking to transform the drabness of her beloved's apartment into a more conducive space to the pleasures of coupledom. She is not just an erotic object for Jeff and the male spectator to look at. She is a very strong and active subject underneath the veneer of her wealth and apparent frivolity. The fact that most critics have seen *Rear Window* as a single-protagonist movie speaks volumes not only about the resilience of patriarchal structures but also about the invisibility among the critical and academic institutions of certain generic configurations, precisely because of their 'femininity'. Slavoj Zizek has recently suggested that this critical tendency to overlook the inside of the apartment has indeed been a serious oversight:

> What happens on *his side* of the window, in the hero's apartment –
> the amorous misadventures of Stewart and Kelly – is by no means a
> simple subplot, an amusing diversion with no bearing on the central
> motif of the film, but on the contrary, its very centre of gravity. Jeff's

(and our) fascination with what goes on in the other apartments functions to make Jeff (and us) overlook the crucial importance of what goes on this side of the window, in the very place from which he looks. (1999: 126)

Lisa spends much of the film and all of her energy trying to get Jeff to look away from the window, to turn his face towards the inside of his apartment, to project his identity onto his relationship with her rather than onto the other windows. When she apparently gives up and decides to join him in his interest and fascination with what goes on in other people's lives, this is not a capitulation but only a strategic move. By joining him by the window and projecting herself onto the opposite side of the courtyard, she is only enlarging the space of the (in more ways than one) diminutive apartment and eventually cancelling out his former fascination by turning the whole space of the film into his (and now also her) apartment.

In what is left of this chapter, I follow Zizek's advice and turn away from Jeff's perspective, not because it is not important in the film but because it has already received more than its critical due, and concentrate for once on Lisa's perspective. Likewise, in spite of the obvious pleasures to be found behind the other windows in the Chelsea block, Jeff's apartment deserves more attention than has been given so far and a generic approach seems an appropriate way to make up for this critical oversight. Obviously, much of what goes on in this location is related to the look, the window and the courtyard, but the action here is not exhausted by the characters' projection towards the outside: there are Lisa's repeated attempts at catching her boyfriend's attention, there are the tense and intense conversations about their problematic relationship, there is Stella's advice on love and marriage, there is Doyle's (Wendell Corey) reaction to the intimacy that he finds between Jeff and Lisa the second time he visits the apartment, there is the violent invasion of this space by Thorwald in the climactic scene of the film, and there is the final scene, whose end, for all the ambiguity tendentiously interpreted as a sign of precariousness by Wood and others, suggests, at least, a change in the status quo (precisely what Jeff resisted) in the direction of Lisa's desire. None of these moments can be seen in isolation from the generic conventions of the thriller that dominate the rest of the action and the space of the courtyard, because in this as in other films generic clusters do not work independently but in close combination with one another. The romantic comedy of *Rear Window* is not all-pervasive or unstoppable, as it is in purer instances of the genre. Its encounter in this film with a non-comic genre such as the suspense thriller makes it more fragmentary, more intermittent, less confident in its celebration of specific sexual discourses than in the two comic films analysed previously. Yet it defines Lisa as a character, accompanies her in her endeavours throughout the film and fights a generic battle that can only be said to be lost if we consider Jeff's perspective exclusively and ignore the most obvious aspects of the film's resolution.

Society calling

Even before Lisa makes her first appearance, Jeff's apartment has become, in spite of himself, a space traversed by contemporary affective discourses. As Elise Lemire has brilliantly argued, Jeff embodies a male reaction to dominant sexual and social discourses in the early 1950s that asked men and women to conform (2000: 66–8). While white middle-class women's conformity consisted in returning to the fast-growing suburban home after the exceptional parenthesis of the war and in becoming good mothers and housewives, men were supposed to marry, settle down and be good providers for their wives and children. The pressures of conformity often became too heavy a burden for both men and women to carry (Ehrenreich, 1983). The emergence of *Playboy* magazine in 1953, which celebrated the sexually promiscuous heterosexual single man, and the gradual proliferation of such books as the novel *The Man in the Grey Flannel Suit* (1955) or the psychological study *Must We Conform?* (1955) indicate that men were resisting heterosexual 'normality' in greater and greater numbers. In their desperate quest for liberation from the 'breadwinner ethic' it was only to be expected that men would see women as the main culprits because of their insistence on getting married. As *Playboy* repeatedly asserted, this was a magazine for men who loved women and hated wives (Ehrenreich, 1983: 42). Jeff's fantasies and fears in *Rear Window* are a direct consequence of this state of affairs. After the title credits and the famous opening panning shot, the film plunges straight into the articulation of these discourses, first through the telephone conversation between Jeff and his editor and then through his subsequent dialogue with the company nurse, Stella (Thelma

Ritter). These discourses revolve, on the one hand, around the issue of marriage, and different contemporary approaches to coupledom, and, on the other, and inevitably related to the former, around constructions of homosexuality as defective masculinity.

Jeff may become increasingly involved in his voyeuristic pleasures as the film unfolds, but it must be remembered that he does not engage in his Peeping-Tom activities as a matter of choice. If we are to believe his own perception of himself as he intimates it to his friend, he is much more interested in resuming his glamorous life of adventure than in ogling the young women in the neighbouring apartments. In this sense, we may consider in some detail the sequence in which Jeff looks at Miss Torso (Georgine Darcy) for the first time, as she dances, scantily clad, around her kitchen. Setting the structure for the rest of the film, Hitchcock provides various shots of Jeff looking and corresponding reverse shots of the young woman from his approximate position. The reverse shots are relatively lengthy, apparently taking pleasure in the woman's gyrating body, and the reaction shots reveal a measure of voyeuristic interest on Jeff's part. Simultaneously, Jeff discusses his situation with Gunnison and the next job he would have taken if he had not had his mobility impaired. When the protagonist finds out what the assignment would have been – the conflict in Kashmir – and that it will be given to somebody else, his interest in Miss Torso immediately dwindles and he starts looking at somebody else, specifically the middle-aged sculptress in the basement.

It is as if a struggle has been taking place between Jeff's voyeuristic pleasures and his professional life. Once he is reminded of the wonderful excitement of adventure, his erotic life recedes into the background and the attractive young woman turns into the matronly artist downstairs. The scene, however, could be read differently: the protagonist's erotic curiosity in Miss Torso remains in place as long as he can see himself as an intrepid adventure photographer. Once it dawns on him that he is, at least temporarily, unfit for adventure, his erotic drive also staggers. Maybe when he recovers he will become again not only a roving professional but also a predatory heterosexual in the *Playboy* mould. The ambiguity of this scene derives from Stewart's performance: while the film's concentration on Miss Torso from Jeff's perspective suggests the importance of the voyeuristic look, his facial expressions in the reaction shots never seem to spell more than a neighbour's curiosity. This impression, in fact, extends to the whole movie and renders Stella's criticisms of his virility and Lisa's growing fears more credible. In any case, this is probably the first and also the last time we can discern something like erotic curiosity in Jeff's gaze, if only because of the textual insistence on his look and the nature of its object. From now on, women will start to mean something different, something altogether less attractive.

Apart from Miss Torso, the only other female characters that appear in the film as would-be erotic objects of Jeff's gaze are the two young women who disappear from view as they undress, ready to sunbathe on the balcony of one of the top floors, but the only time Jeff sees them he seems to be more interested in the hovering helicopter whose pilot is ostensibly looking down at the women than in the women themselves. In general, the sunbathing beauties and dancing female bodies that materialise on the screen through Jeff's gaze, as he utters his frustration, are less an expression of the protagonist's *Playboy* mentality than an early textual disclaimer of any danger of homosexuality, which was at the time, as cultural critics have pointed out, the devilish quagmire into which men would inevitably fall if they were not to follow the rules. *Playboy* defended that there could be healthy male heterosexuality outside marriage but cultural constructions of the time, such as this film, suggest that the battle had by no means been won. Bachelorhood beyond a reasonable age was surrounded by fears of homosexuality while male desire for other men was seen as a shortcoming to be overcome, very close to the 'hormone deficiency' that Stella will soon accuse Jeff of suffering from.

Why doesn't Jeff want to marry Lisa? This is the question around which most of the sexual discourses of the film revolve. From the perspective of romantic comedy it is a very familiar question and one which directly links *Rear Window* with many of the sex comedies of the period. On the other hand, what separates the film from a sex comedy like, say, *Indiscreet* (1958) or *Pillow Talk* is a slightly different question: why doesn't Jeff want to have sex with Lisa? Two general types of answers have been given to these questions, one related to Jeff's preference for a life of adventure and negative attitude towards women and marriage, and the other revolving around his more or less latent homosexuality. Critics like Juan Suárez or Robert Samuels, among others, have explored the latter avenue, in both cases proposing psychoanalytic interpretations of Jeff's reluctance to accept Lisa's advances. Suárez activates the structure of paranoia and usefully explores Jeff's identification with Mrs. Thorwald, which he interprets as his desire to be nursed by a man (1996: 365), while Samuels revises Mulvey's theory of the Lacanian gaze in order to read Jeff's voyeurism differently, concluding that, in their fascination with Grace Kelly, earlier critics have 'missed the hairy athlete who hides behind the curtain' (1998: 121).

Convincing though these symptomatic readings are, it has not been sufficiently emphasised that the film itself seems to have no difficulty referring to the protagonist's problematic sexual orientation in relatively open terms. It is not only that, through much of the narrative, Jeff is much more interested in Lars Thorwald (Raymond Burr) than in Lisa. Both his girlfriend and Stella constantly taunt him with his being less than a man. When he explains to Stella that Lisa wants to marry him, the nurse's reply – 'That's normal' – is simply commonsensical, but when Jeff says that he does not want to get married, Stella's question – 'Is that normal?' – immediately recalls the 1950s horror of homoerotic desire. Normality in sexual matters is the opposite of homosexuality, the 'normal' cure for which is marriage. Homosexuality remains unutterable but the very resistance to name it on the part of the characters increases its visibility. Stella seems aware of this when, in response to his attempt to explain that Lisa is not what he wants at the moment, she asks: 'Is what you want something you can discuss?' Similarly, later on, Lisa tries to draw her boyfriend's attention once again with a second shower of passionate kisses but Jeff, forgetting to kiss her back in mid-action, returns to what really interests him, the Thorwald case, and, after mentioning some incriminating evidence, asks for her opinion: 'What do you think?' Lisa, pulling away from him in despair at his lack of responsiveness, replies: 'Something too frightful to utter.'

While this dynamic of representing but not saying ensures that the 1950s spectator understands what is at stake and allows the contemporary spectator to examine topical definitions of homosexuality, the film is less interested in the exploration of alternative sexual orientations than in the problematisation of patriarchal masculinity (Fawell 2001: 6 and *passim*). Jeff's potential for homoerotic desire is part of an often confusing amalgam in the construction of his character that includes the *Playboy* mentality, anxieties about

7 'Is that normal?': Stella questions Jeff's masculinity. Thelma Ritter and James Stewart in *Rear Window* (dir. Alfred Hitchcock, 1954, Paramount)

female sexuality, the love of adventure and the great outdoors and, as Suárez suggests in the title of his essay, homosocial desire (1996: 359). Like his look at Miss Torso in the first scene, stranded between the camera's concentration on the woman's body and Stewart's non-committal performance in the reaction shots, Jeff's refusal to marry is overdetermined in a way that does not necessarily make narrative sense. The film throws in various possible reasons why the protagonist does not want Lisa but is not particularly interested in integrating them into a coherent characterisation of Jeff, thus prompting spectators to make connections – such as homosexuality and the fear of women, or homosociality and homosexuality – which the text itself does not take very seriously. Rather, *Rear Window* is more concerned with building as formidable as possible an obstacle to the heterosexual union, and this obstacle is completely inside Jeff's mind.

The discourse on homosexuality as 'hormone deficiency', then, is subordinated to the discourses on heterosexual desire and marriage. Jeff's temporary interest in Miss Torso in the first scene is a consequence of his boredom after spending six weeks with nothing to do but look out of the window (no DVDs then and Jeff does not seem to be the book-reading type). This boredom has gradually turned into restlessness and it is as a consequence of this that he becomes vicariously involved in other people's lives. But, as he says to Gunnison, there is something worse that his frustration could lead him to if a change does not happen soon: he might do something drastic, like getting married. Marriage, the 'normal and healthy' choice for an adult man like Jeff in the 1950s, is transformed into a desperate measure, a nightmare of household appliances and nagging wives. The familial bliss of contemporary suburban life bleakly evoked here has soon turned awry, opposed as it is to the fantasy of the great outdoors, of the man in the Roosevelt and John Wayne tradition (Lemire 2000: 67). As he utters his threat of getting married, and Gunnison, the institutional voice of society, replies that it might be a good idea, Miss Torso is instantly replaced by the Thorwalds and a story that sparks Jeff's imagination much more vividly. As if to confirm that in his neighbourhood wives do not discuss but just nag, the first glimpse we get of the married couple shows the bedridden wife pretending to feel worse than she obviously does when she hears her husband coming home, and mercilessly shouting at him as he tidies up around her. Jeff's anxieties about conforming could hardly have been expressed more plainly. Since we never see his editor and he never appears in the narrative again, his advice to marry goes obviously unheeded and the nightmare of married life that the film has just visualised registers much more powerfully with the spectator.

In terms of affective discourses, therefore, *Rear Window* initially sets itself outside the dominant order, expressing through Jeff the superiority of a life of bachelor adventure and excitement over suburban or lower-middle-class urban family life. Thus, the film can be seen as one more symptom of the emasculation that conformity was threatening the U.S. male with, and one more dream of escape from the increasing oppression of family life. Lisa will soon become, in spite of Jeff's efforts, a powerful antidote to this view, but even before she appears Stella already anticipates the lasting validity of what at first sight may be seen as a traditional discourse: the discourse of romantic love and sexual attraction leading to marriage. Thus she becomes the film's first spokesperson for romantic comedy.

Stella articulates not one but two alternative discourses on sexual desire and marriage. She starts by contradictorily accusing her patient of an unhealthy interest in the people across the yard (particularly the young women) and doubting his virility. The not so veiled references to homosexuality become part of her defence of marriage when Jeff introduces the question of marriage to Lisa

Fremont in the dialogue referred to above. As has been suggested, Stella's words are not so much an attack on Jeff's sexual ambiguity as part of a normative defence of marriage as the guarantee of sexual health besides emotional and personal happiness. At the same time, virility on the man's part and, more generally, the acknowledgement of the power of sexual desire are important ingredients of the type of marriage that she defends. Jeff does not want to get married but for Stella this is not only evidence of the danger of perverse sexuality but also of a 'modern' approach to marriage that she – and the film – profoundly dislikes.

From the way in which it is constructed through Stella's words, fashionable 1950s marriage reads as an early articulation of the discourse of intimacy that, according to David Shumway, emerged in the last third of the twentieth century and came to partially replace romantic love (2003: 3). While the love proposed by Stella is based on sexual infatuation – people coming together like two taxis on Broadway – and marriage and a happy life together should be a consequence of this initial moment of passion, Jeff argues that there is an intelligent way to approach marriage, that we have progressed emotionally and that people have different emotional levels. This summarises the discourse of intimacy as opposed to that of romantic love. Whereas, as Shumway argues, romantic love was only interested in the build-up to marriage but never in the reality of a life together after the wedding, producing as a consequence frustration and successive marriage crises, the discourse of intimacy provides a model for the continuing expression of emotion through-out the duration of a relationship. Passion is replaced by emotional closeness, deep communication, friendship and sharing, all feelings that outlive and replace the thrill of new love (27). This is the dis-course that has coexisted with romantic love for decades but has steadily gained ground and credibility.

It is odd that the representative of this new discourse in *Rear Window* is a character who is not interested in women or marriage at all and relishes instead a life of independence and permanent travel, with no more than casual relationships. We may speculate that this unlikely association is made because the concept of inti-macy was an emergent discourse, familiar enough to 1950s specta-tors to be understood, but not one that had reached wide levels of acceptance and clearly not the film's choice. A lasting relationship sanctified by marriage and based on the violent passion of romantic love is what Stella, the dominant voice of wisdom at this point, is proposing in her discussion with her patient. The central paradox of the discourse of romantic love – how can a relationship based on a moment of passion last a lifetime – is not even hidden in Stella's words: she and her husband were 'a couple of maladjusted misfits' when they met and still remain the same but their relationship has been successful. While the contradiction is so glaring that the spectator can hardly fail to record it, the alternative discourse of emotional levels of engagement, profound knowledge of each other and pre-marital communication, uttered as it is by such an unlikely spokesperson, does not stand much of a chance of succeeding. Rather, the discourse of intimacy seems to be no more than a weapon in the hands of the nurse to castigate Jeff's reluctance to marry.

The scenario is, therefore, set for the ideological struggle to take place through the narrative confrontation of wills that is about to start. Inside the room, as in the social space of so many romantic comedies, male independence and romantic love have staked out their positions. Significantly, Stella's first visit is bracketed by two corresponding views of marriage in Jeff's look at the apartments opposite: the Thorwalds' married life, dominated by disappointment, constant arguments, deception, infidelity and, as we will find out later on, violence, just before Stella comes in, and the newlyweds, who make their first entrance as the nurse is leaving, showing the excitement of first love. Since, as has been mentioned before, the protagonist's interpreting activities can be seen as projections of his own psychological life, it may be surmised that, at this point, Stella's rhetoric has made some progress and the excitement of marriage is at least contemplated as a possibility by the reluctant hero. This is only temporary and at the film's conclusion this new couple has already started to resemble the Thorwalds (like, perhaps, Jeff and Lisa). In any case, the two terms of the debate have been powerfully stated inside the social space of the room.

It started with a kiss

Stella's comic defence of a romantic love based on desire and sexual passion has brought the film closer to the conventions of romantic comedy and now the stage is set for the introduction of a comic space that will allow the characters to play out its scenarios of desire. As has been suggested, the generic configuration of *Rear*

Window does not allow completely free rein to the comic space, compromised as it is by the projection of sexual and social anxieties through its suspense thriller dimension (Suárez 1996: 366), and by Jeff's (and the spectator's) insistence on looking the other way. Yet the first fade out, which follows Stella's departure after the newly-weds' first kiss, openly transports the spectator and the narrative to a different level of reality, if only temporarily. The subsequent fade in signals a temporal ellipsis – it is now evening – and the *mise en scène* has been noticeably transformed: the new long shot of the courtyard is now suffused in an artificial orange light, which beyond denoting the sunset turns the screen into a veritable *mise en scène* of desire (Cowie, 1984). The spectator may vaguely relate this change on the screen to the blind being pulled down in the newly-weds' apartment a few seconds before and mentally construct a space of sexual fantasy, or, more plausibly, to the charged atmosphere of other Hitchcockian murder stories, filmed in similar arti-ficially manipulated sound stages, like *Rope* (1948).

The impossibly orange sky, as the camera pans around the now quiet courtyard, is accompanied by an unidentified female voice rehearsing a song. The fact that the whole of the film's soundtrack is composed of diegetic sound and that, as a general rule, the spec-tator is always aware of the source of a melody or a sound effect, makes this snatch of musical rehearsal more remarkable, especially if we consider that, as in the first shot, the camera pan ends on a medium close-up of a now sleeping Jeff. The impression is, once again, that he may be dreaming this world of intense orange light and beautiful female voices, a radically different fantasy from the one he will soon start constructing around the window of the Thorwalds' apartment. Given what has just happened in the previ-ous scene, this fantasy seems to have been conjured up by Stella's paean to romantic love and passion or even by what he may imagine is going on beyond the newlyweds' window. In a different sense, the way in which Lisa is introduced at this point may, in retrospect, be read as a Hitchcockian false clue, a threat of a crime about to be performed which does not materialise but anticipates the murder that will actually take place later on. This dimension of the scene as leading nowhere for the Hitckcock fan, avidly looking for a murder story, may partly explain why critics have insisted on ignoring the inside of the apartment as a secondary, unimportant appendage to 'what really matters' in a Hitchcock film. On the

other hand, given Jeff's opinion of marriage and his unusual aggressiveness towards Lisa, the manner of her appearance here may
indeed be announcing a different type of crime against Jeff, maybe
one of even more serious consequences than the murder he will
later investigate.

Let's look at the visual articulation of what is probably one of
the most spectacular character entrances in the history of cinema.
The medium close-up of Jeff, now asleep and therefore unaware
of the activity outside, suddenly incorporates a cast shadow over
his face, anticipating danger. As Fawell suggests, the film's romance
story is introduced as a threat, a dark shadow in the protagonist's
life (2001: 63). That this shadow does not correspond to a *femme
fatale* out of a contemporary *film noir* is immediately revealed by
the reverse close-up of Lisa's face approaching Jeff. A new cut to
him, now in close-up with his face completely covered by her
shadow, confirms the absence of immediate danger and anticipates
the next shot of Lisa, moving in slow motion to extreme close-up
distance, practically kissing the camera (and metaphorically the
spectator). A change of angle still in extreme close-up shows the
kiss in profile as the slow motion is replaced by a different manipulation of speed in post-production, the step-print, a method which
suggests motion by means of a succession of stationary stills (Fawell
2001: 153), producing an effect of great intensity in the rendering
of the kiss. Hitchcock here uses cinematic technique in a radical
way to involve the spectator in the kiss in such a way that, by the
time the characters' lips touch, we cannot help feeling part of the
scenario thus created. The static shots and Jeff's stasis are counter-
pointed by the overwhelming sensation of movement as Lisa closes
in on him. There is no way in which the male protagonist, and
through him the spectator, can escape from Lisa's 'assault' in what
feels like an extreme manoeuvre to conquer an unattainable fortress, openly reversing the pattern of male–female relationships in
a patriarchal society where the man is usually the conqueror and
the woman the fortress. Simultaneously the voice of the singer and
all other background noise has suddenly disappeared and been
replaced by a pregnant silence which confirms that the film's space
has been transformed into a magic space, one clearly differentiated
from the social space articulated before.

This is one of several intensely filmed kisses in Hitchcock's career
but what is unusual about this one with respect to comparable

8 'Anything bothering you?': Lisa starts her campaign to subdue the fortress of reluctant 1950s masculinity. Grace Kelly and James Stewart in *Rear Window* (dir. Alfred Hitchcock, 1954, Paramount)

moments in *Notorious* (1946), *Vertigo* (1958), *Marnie* (1964) or even *To Catch a Thief* is that it does not come as the culmination of a process of romantic attraction between a man and a woman, representing the moment of final liberation of inhibitions, but is, rather, only the introduction to their relationship. Given the position that it occupies in the narrative, this spectacularly visualised kiss can be interpreted as the index of Lisa's sexualised approach to romantic affairs. Made in the year after the publication of Kinsey's report on the sexual habits of U.S. women and the launching of *Playboy* magazine, *Rear Window* constructs a heroine who may still want to get married as her ultimate goal in life but who, at the same time, is not only active in a social sense, probably a former model turned business woman (see Lemire 2000: 69–70; Street 2000: 102–3), but also in a sexual sense, taking the initiative at every moment, as her subsequent behaviour in the film repeatedly proves. As 1950s films as varied as *Love in the Afternoon*, *An Affair to Remember* (1957), *The Girl Can't Help It*, *Indiscreet*, *Pillow Talk* or even *The Seven-Year Itch* show, sexuality had come to the forefront in the representation of love in the comedy of the decade, but the woman's attitude, whether resistant or willing, was generally one of waiting for the man to make his move. The kiss in *Rear Window* may be far from transgressive sex by early twenty-first-century standards but it still suggests a relatively unusual female behaviour and one which the film consistently endorses. Stella had already introduced the erotic power of romantic love through her image of the crashing Broadway taxis and Lisa's kiss now confirms that what the comic space so forcefully introduced by her at this point is going to protect is not so much the emasculating post-war version of marriage that Jeff and the spectator have become extremely anxious about but the openly sexualised expression of heterosexual desire that she stands for.

Lisa, then, has brought into the apartment the space of romantic comedy and clarified the kind of intimate behaviour promoted by that space, but we soon realise that in a film like *Rear Window* it takes more than a sequence like the one described above to consolidate the presence of this genre. The second thing that impresses the spectator after the exceptional filmic construction of the kiss is Jeff's cool reaction to it and to subsequent attempts on the part of his girlfriend. The next time we catch them in the middle of an intimate kiss, for example, he manages to divert her attention to the Thorwalds' apartment, making her worry about his sexual orientation. Here the verbal exchange which follows her self-introduction while she turns on various lamps and parades her expensive designer's dress could still be recuperated as the erotically-charged sparring that Greenblatt places at the origin of romantic comedy's representation of sexual desire. Yet, as the scene develops, we soon realise that the viciousness of assertions like Jeff's association of Miss Torso (or what he thinks of her) with Lisa cannot be easily assimilated and interpreted as an expression of his desire for Lisa but rather of his repulsion towards her femininity and, specifically, her sexuality. In the following scenes, the force of Kelly's performance and the filmic construction of Lisa as a strong-willed and sexually active woman who knows what she wants, together with her adaptability to changing scenarios in order to achieve her objective, will be counteracted by Jeff's unusually violent resistance and his insistence on constructing women and sex as dangerous and undesirable. This struggle will be narratively carried out through the generic confrontation between romantic comedy and the gothic suspense thriller, with its attending sexual anxieties, a confrontation between two spaces that stage opposed 1950s discourses on masculinity, femininity and sexual desire.

The encounter between the two generic configurations starts from this very moment. The stylised evening atmosphere that pre-

cedes the kiss can, as we have seen, signify the articulation of the
space of comedy in which a compatibility of desires can be represented in a magically transformed social space, or the gothic space
of the thriller in which murderous drives often signify sexual obsession and repression. The kiss itself is ambiguous enough: first, we
see a frightening shadow, full of threat and foreboding, and the
next second, Lisa's desiring face fills the screen. Desire and anxiety,
romantic comedy and the thriller, have staked out their positions
and their claims for the spectator's attention. In the rest of this
scene, Jeff keeps letting his gaze wander across the window and
nastily resisting Lisa's repeated attempts to make him look at her
instead. Their subsequent dialogue turns from the lively screwball-
like banter signifying sexual friction to the more serious argument
about the impossibility of living together. By the end of this exchange
Lisa leaves the apartment, apparently in despair, yet her promise/
threat not to return for a long time, at least not until tomorrow
evening, suggests that the battle is far from over.

Romantic comedy conveys an optimistic attitude to the feasibility
of affective and sexual relationships, which in this case are dominated by the image of the socially and sexually active post-war U.S.
American woman. The thriller suggests a heterosexual scenario
dominated by male–female incompatibility, lack of communication
and violence, whether traceable to repressed homoerotic desire or
to other causes, and is here represented by the aggressive and reluctant Jeff. Romantic comedy, on the other hand, has, throughout its
history, explored various ways of reconciling gender difference with
desire. From the point of view of this genre, *Rear Window* incorporates emergent 1950s discourses on male and female sexuality
and takes advantage of their increasing visibility in U.S. society
(Ehrenreich, 1983; Dyer, 1986: 24–34) in order to put forward a
view of romantic love which, while based on traditional patriarchal
views of marriage as women's 'natural' goal in life, also returns to
Shakespearean definitions of love as openly ruled by sexual desire.
As a result, those who love, like Lisa, are sexually forward, and
those who are reluctant to love, like Jeff, are afraid of sex. Thus,
the two genres can meet on a common ground: the representation
of sexuality and, more specifically in this case, male anxieties about
female sexuality. The thriller tends to pathologise those anxieties
whereas romantic comedy seeks to overcome them through the
power of desire.

It can, therefore, be concluded that the film activates the space of romantic comedy in order to celebrate the type of femininity represented by Lisa. She embodies both a resistance to dominant discourses which construct the ideal woman as middle-class suburban housewife and contemporary debates about women's strong sexual appetites. Faced with this far from submissive woman, Jeff displaces his unbearable anxieties about his own masculinity onto the investigation of a murder story which not only constructs marriage as riddled with guilt, deceit and murder but also allows him to keep the formidable Lisa at a distance, first replacing her passionate kisses with speculations about the Thorwalds, and then literally sending her away to become part of his murder story, thus plunging the spectator in the generic world of the Hitchcockian thriller. Romantic comedy strives to bring the protagonists together, and the thriller, siding with Jeff, pushes them apart because, in this generic configuration, Lisa conjures up the shadow of feminisation and unmanning. As Lemire graphically puts it, 'when faced with Lisa and her desires, Jeff can't get it up' (2000: 75).

Once the encounter between the two genres has been brought to the fore, issues of Jeff's potential homosexuality recede into the background, at least momentarily, and our attention is shifted to specific aspects of the war of the sexes. The threat of latent homosexual desire is resolved in the final confrontation between Jeff and Thorwald, one in which, on the one hand, Jeff comes into contact for the first and only time with the repressed object of his desire – Thorwald manages something that Lisa has repeatedly failed to do: move her boyfriend from the wheelchair to the bed – and, on the other, violently rejects such a desire by defeating the murderous villain. However, as we will see in the next section, both before and after this climactic confrontation, the generic struggle between the two ways of conceiving heterosexual desire is also resolved, or rather, highlighted without achieving a clear resolution. The thriller ending is riddled with ambiguities but so is the romantic comedy ending which occupies the film's epilogue.

The neverending story

The film's climax starts with a rather confusing telephone call: Lisa decides to sneak into Thorwald's apartment, instructing Stella to get Jeff to ring the apartment when they see the villain approaching. Jeff unhooks the telephone but is asked by the nurse to give his girlfriend one more minute to find some incriminating evidence. Then, unexpectedly, both Jeff and Stella's attention gets diverted to Miss Lonely Hearts in the apartment downstairs. When Stella realises that the lonely woman is about to commit suicide, she urges Jeff to ring the police. At this point the composer's finished song is heard in the courtyard and this stops her from swallowing the pills, in the nick of time. In the meantime, Lisa has been all but forgotten, and when the two onlookers shift their gaze back to the flat upstairs, it is too late: Thorwald has already come up to the landing leaving them no time to warn Lisa. At this point, Jeff, who had started ringing the police for Miss Lonelyhearts, changes the content of his call to report that another woman is being attacked.

In the course of this sequence, therefore, Jeff lifts the telephone receiver to ask Lisa to leave the apartment immediately, which he does not do, fails to warn her when Lars arrives, starts calling the police to stop another woman from committing suicide and finally succeeds in saving Lisa by using the same telephone call, as a kind of afterthought, once he has confirmed that the other woman is safe. It is as if, at the moment of maximum danger for his girlfriend, he still cannot make up his mind between the two women – the real one and the projection – and only settles for Lisa when his help is not needed by the other one. Or, to put it in a different way, the protagonist can still not decide whether Lisa should be murdered or not. His (and Stella's) wandering eye suggests that, in spite of her effort to ease herself into Jeff's adventure, Lisa has not yet managed to command his undivided attention. Rather, by having moved over to the other side, she has become one more actor in her boyfriend's pleasure theatre, and, inside this scenario, the woman downstairs, who in her solitariness had always been something of a favourite with the photographer anyway, can claim seniority. The text has structured the events in such a way that the spectator may not even notice the unconscious hierarchies operating in Jeff's mind but it can be surmised that he still has not learned to prefer the 'real Lisa' to his constructed fantasies, figments of his anxious imagination. At this very late point in the narrative, he keeps up his battle against marriage, or, as has been argued before, heterosex.

Various commentators have noticed that when Lisa reveals Mrs. Thorwald's wedding ring to Jeff, now safely lodged in her own finger, she is both signifying the success of her mission and her 'threat' that she still aims to marry him and, sooner or later, to have sex with him. The suspense thriller operates here with maximum potency not only to bring about the longed-for narrative climax but also to reinforce the male anxieties about commitment and about female sexuality that the genre has represented in this film. If the physical resemblance between Mrs. Thorwald and Lisa suggests that Lisa has already been metaphorically killed once, now Jeff conjures up the incarnation of his unconscious desires, to, once again, in a feast of overdetermination, get rid of his girlfriend. The telephone call finally prevents the second murder when Thorwald has already started his gruesome commission, as if Jeff had finally been shaken out of his dream. After this awakening, faced with the possibility of losing Lisa forever, Jeff seems finally ready, as Sander Lee suggests, to engage with the embodiment of his darkest impulses and, therefore, with his fear of marriage and commitment (1988: 24–5), a readiness which is dramatised through his struggle with Thorwald. As a result of this, not only is the murder case resolved, but Jeff finally accepts Lisa as his lover and life companion, even if, ambivalently, this signifies a second broken leg.

Lee suggests that the conflict is not resolved but is, at the end, at least resolvable. There may have been earlier hints of Jeff's incipient change of mind with respect to Lisa, but, as the evidence of the ambiguous telephone call confirms, only a few minutes before his unconscious was still violently rejecting her and wishing her dead, so we cannot expect the protagonist to become all of a sudden the champion of women's rights and the possessor of a deep knowledge of female sexuality. In any case, his surrender to Lisa's caresses and ministrations, lying in her lap after the fall in the courtyard, is a beginning, and one that should be seen as proof of the film's hope, however hesitant, in heterosexual compatibility. As if to confirm this, the final scene, a sort of textual coda, returns the spectator firmly to the space of romantic comedy.

The generalised critical and cultural contempt towards the genre is nowhere more clearly seen than in assessments of the conventional happy ending, which has come to encapsulate everything that is wrong with romantic comedy: facile erasure of conflict, lack of innovation and originality, patriarchal conservativeness and staunch defence of the obsolete institution of marriage. This has led, as I argued before for the genre as a whole, to inclusion in the genre of only those 'happy endings' that can be assimilated as standard and unproblematic and consideration of the rest as occasional subversions of or deviations from the conventions. However, a closer look at this generic convention proves that ambiguity and variety are relatively frequent and, one would say, even part of the convention itself (Deleyto, 1998). The ending of *Rear Window* is one such case, not particularly exceptional in its ambiguity, and not very different from, say, the endings of *Bringing Up Baby*, *The Lady Eve*, *An Affair to Remember*, *Pillow Talk* or *The Apartment*. Uncertainties about the future of the relationship are there in *Rear Window* as they are present, to a lesser or greater degree, in many other instances of the happy ending: Jeff continues to be prostrate in his wheel chair, now with not only one but two broken legs, and Lisa, at first showing willingness to learn to be the adventurer woman he wants, soon replaces the book she is reading, *Beyond the High Himalayas*, by the latest issue of *Harper's Bazaar*, thus signifying that neither she nor Jeff will eventually change, and casting a shadow on the possibility of their ever meeting on common ground, even reinforcing their parallelism with the Thorwalds.

Yet, the two have come together, Lisa seems to have moved in, attaining her objective, and she seems happy enough, as does Jeff, whose contented dreams now show on the blissful expression of his face. No doubt there will be problems ahead, but those are not part of the film, which, unlike life but like other films, finishes the moment the final credits start to roll. At this moment, the two characters are powerfully protected by the magic space of romantic comedy and the particular details of the two characters' positions in this scenario can now be interpreted within the specific contours of the film's discourses on heterosexuality: Lisa's choice of reading matter suggests that the type of heterosexual relationship envisaged by the film is not one in which either of the partners needs to lose their identity and become a mirror image of the other person, but rather can continue to be themselves within the relationship. Jeff's two broken legs may be interpreted as a metaphor of his necessary debasement in front of Lisa, a form of positive male humiliation that this film shares with many other romantic comedies. On a more explicit sexual level, he may now have accepted Lisa's sexual forwardness and begun to learn to acknowledge it as a normal, although to him perhaps novel, expression of female sexuality. It was Jeff that most needed to change and, in this as in other films, change involves a process of feminisation of some sort and a reversal of gender roles. As Lemire has pointed out, *Rear Window* does not endorse 1950s gender ideals but both exposes them and offers a way out (2000: 85). Lisa's personal masquerade of masculinity in this scene may be disturbing, as Street concludes (2000: 107), but, given the way in which her character has been constructed throughout the film and given her sustained commitment to the conventions of romantic comedy, her powerful femininity remains wholly within the boundaries of the genre.

This final evocation of romantic comedy in *Rear Window* does not cancel out the impact of the thriller. In fact, the ambiguities of both endings are a consequence of the interaction between the two genres. From a narrative viewpoint, it may be said that the romantic comedy ending predominates since it comes last, but in terms of generic analysis, what matters is not so much the narrative resolution but the way in which the interface between the two genres has constructed an early 1950s scenario of male anxieties about women and marriage, of criminalisation of homoerotic desire and of a hope in heterosexual compatibility based on male acceptance of female sexuality. Romantic comedy is not here to predominate over other genres but rather to contribute a comic perspective and a protective atmosphere which intimate that all problems in matters sexual have a solution and that desire, in this case heterosexual desire, will not be interfered with.

II. The space of comedy and beyond: *Crimes and Misdemeanors*

Near the beginning of Allen's film, Alfred Hitchcock is quoted in typical postmodern fashion. A classical two-shot shows Judah Rosenthal (Martin Landau) trying to dissuade his lover Dolores Paley (Anjelica Huston) from disclosing the details of their affair to his wife. After a straight cut, this is followed by a similarly framed shot of the protagonists of Hitchcock's screwball comedy *Mr. & Mrs. Smith* (1941), in which husband and wife (Robert Montgomery and Carole Lombard) are having a comparable fight which ends with the male protagonist being thrown out of his house. On a first viewing, the Allen fan may interpret this allusion to a classical comedy as an indication that the tone of *Crimes and Misdemeanors* will soon lighten up and that it will eventually become another comedy of contemporary love and desire portraying modern women's and especially men's anxieties about sexuality, commitment and moral responsibility. Fragments from *Mr. & Mrs. Smith* are then interspersed with shots of Clifford Stern (Woody Allen) and his niece Jenny (Jenny Nichols) watching the old movie in a Manhattan cinema. The presence of Allen's by then well-known *schlemiel* character this early in the film's diegesis seems to confirm the first impression. So does, for those in the know, the fact that Jenny is played by the daughter of stand-up comedian and theatre and film director Mike Nichols, a predecessor of Allen in ushering in the contemporary comedy of the sexes through such films as *The Graduate* (1967) and *Carnal Knowledge* (1971) and, the year before *Crimes, Working Girl*. In retrospect, however, this intertextual hypothesis turns out to be less than accurate and the reference to *Mr. & Mrs. Smith* a little more complex.

Crimes and Misdemeanors features two stories which only come together in the final scene and, while the story of Judah and Dolores is never even slightly touched by comedy, Clifford's becomes gradually darker, as if contaminated by its contact with the other strain of the plot. The film brings together the murder plot of a Hitchcockian thriller and the comedy of manners of desire and infidelity among mature middle-class New Yorkers typical of earlier Allen films, but there is in *Crimes* a gloomier strain in the representation of desire and a more precarious presence of romantic comedy than, for example, in *Rear Window*. In terms of Allen's career, the movie may be seen as the central piece in an unofficial trilogy of increasingly more pessimistic multi-protagonist explorations of contemporary love initiated with *Hannah and her Sisters* (1986) and culminating three years later with *Husbands and Wives*, before *Manhattan Murder Mystery* (1993) changed the trend and introduced the generally more optimistic comedies of the 1990s.

By referring to Hitchcock's film, therefore, Allen is not anticipating a generic shift towards comedy but, rather, calling our attention to a generic contrast and evoking the better-known and more frequent allegiance of the English director to the thriller: if *Mr. & Mrs. Smith* was the only 'pure' romantic comedy directed by 'the master of suspense', the dramatic plot of *Crimes* is Allen's attempt to make a thriller *à la* Hitchcock. This experiment with a new genre, however, is not arbitrary. Allen uses the thriller in so far as it can affect the evolution of his brand of romantic comedy. If, in the late 1970s and early 1990s, the New York director had played a crucial part in the introduction and consolidation of the nervous romance

(Krutnik, 1990), and thus contributed important texts to the history of the genre such as *Annie Hall* (1977), *Manhattan* (1979) or *A Midsummer Night's Sex Comedy* (1982), ten years later we find him exploring the limits of the genre. The reference to *Mr. & Mrs. Smith* suggests that the film we are about to see will exist in the same generic framework as Hitchcock's but will be crucially influenced by its encounter with the Hitchcockian *thriller* in a way that the master's own comedy was not.

The general tone of *Crimes and Misdemeanors* is pessimistic. The love triangle is doubled and Judah and Dolores's story of murder and despair becomes an inverted mirror of the relationship between Cliff and Halley (Mia Farrow) in the 'comic' plot. Love and desire, Allen's and romantic comedy's favourite subjects, are never given free rein in a comic space but are, instead, defined by boredom, selfishness and infidelity. The alternatives to coupledom are equally hopeless, as proved by the sexual experiences of Cliff's widowed sister, Barbara (Caroline Aaron) and by the predicament of the unhappy, neurotic Dolores. Gender relationships in this film move between the extremes of superficiality and betrayal. The few jokes afforded by the text are more anxious and morbid than usual. Professor Louis Levy (Martin Bergmann), who brings some hope to the film through his neo-Sartrean philosophy based on the importance of love for the human being, ends up committing suicide without any explanation many years after having survived Nazi concentration camps. The most generous character in the film, Rabbi Ben (Sam Waterston), is 'rewarded' with the loss of his sight even as his daughter is getting married. And yet all the ingredients of romantic comedy, as they had appeared in previous Allen movies, are still in place: the contemporary chronicle of sexual mores and protocols, the Allenian brand of humour and even the transformative space of comedy, present here through Ben's humanity, Professor Levy's optimistic philosophy of life, and Lester's (Alan Alda) theories of comedy, as well as in the setting of the final scene.

The generic uncertainty found in *Crimes* is a consequence not only of the special juxtaposition it proposes of thriller and comedy but, more specifically, of the permeability of the latter with respect to the former, the elasticity it shows in allowing itself to be transformed by the thriller. While previous critical work on the film has almost exclusively concentrated on its 'serious' dimension and on the philosophical underpinnings of the thriller plot, this analysis will try to show, from the perspective of romantic comedy, that its devastating representation of love and sexuality is the result of the unworkable fit between the social and the comic space. Consequently, the film cannot be properly understood without due attention to its use of romantic comedy from the margins of the genre. The genre's transformative space is constantly visible in multiple forms but never manages to affect the social space, dominated here by decadence, coldness and cynicism and therefore closer to the space of melodrama and existential tragedy. Existing in the interstices between two spaces which never come together, humour often becomes heartbreaking and tendentious in the Freudian sense. It is only what could be described as a narrative afterthought that finally saves the film from total darkness and despair. Yet this final coda becomes, almost from outside the story, a fitting culmination of the film's ideology and, along with the rest of the *dénouement*, one of the most brilliant moments in the whole of Allen's filmic career.

Love, faith and the comic space

Crimes ends with a wedding celebration, but the fact that the spectator knows neither the bride nor the bridegroom suggests that there may be a romantic comedy here but it is somebody else's, not ours. As the genre dictates, there is a final reunion of sorts, with most of the characters of this multi-protagonist movie attending the ceremony and the two consolidated couples – Halley and Lester, and Judah and Miriam (Claire Bloom) – also present. Lester can finally introduce Halley as his girlfriend to his family and friends and, at one point in the scene, we see Judah and Miriam kiss for the first time, in a long shot which underlines the social dimension of their happiness – they are planning their daughter's wedding – but simultaneously separates the spectator from them emotionally. However, neither the formation of the new couple nor the confirmation of the old one, after a crisis of which the wife has not even been aware, constitute the story's true resolution, which consists, rather, of a double event: Cliff's shock at Halley's choice of Lester over himself and Judah's veiled confession of his crime and revelation that he feels no remorse. Both events, signifying disappointment in love and the absence of a moral structure in the universe, are alien to the world of comedy. Yet, there are important compensations, namely the presence, physical or narrative, of Rabbi Ben and Professor Levy, whose views of the world and the human being are spectacularly summarised in the final montage sequence and work as a counterpoint to the chilling experiences of the two protagonists. If Cliff and Judah remain the main characters to the end, it is the other two that articulate the space of comedy, a space both extremely precarious and vigorous.

Ben and Levy coincide in defending the need to encourage a moral attitude in people's lives whether from a religious or a secular perspective. Professor Levy is the subject of a documentary that Cliff is making and his philosophy is revealed to the spectator through four fragments of this documentary. The common denominator of these four interventions is the importance of love in our lives and its role as a substitute for the idea of God. The notion of God as an invention of the human being places Levy within an existentialist philosophy in which the norms of ethical behaviour are the sole responsibility of humans and the idea of God a distillation of those norms and, therefore, of our own choice. However, this knowledge makes for a very cold and inhospitable universe and it is human beings that make it liveable with our feelings. From our infancy, we need great doses of love to face God's silence and it is love, in spite of its contradictions, that prevents us from ending our lives prematurely and from falling into despair. Levy's philosophy is very inspiring for the spectator and, especially, for Cliff, who is therefore devastated when he learns that the philosopher has committed suicide. Yet the film reserves the professor's most hopeful words for the final scene. We know that after saying this he killed himself but, from a narrative viewpoint, his suicide is not the end. After the story proper has ended, we hear him again, in voice-over, emphasising the importance of both the big and small decisions that we make in our everyday lives and pointing at the lack of correspondence between the morality of our actions and the reward we get from them, a good summary of his allegiance to the doctrines of existentialism (see Lee, 1997: 287 and *passim*). He then returns to his favourite subject, love: since life is unfair for the authentic person, unhappiness is our constant companion and we are the only ones that can give meaning to our lives with our capacity for love. In the face of repeated disappointments, most people keep trying and manage to find great satisfaction in the little things, in our families and work, and in the hope that in the future our children will understand the universe better. Mary Nichols argues that

Professor Levy's theories articulate a comic view of the world: Allen has his philosopher commit suicide but keeps his most affirmative words for the ending, with an invitation to endurance, survival and hope (1998: 153, 163).

Rabbi Ben, for his part, makes his views manifest through the generosity that characterises his relationships with others and the advice that he offers Judah earlier in the narrative. For him faith in God is reason enough to believe in the existence of fairness in the world. He has performed the Kierkegaardian 'leap of faith' which gives meaning to his life and makes him happy. He resembles Judah's father, who in an earlier flashback had admitted that he would rather believe in God, even if he knew He did not exist – God is more important than truth. He also evokes, outside Allen's *oeuvre*, Pascal's concept of *le pari* (the bet) and, within the history of cinematic comedy, the religious belief of two characters in Eric Rohmer's *Ma nuit chez Maud* (1969) and *Conte d'hiver* (1991). According to Loic (Hervé Furic), the catholic intellectual of *Conte*, living in the hope of the existence of God is preferable to living without it, even if we are sure that that hope will never materialise. The benefits that faith affords us compensate for the possibility that we may be misguided, and even if the soul turns out not to be immortal, those who believe have a much better life than those who do not.

In spite of the distance between the cultural and religious traditions that inspire them, Rohmer's and Allen's comedies share more than one element in their analyses of interpersonal relationships in contemporary Western societies, including similar moral structures for their worldviews. However, the *dénouements* of their films are not necessarily analogous: while the female protagonist of *Conte*, who embodies Pascal's notion in her lived experience, is finally rewarded for her absolute faith with the return of her beloved, the reward *Crimes* has in store for Ben is his final blindness, in a story in which eyesight has great symbolic importance. His intense faith and his goodness have not been enough to cure his illness and the centrality of blindness as a metaphor in the movie highlights the text's scepticism towards the character's devotion. And yet, Ben keeps his faith to the end, against all odds, while Levy's final resounding words remain in our minds beyond the credits. The film does not offer easy solutions but also refuses to give up hope or, in generic terms, to deny the transformative power of comedy.

It is as if, in one of his darkest movies, Allen found it difficult to discard his comic view altogether. Yet the comic atmosphere and Levy's final observations appear too late in the story and remain curiously isolated from the characters and events, remaining inside a fictional documentary which will perhaps never be finished. On the other hand, this split between theory and life and the painful inability of the comic space to affect the lives of the characters help clarify the nature of one of the genre's central features: the comic space consists of an abstract concept of love, an optimistic attitude to life based on the wonders and mysteries of desire. Specific manifestations of love and desire, such as those present in Allen's film, have an ideology, reveal certain power relationships and reflect hopes and anxieties belonging to a historical moment, but in romantic comedy, from the sixteenth century to our times, they are simultaneously used as a magic force, capable of transforming the world. In other words, love as lived experience, with its demands, imperfections and contradictions, constitutes both the social space of romantic comedy and, simultaneously, the stuff from which its utopian comic space is made. *Crimes*, a film in which love and desire only bring about frustration and despair, invites the spectator to consider these two versions of love and the way in which they allow romantic comedy to combine reality (real love) and fantasy (utopian love). Allen's text suggests that, while in most films the fit between the two is taken for granted, it sometimes may be difficult, even impossible, to bring them together. This insight helps to understand the genre's dynamics better. In other instances of romantic comedy, the comic space enables the characters to readjust their attitude towards love and desire in various ways, while the lifting of their sexual inhibitions often helps them change their identity, mature psychologically and/or approach social problems in a more positive way, but in this film there seems to be no hope of transformation, even if the comic space appears to be in place. Following Babington and Evans's description of *Carnal Knowledge*, we could define this as a dystopian comedy, that is, a comic text in which relations between the sexes have become impossible (1989: 277).

Inside the Statue of Liberty or love in the time of cholera
Jenny and Cliff come out of the cinema where they have been watching *Mr. & Mrs. Smith*. It is cold and rainy outside and they are looking for a taxi, always a difficult endeavour in Manhattan.

Allen allows the spectator one of the film's few jokes, when his character says: 'I think I can see a cab. If we run quickly we can kick the crutch from that old lady and get it.' Aggressiveness towards women characterises much of the humour in the film. This aggressiveness is often directed at Cliff's wife, Wendy (Joanna Gleason), who, for example, is at one point compared with Hitler. While the old lady of the joke obviously has little to do with the problems of the married couple or with the bleak view of marriage offered by the narrative, the film's rhetoric reveals its 'true colours' when an ellipsis immediately after the joke transports the spectator to Cliff and Wendy's apartment, where he is just arriving after dropping Jenny at her house.

That the old lady joke unconsciously vents the protagonist's frustration at his married life is not only suggested by editing – the straight cut that signifies a temporal ellipsis – but also confirmed by the *mise en scène* and framing of this and the other scenes in which we see the two together. Most of the time we see them arguing in the suffocating space of their flat, their intimate life apparently made up of accusations, reproaches and disagreements which are barely concealed by the veneer of civility that they show on social occasions. Visually these scenes resemble both some of the marriage scenes of *Hannah and her Sisters* and similar situations in *Husbands and Wives*. Doors, walls and corridors turn the home into a labyrinth full of obstacles in which communication is impossible. In their first scene together, Cliff and Wendy hardly ever share the frame and when they do they constantly argue, without even looking at each other, standing on the edges of the frame with a big gap between them. If they fleetingly look in the other's direction, their eyes are full of anger and resentment and the overall impression is that, rather than live together, they are permanently in each other's way. This is the representation of a rapidly dissolving relationship but, in terms of sexual politics, it is not neutral. The spectator is never afforded the possibility of sharing Wendy's perspective while Gleason's performance constructs one of the most negative, unsympathetic female characters in Allen's *oeuvre*. By the final scene, the two have decided to split up and Wendy tells her beloved brother Lester that she has met someone else. Again, although it had been made sufficiently clear that the relationship had no future, the text continues to hold on to the view that it is all her fault, even indirectly accusing her of infidelity, although we

9 The *mise en scène* of the end of love: Women take the blame.
Woody Allen and Joanna Gleason in *Crimes and Misdemeanors*
(dir. Woody Allen, 1989, Orion)

know that it is Cliff who has been trying to be unfaithful for much
of the film. The general impression that we may draw about contemporary relationships is that marriage as an institution does not
work any more and that women are to blame.

Before Wendy tells her brother about the break-up, Cliff has
already told his sister Barbara. Their short dialogue includes the
film's last joke. When Barbara says that a relationship in which sex
does not work has no future, her brother agrees and adds: 'The last
time I was inside a woman was when I visited the Statue of Liberty.'
This line summarises the textual attitude towards women and is an
almost literal illustration of Freud's theory of humour and the
comic. Freud argues that the most effective jokes are those he calls
tendentious, which make possible the satisfaction of an impulse by
overcoming an obstacle. The obstacle is always the same: woman's
incapacity to tolerate uninhibited sexuality due to her social repression. Tendentious jokes allow us to recover what used to be ours
and we have had to repress. The Viennese thinker reveals his traditional view of women's inferiority and weakness, as well as his
sexist attitude towards male and female sexual desire, in his use of
the term 'incapacity' to define women's attitude to sex. As he
elaborates in other writings, for Freud women's resistance to sex is
not only part of their sexual development but also crucial to rein
in men's drives. The pleasure afforded by the tendentious joke
consists precisely in demolishing the female obstacle and includes

an important element of hostility towards women for not allowing the consummation of men's desire (Freud, 1983: 144–5).

Although Freud's theory originates in a cultural context in which women's sexual desire was almost unthinkable and certainly reprehensible, Allen's joke, uttered in a very different historical context, accurately reflects all the elements of the theory: man's impotence in the face of repression of his sexual drive, the conversion of impotence into pleasure through laughter, and explicit hostility towards women. For Freud pleasure in the joke consists of two stages: the fore pleasure, resulting from the joke's linguistic strategies to achieve the comic effect, and the real pleasure, consisting in overcoming the female barriers to sex. In this case, Cliff is ostensibly conveying his view of his relationship with Wendy: she, with her disdain towards masculinity and her refusal to have sex, is to blame for their estrangement. The woman says no, the man represses himself and then vents his frustration through humour. Cliff becomes, therefore, a Freudian man – the uncomprehending victim of women's forever resistant sexuality.

But the joke does not only express the protagonist's hostility towards his wife. Just as the reference to the old lady's crutch was immediately followed by a scene between Cliff and Wendy, the Statue of Liberty line anticipates the arrival of Lester and Halley at the party and Cliff's shocked realisation that the two are together. Narrative sequentiality facilitates the interpretation of the joke as an unconscious displacement of the character's hostility not towards his wife but towards Halley, for rejecting his desire for her and, especially, for choosing Lester, the embodiment of the values he most detests in life. Thus, Lester's superficiality, dishonesty and materialism are tendentiously displaced onto the female character, a displacement which had subtly started earlier on, when Halley had revealed an excess of interest in her job and a readiness to sacrifice everything to professional success. It is within this context that her final preference for Lester over Cliff must be understood and it is also within this context that the movie's last joke makes complete sense.

It is, therefore, not the wife but the professional and desiring woman that becomes the ultimate embodiment of the film's grim view of heterosexual relationships. The Freudian interpretation suggests not only, as William Pamerleau argues, that the text's fundamental tension is that between love and economic and social success

(2000: 107), but, more insidiously, that the real problem, as constructed by the text, is that a woman should choose the latter over the former. This dimension of its ideological structure places *Crimes* within the neo-conservative discourses of the 1980s, which openly blamed feminism, women's demands of equality and their massive presence in public life for the growing unhappiness in their private lives. As Susan Faludi has explained, however, it was not women's unhappiness that was really at stake but the consequences for men of the profound social changes that were taking place (1992: 9). In this film, patriarchy's undeclared fears once more come to the surface: while Halley appears to be reasonably happy at the end of the film, Cliff ends up disappointed in love and his private life is deeply affected by women's decisions. Halley's choice is presented as the wrong choice and even as a form of betrayal, although she had never made any promises to him and, therefore, she has not betrayed anybody. We can only understand this once we manage to distance ourselves from the text's rendering of the story: as with Wendy, the only access we ever have to Halley's subjectivity is through Cliff's perspective and idealised construction of her. This construction becomes so powerful that critics have concluded that her betrayal surpasses all previous betrayals in Allen's films (see, for example, Lee, 1997: 284). In terms of the representation of heterosexual desire, Cliff's interest in Halley is initially presented as a counterpoint to his marriage and as a consequence of its crisis, but the text finally reveals what could perhaps be described as its hidden ideology: that Wendy is just an exaggerated version of Halley in her desire of material wealth, in her disregard for her husband's job and affective and sexual needs and, as it turns out, even in her reverential admiration of her brother Lester.

In general terms, therefore, the film's humour has no contribution to make to the implementation of the comic space. Rather, it highlights its impossibility and becomes closer, in generic terms, to the type of humour that can be found in satire. As in that genre, its main objective is not to create a festive atmosphere that will facilitate the temporary abandonment of social norms and repressions but to attack society. On the other hand, while satiric humour is often conscious and direct, *Crimes* is a lot more reluctant to admit the nature of its critique. It expresses pessimism at the social evolution of intimate matters in U.S. society in the 1980s and blames it on the relative gains of feminism.

Splitting genres

The film's double plot, dual structure and double generic allegiance is replicated by the final scene's two clearly differentiated spaces, both in terms of physical location and cinematic rhetoric. On the one hand, there is the main hall of the Waldorf-Astoria hotel in which the wedding celebration is taking place and, on the other, the adjacent room to which Cliff withdraws after the ceremony in order to nurse his distress at the unexpected ending of his desire for Halley. In the first of these two spaces, to which most of the scene is devoted, life goes on: Barbara is still looking for a partner, Judah and Miriam return to their previous comfortable life together after their muted crisis, Lester celebrates his conquest of Halley with his usual sense of humour, Wendy begins to savour her recently gained freedom, and unknown guests praise Lester, the successful film director, for his generosity in financing his niece's expensive wedding. Meanwhile, illustrating Lester's theory of comedy – comedy is tragedy plus time –, time has stopped in the second space. Here the end of the relationship between Cliff and Halley is staged as she gives him back his only love letter and asks for his understanding, which he refuses on moral grounds. Then we witness Judah's confession of sorts, which is presented as his last nod at the ethical universe which he has definitively abandoned.

The end of the love affair even before it had started and the revelation of a morally empty universe place the characters outside comic time: without love and without the hope that life may make some sense, there is no future for humankind. The framing used to visualise both spaces is also significant: while the action in the main room is presented by means of a relatively high number of brief shots, including a very unusual series of shots/reverse shots at this stage of Allen's career, for the second space the director resorts to his favourite no-cuts rhetoric in which the uninterrupted intensity of the spectator's look at the characters corresponds to the importance of the narrative event. Judah's narration constitutes the culmination of this stylistic option. Allen presents this protracted moment through just two long takes, totalling more than four minutes between them, only briefly broken by one cut to the main room. During the confession, the camera closes in on the character's face very slowly until he is framed in an asphyxiating close-up which offers a brilliant visual counterpoint to the overcoming of the moral crisis that he narrates. This stylistic option suggests that his liberation from guilt has brought about a more horrible type of imprisonment.

The formal and dramatic contrast between the two spaces underlines the predicaments of two characters whose narrative experiences have literally set them apart from the social space of comedy and have therefore prevented their eventual transformation. Life goes on and the power of comedy remains visible in the next room but the two protagonists do not belong to that space anymore. This split is emphasised by a contradiction in Judah's speech: the character starts by conveying his own experience in the third person, as if it were the plot of a film, but when at the end Cliff confronts him with his moral objections to this plot, Judah replies that he is not talking about cinema but about reality: 'If you want a happy ending, you should go and see a Hollywood movie.' The spectator, of course, knows that this *is* a Hollywood movie and that the happy ending is actually taking place next door. The space occupied by these two characters, therefore, is the space of a world that is impervious to the regenerative mechanisms of comedy.

What is Cliff thinking about at the end of the film? How can we interpret the sadness and resignation of his countenance? It could be argued that he is meditating on the difference between cinema and reality mentioned by Judah before leaving. The world in which he has tried to live his romance with Halley is a film world, not only because of its utopian view of relationships but also because of its moral structure, which is lacking in a contingent and unpredictable reality. In the real world, crimes are not punished, love is hardly ever reciprocated and social appearance and dishonesty generally triumph over the goals of the Sartrean authentic person. Judah has speeded up Cliff's fall from his cinematic cloud and has metaphorically closed one more door to comedy. Yet, a wedding between two people, the traditional symbol of the ritual of renewal proposed by comedy, has just taken place, while a bustling group of guests provide the traditional comic environment, sanctioning once again the communal dimension of marriage and the triumph of love and youth over death. Two fleeting shots of some children among the guests at the wedding anticipate the hope in the future that Levy will soon spell out in his final words. The benevolent space of comedy, inaccessible as it has proved to be for the protagonists, seems to have finally found its place in the social space. The division of the setting in two locales reinforces the impression that we are being told a tragic story while a romantic comedy is taking place next door, a romantic comedy that we are only allowed to glimpse in the final moments. One could even speculate that in a different film, told from a different perspective, Lester and Halley, Wendy and her new friend or even Barbara, if she ever meets somebody she likes, might become protected by the comic space, but that would be another story, one in which romantic comedy would not have to fight the losing battle it has fought here.

The wedding and Cliff's conversation with Judah are the last events narrated by the film but not the text's final word. Once the separation between social and comic space has been confirmed, the movie closes with the last fragment of the documentary on Professor Levy, who for the first time is heard in voice over while a montage sequence of ten shots takes us back to the highlights of the story, bracketed by shots of Ben dancing with his newly married daughter. Sam Girgus argues that the flashback is a crucial element to express interiority in this film. The combination of a close-up of a character and a flashback that indicates a memory articulates an interior space which visualises one of the most important themes of the movie: the presence of the past in our lives (2002: 118–19). However, this time the successive flashbacks represented by each of the ten shots are not narratively motivated by a character's memory but are totally external and only justified by Levy's words. It should also be said that this is the only occasion when the philosopher's dissertation is not accompanied by footage from Cliff's documentary, i.e. him talking to camera. These characteristics set the scene apart from the rest of the film, a scene in which only the first and last shots (both of the wedding ball) are anchored in the narrative present. It is, therefore, not a character but the text itself that merges the philosopher's conclusion about life and love with a selection of images of earlier moments in the story in order to offer its own conclusion. It is now that reality definitively becomes film and the social space becomes comedy.

The sequence starts with images that illustrate the fundamentals of Sartrean philosophy: when Levy talks about the important decisions that human beings have to make from time to time we see Judah and Dolores arguing, in anticipation of his crime, and when he mentions the small decisions, we see Cliff kissing Halley. As we hear him say that we define ourselves by the decisions we make, we are given a shot of Judah 'commissioning' Dolores's murder over the phone, and when Levy affirms that our identity is the total sum of our choices, we go back to shots of Mussolini and Lester edited together in Cliff's mock documentary. The sequence continues along this line until a tracking shot shows Dolores walking back to her apartment before dying, while the philosopher argues that human happiness does not seem to have been included in the structure of creation. This is a visual summary of the calamities and misfortunes of life which have been the subject of the narrative, but, unlike the film's story, Levy's final words now go on to celebrate the pleasures that can be found in the little things, in human tenacity in the face of an indifferent universe, and in the hope that our children will one day discover the mysteries of existence. These optimistic words are accompanied by the last three shots: when Levy reiterates humans' capacity to love, we see a shot of the wedding service; when he explains that, in spite of the obstacles, human beings keep on trying, the film goes back to a shot of Cliff and Jenny walking in the street after going to the cinema; and when he mentions the small pleasures and the hope in the future, we are shown one more shot of Ben dancing in the dark with his daughter until the dance ends with the applause of the guests, followed by a fade out to black and the final credits.

This is an exceptionally moving scene as the spectator, even after repeated viewings, gets caught once and again in the resigned optimism conveyed by the combination of Levy's words and the image of the happy blind father being tenderly led over the dance floor by his daughter. Their expressions reflect the powerful love they feel for each other but, simultaneously, we cannot help feeling sad about the blindness that has overpowered the only totally good character in the story. His hesitant movements evoke the ending of a contemporaneous film, *Ran* (1985), in which a succession of shots of a solitary, blind young man walking uncertainly on the edge of a cliff translate into images the end of social relations and of the bond that joins human beings to the world to be found in Shakespeare's *King Lear*, the play adapted in Kurosawa's film. Similarly, Ben's total loss of vision metaphorically suggests the end of the moral universe represented by this character. At the same time, however, Levy's words in the soundtrack offer a comic counterpoint to Shakespearean despair. Within the story of *Crimes* it may prove difficult for the spectator to feel close to Ben's daughter, since we have not been given the chance to identify with her, but the one character who has so far represented the future generation is Jenny, the protagonist of the last but one shot.

The fisher king and the future generations

In a recent analysis of Allen's *Manhattan*, Lee Fallon argues that the film's central theme is not the dubious morality of the relationship between the older man and the younger woman, but the spiritual rejuvenation of the city of New York through the character that best embodies it. As in the legend of the fisher king, *Manhattan* and *Husbands and Wives* deal with the spiritual decline of the king of the city, whose only hope lies in the spiritual renewal he pursues through repeated and often failed sexual encounters. Fallon asks the spectator to abandon the dictates of bourgeois morality and to interpret the films not on a realist level but as symbolic quests for spiritual redemption. *Manhattan* is, for him, a fable about a mature man who identifies himself with a vibrant but corrupt city and who considers that his only hope of rejuvenation is a young woman, free of pretence and neurosis, who will, if he lets her, return his faith in humanity (2001: 54). In *Crimes*, Cliff is also the fallen king, grieving over a society he does not understand any more. Unlike in earlier films, sexual relationships are now too much part of the social crisis and cannot help to overcome it. In this social world, Barbara's sexual experience and the Statue of Liberty joke represent the limits of a sexuality which is part of the problem rather than, as usually in romantic comedy, its solution. Cliff has looked for spiritual renewal in sexual desire but has resoundingly failed. The way out must come from a different quarter.

The protagonist's failed relationship with Halley is the clearest symbol of the negative perspective offered by the film on the position of sexual desire in the 1980s, and of the dead end into which recent social changes in this field had led men and women. As we have seen, this discourse coincided with contemporary neo-conservative responses to those social changes, but, as Seidman argues, the cultural consensus on the dangers of a liberated sexuality was much broader in the United States and also included liberal discourses, tempered and transformed by the devastating consequences of Aids (1992: 61–76). In generic terms, it is significant that Allen has chosen the thriller as a generic counterpoint to comedy. In the mid-1980s a group of films had started to appear, labelled by critics as family thrillers or erotic thrillers, which routinely associated an (almost always female) uncontrolled sexuality with death. Films like *Fatal Attraction* (1987), *The Hand that Rocks the Cradle* (1991), *Cape Fear* (1991), *Basic Instinct* (1992) or *Single White Female* (1992) convey as problematic a view of sexual desire as the one that can be found in *Crimes* (see Williams, 2005). Romantic comedy had continued to be popular with its more optimistic discourse about love, but even in this genre romantic love and sexual desire would soon begin to be displaced, during the 1990s, by other types of relationship. Films like *White Men Can't Jump, Clueless* (1995), *Walking and Talking* (1995), *The Truth about Cats and Dogs* (1996), *If Lucy Fell* ... (1996), *My Best Friend's Wedding* or *The Object of My Affection* suggest that love and sex need not control all types of interactions between men and women and friendship is increasingly posited as a more reasonable option (see Deleyto, 2003). More recently, the genre has followed the lead of *White Men* and *My Best Friend's Wedding* in offering happy endings in which the heterosexual couple do not end together, in comedies like *In Good Company, Prime* or *The Break-Up*. The crisis of love and traditional attitudes towards sexual relationships appears to have installed itself quite comfortably in the realm of romantic comedy. *Crimes* is, therefore, not an isolated case but part of a broader tendency both inside and outside the genre. In this film, it is not an abstract concept of love – the love defended by Levy as an antidote to loneliness and despair – that is attacked but, more specifically, romantic and sexual love. For this reason, a sexual relationship between Allen's protagonist and a much younger woman like the one in *Manhattan* would not make any sense.

The absence of viable instances of romantic love, however, does not preclude the presence, even the abundance, of other types of love: Cliff's love for his sister and Wendy's admiration for her brother, the intimate friendship between Ben and Judah, the close-knit family of Judah's childhood, the love between Ben and his daughter, or Cliff's affection for his niece. Filial love, parental love, friendship and love for one's family permeate the story from beginning to end and represent feelings that are not affected by the sarcastic humour and the moral indictment that the text has in store for heterosexual love.

Of all these relationships, the one that is most clearly protected by the comic space is that between Cliff and Jenny. 'I'm crazy about that kid', enthuses the protagonist at the beginning of the movie.

The best moments of his everyday life are those he shares with her: at the cinema, walking in the streets of Manhattan, buying her presents, teaching her 'practical' lessons about life, explaining to her his love for Halley. It comes as no surprise that, in order to illustrate the human being's perseverance in the face of adversity, the text chooses a shot from one of the scenes featuring these two characters. Once sexual desire has been discarded as a source of regeneration for the fisher king, affection for Jenny appears as the best option for the future. The girl represents the purity of youth and the hope of adapting better to a fast changing world, a world Cliff cannot understand anymore. She symbolises the superiority of future generations. Cliff may have been bitterly disappointed in his desire for Halley and he may be demoralised after the break-up of his marriage, but the love celebrated by Levy is still present in his life through his relationship with Jenny. A few years later, in a more optimistic period of Allen's *oeuvre*, Dj (Natasha Lyonne), the internal narrator of *Everyone Says I Love You* (1996), fulfils a similar role and has a similar relationship with her father, Joe (Allen), and it is the intensification of her perspective, through her narrating voice, over those of the other characters that gives the film a more optimistic tone, which extends to the older characters, as well. In *Crimes*, on the other hand, her influence is more limited.

It may be no coincidence that Cliff's niece has the same name as the protagonist of *Portrait of Jenny* (1948), the film wildly praised by the surrealists for its subversion of the bourgeois morality also criticised by Fallon which narrates the fantastic story of the love between an adult man and a little girl who grows up while he waits for her without ageing until their love can be consummated. More recently, *Beautiful Girls* (1995) also features a similar relationship, this time between the male protagonist and a young teenage girl played by Natalie Portman in a fascinating combination of adolescent vulnerability and postmodern precocity, who also asks him to wait until she grows up so that they can get married. The parallelisms with these films might tempt biographical critics to posit a morally reprehensible subtext in Allen's film but such an interpretation is not justified by the text and would lead nowhere. *Portrait of Jenny* and *Beautiful Girls* are, like *Manhattan*, versions of the legend of the fisher king though they reveal, to a greater or lesser extent, a belief in the viability of romantic love. This belief is conspicuously absent from *Crimes*. Rather, the similarity lies in the

10 Alternatives to romance: Jenny widens the space of romantic comedy. Woody Allen and Jenny Nichols in *Crimes and Misdemeanors* (dir. Woody Allen, 1989, Orion)

mixture of purity and wisdom of the young female characters and in their ability to represent a better future for the male protagonist. Jenny, therefore, embodies the confluence of the superiority of family love over sexual desire and the transformative power of comedy.

To sum up, in *Crimes* all the elements of romantic comedy, as it has been described here, are in place: a social space formed by certain ideological discourses on love and sex, masculinity and femininity; the presence of humour in order to offer a specific perspective on those discourses; and the transformative space of the genre. Yet, the pessimism of the ideological discourses, the aggressiveness and precariousness of humour in the film and the distance between the social space and the comic space separate the film from romantic comedy. The discourses on romantic love and their relationship with sex correspond to a feeling of disillusionment towards social changes in this field which became typical of the cinema and culture of the late 1980s. These discourses combine a neo-conservative critique of the libertarian attitudes of the previous decade with the difficulty to find workable alternatives. The film articulates a point of view which is not only monolithically male but openly sexist, and it consequently demonises feminism and women's demands of gender equality as the source of all evil. The humour deployed by the text does not contribute to the construction of a comic space but, in a more satirical vein, criticises social mores and, in many cases, constitutes an almost literal illustration of the type of male hostility towards women theorised by Freud.

The elements for the articulation of a comic space are not only present but are even verbalised, from an existentialist perspective, through professor Levy's philosophy, and yet his words never manage to make an impact on the relationships between the main characters but remain latent, metaphorically speaking, in the next room, until, in the final montage sequence, they end up promoting different types of love, especially family love between different generations. This final message certifies the crisis of romantic love and suggests new avenues of social regeneration. From the perspective of genre history, *Crimes* stands on the interface between two of the most popular Hollywood genres of the late 1980s, the romantic comedy and the family thriller, underlining the cultural and narrative links between the two that make their combination not only possible but also culturally relevant. Within Allen's career, the film belongs to a period of existential crisis and formal experimentation which extends to his constant exploration of the limits of romantic comedy – the genre that he had crucially helped revive at the end of the earlier decade. Thus the film may be seen as a theoretical lesson on the genre's limits: the representation of love and sex and the positing of a comic space are not enough for romantic comedy to be active if humour does not contribute to the construction of the comic space and if the comic space remains isolated from the social space of sexual and gender discourses. Finally, from the perspective of the history of romantic comedy, *Crimes* anticipates, in spite of the precariousness of the genre's presence in it, ideological positions which will become increasingly familiar in the next two decades: the growing preference for other types of relationships over romantic love and the 'happiness' of an ending in which the traditional heterosexual partners do not end up together.

4

Contemporary romantic comedy and the discourse of independence

The history of romantic comedy in Hollywood has been seen as a series of popular cycles followed by periods of dearth or, at least, transitions in between peaks. While, as I have argued in this book, there is much more to the genre than has been included in previous accounts, there is no denying that romantic comedy, perhaps more than other genres, has had its ups and downs in the last century or so. The situation, however, seems to have changed in the last three decades. When, in the early 1990s, Neale and Krutnik identified first the nervous romances of the late 1970s and then the new romances, starting around the mid-1980s, as two distinct cycles, they could not predict that the popularity of the genre would continue unabated well into the twenty-first century. Today romantic comedy remains as strong at the box office as it has been for the last twenty-five years. Neale's definition of the new romance – the 'persistent evocation and endorsement of the signs and values of "old-fashioned" romance' (Neale, 1992: 295) – has become clearly insufficient to encompass everything that has happened in the genre.

More recently, Krutnik has enlarged the scope of the new romances into the 1990s by adding to their initial characteristics the postmodern scenarios of deception and fabrication that he finds in several films of the decade (1998: 28–33, 2002: 140–4). At the same time, however, he acknowledges the bewildering variety shown by the genre in the last twenty years (2002: 139–40) and lists various subgroups, hybrids and developments which fall clearly outside the narrow definition offered by Neale, a definition based on the ideological apriorism of the cycle's neo-conservative return to a past of traditional patriarchal heterosexuality and monogamy. Leger Grindon (2007) is also dissatisfied with the notion of the new romance as the prevalent trend in contemporary romantic comedy. Taking his cue from William Paul's theory (2002) of the integration of the grotesque in the genre since *There's Something about Mary*, he finds two prevailing modes in post-1997 instances of the genre: ambivalence and the grotesque. For him, contemporary romantic comedy lovers find themselves so mired in ambivalence that the grotesque, which highlights the power of sex to disturb, distort, humiliate and infantilise, is called upon to destroy the obstacles between the couple, a dangerous operation because the grotesque, with its potential for parody, puts at risk the affirmation of romantic love. While for Grindon only those films that deal directly with the traditional concept of romantic love can ultimately be included within the corpus of romantic comedy, the new tendency he posits points rightly towards the lack of fixity of the ideology and form of the genre. More generally, the evidence of the genre's abundance and sustained popularity in the last three decades suggests that it has expanded significantly, not because of the cultural importance of the new-romance ethos as a contemporary articulation of modern heterosexual love but, more generally, because of the great diversity of approaches to intimate matters that it has been able to encompass.

Thus, romantic comedy has not only dealt with the tension between modern fear of commitment and a fantasised past in which relationships were easier, or with more unambiguous idealisations of old-fashioned romance coinciding with the rise of the New Right in the 1980s. It has also featured, in ways that have proved significant for millions of spectators around the world, the slow but unstoppable increase in visibility of gay and lesbian romance; the contingency of love and the proliferation of relationships depicted in multi-protagonist comedies; the liberatory dimension of sex within or outside romance; the frequent preference of friendship over love and sex on the part of romantic protagonists; love and desire in the context of teen group pressure; the erotic potential of the workplace in the era of late capitalism; the complicated adjustments of men and women to the new 'post-feminist' sexual politics; interracial, interethnic and transnational romance; the ever-growing generalised anxiety about heterosexuality and the open preference of an increasing number of film couples for short-term relationships – the 'happy right now', to borrow Kelly McWilliam's phrase (forthcoming) – over the always and forever.

The inadequacy of the traditional generic formula based on the formation and consolidation of the special heterosexual couple is today more blatant than ever as much in our culture as in romantic comedy, and the 'neo-traditional romantic comedy' (Jeffers McDonald, 2007: 85) is not the only or, in my view, the most relevant tendency within the contemporary panorama. The genre has been unusually busy in the past three decades, and the variety of sexual and intimate scenarios broached here, as well as their continuing relevance in the construction of contemporary identities, may be sufficient to explain its current popularity and why this popularity has lasted so long.

It may be no coincidence that the first stirrings of this extended period of visibility took place approximately at the same time as other stirrings of a different kind were beginning to be felt: those of the new independent cinema. Although the overwhelming majority of the examples mentioned in theorisations of contemporary romantic comedy are not only generically more or less 'pure' but also commercial films, there has also been life for the genre, and a very exciting one, outside the mainstream. In this chapter, I would like to argue that the variety of narrative and ideological approaches to intimate matters articulated by the genre in recent years may be, at least in part, attributed to the growing impact of independent cinema on the mainstream and the subsequent all-but-complete absorption of the former by the latter.

Originally taken to signify simultaneously financial and industrial independence from the Hollywood majors, stylistic and narrative originality, cultural marginality and alternative points of view, the concept of contemporary independent cinema has had to change in recent years in order to adapt to shifts in its relationship with the mainstream. At the beginning of the twenty-first century, most of the independent companies of the 1980s and 1990s have either disappeared or been absorbed by the big studios; the term is now routinely applied to films distributed by the 'classics' divisions of the majors, and the aspiration of the filmmakers of most independently produced features is to be noticed by one of these 'classics' divisions in order to secure worldwide distribution.

'Has "indie" become merely a brand, a label used to market biggish budget productions that aim to please many by offending few?', wonders Chris Holmlund, who later concludes that, although independents are now in a position of dependence, 'creative

imagination, determination, and courage continue to be present'
(2005: 1, 11). For Geoff King independent cinema is not a phenomenon with clear margins but a wide spectrum which touches on the
experimental, the avant-garde and the amateur at one end and the
mainstream at the other. The variety of forms of financing, production and distribution, as well as the multiple combinations of industrial arrangements with aesthetic forms and cultural positioning,
make it impossible to restrict the label to just one type of film,
especially when the panorama remains extremely volatile. At industrial as well as aesthetic and ideological levels, 'independence' is a
relative rather than an absolute quality (2005: 9). Similarly, Yannis
Tzioumakis argues that the distinction between independent and
mainstream filmmaking is ultimately impossible to make both in
terms of economics and aesthetics, and suggests that the term
'American independent cinema' is best understood as a discourse
which is constructed indistinctly by filmmakers, producers, trade
publications, academics and film critics, an object of knowledge
through which the various institutional forces involved in the cir-
culation of film texts highlight specific practices and procedures
(2006: 9–11). In this sense, the discourse of American independent
cinema has influenced the way in which we look at and make sense
of contemporary films, whether these are 'truly' independent or, as
is the case with the vast majority of them, not.

King argues for the existence of a dialectical and dynamic relationship between 'independent' films and the output of the big
studios (2005: 57). Contemporary romantic comedy, however, has
been identified almost exclusively with the mainstream, possibly as
a way to prevent the ideological variety and progressiveness associated with the discourse of independence from affecting the patriarchal heterosexual determinism for which it has been generally
criticised. Although, as has been argued here, they are ideologically
more complex than they have been given credit for, films like
Splash, *Pretty Woman*, *Sleepless in Seattle*, *Notting Hill* or *Maid
in Manhattan* are easier to fit into the dominant discourse of romantic comedy than not-so-mainstream Hollywood products such as
Desperately Seeking Susan (1984), *Gas Food Lodging* (1991), *Go
Fish* (1994), *Bar Girls* (1994), *The Daytrippers* (1995), *Walking
and Talking*, *Chasing Amy* (1997), *The Opposite of Sex* (1998) or
Splendor (1998). Woody Allen's disappearance from the forefront
of romantic comedy discourse after his first two hits, *Annie Hall*

and *Manhattan*, may be related to his deal with Orion in the 1980s, a company which, as Tzioumakis has argued, chose to pursue independence at a time when the industrial context demanded alliances with the majors, a choice that led to its final demise (2006: 228–40).

The fact that one of the characteristics most often adduced in definitions of independent cinema is its transgression of generic conventions, its 'anti-genericity' – which has led some commentators to describe the label itself as a genre (King, 2005: 167) – has not facilitated the consideration of the existence of a strand of romantic comedy, one of the most highly codified of genres, within independent cinema. However, the more flexible approach to the genre proposed here allows us to do so. While it may be true that the discourse of independence, with its connotations of ideological progressiveness and transgression, has not often found it useful to associate itself with romantic comedy's culturally accepted conservativeness, the texts themselves tell, as usual, a different story. The short selection of independent movies mentioned above may serve as an illustration of the ways in which romantic comedy has developed through the discourse of independence, while mainstream films as diverse as *My Best Friend's Wedding*, *The Object of My Affection*, *High Fidelity* (2000), *Rumor Has It . . .* or *The Break-Up* show the influence, both stylistically and ideologically, of independent cinema.

Cross-fertilisation with other genres has continued to exist in contemporary Hollywood cinema as energetically as in the past, as is proven by the briefly discussed cases of *Speed* or *Out of Sight*, but also by many other examples mentioned by Mernit (2000: 21–2) and Krutnik (2002: 134–5), including *Romancing the Stone* (1984), *Back to the Future* (1985), *Prizzi's Honor* (1985), *Something Wild* (1986), *Married to the Mob* (1988), *We're No Angels* (1989), *White Men Can't Jump*, *The American President* and a long list. However, another type of relationship – the crossover and mutual influence between mainstream and 'independents' – may be just as characteristic of this period, among other reasons, because so-called independent cinema, no matter what compromises and limitations it may have been subjected to, has found it easier to provide a platform from which to 'translate' recent cultural developments in the field of intimacy and sex into filmic texts. Among these cultural developments, I would like to mention the predominance of a female point of view on intimate matters, the growing preference for friendship over love, especially among female romantic protagonists, the emergent visibility of lesbian and gay love, the presence of unconventional forms of heterosexual desire and the use of a rhetoric of realism in the representation of heterosex.

Although authors like Jeffers McDonald have noticed a recent increase in male-centred romantic comedies, which she labels *hommecoms* (2007: 107), the focus on female perspectives and experiences has been more prominent in the genre as a whole than ever before. The centrality, among romantic comedy stars, of Julia Roberts, Meg Ryan, Sandra Bullock, Jennifer Lopez or Jennifer Aniston already points to the prevalence of a female point of view in the mainstream, but independent cinema has led the way in incorporating into the genre cultural changes and contemporary protocols related to women's new position in society. This has often brought about a more distanced attitude towards romantic love and heterosexual relationships and an increased relevance of friendship in the characters' lives. *Desperately Seeking Susan*, for example, features female heterosexual desire in its story of modern love, but the erotic interests of the two women leads are ultimately subordinated to the special relationship that is established between them. Roberta (Rosanna Arquette) is from the beginning more concerned with finding Susan (Madonna) – and, later, with becoming Susan – than with any of the men she meets during her adventure, including the man she falls in love with, while Susan playfully replaces Roberta as a wife for a while not out of any interest in the latter's husband but in order to adopt a different social identity. The film's ending is ambiguous about the exact nature of the women's relationship but it is definitely their friendship that the comic space protects and encourages.

Films like *Gas Food Lodging* and *Walking and Talking*, among many others, also have heterosexual protagonists for whom female homosocial desire, to adapt Eve Kosofsky Sedgwick's term, is more fulfilling and more central in their lives than the men they are involved with. The wedding that *Walking and Talking* narrates, for example, is more important because of the consequences it has for the two female friends than because of the two people that are getting married. *Friends with Money* (2006) uses the structure of the multi-protagonist movie to explore the disappointments, frustrations and compromises in the love lives of four female friends. By means of this structure the film endeavours to offer a not-too-optimistic canvas of the contemporary white middle-class hetero-sexual scene from a female perspective: the woman whose previous relationships with men have all but annulled her ability to choose and have led her to an inertia that seriously curtails her capacity to function from day to day; the unhappy married woman on the brink of a divorce; the extremely wealthy and apparently fulfilled woman whose marriage is based on alarmingly superficial protocols; and the clothes designer whose husband and father of her child is probably gay and yet enjoys the most satisfactory relationship of the lot, even if the sex may not be dazzling. These relationships, however, are not as important in themselves as for the ways in which they feed into the dynamics of their friendship, which never becomes idealised but is clearly the centre of their lives and constitutes the film's main interest. Given the various anxieties and dissatisfactions surrounding heterosex, it may be concluded from the film that female friendship is the new love. In general, the filmic blossoming of same-sex friend-ships, like, to a lesser extent, the gay-friend convention in *My Best Friend's Wedding*, *The Object of My Affection* or *As Good as It Gets* (1997), analysed by Baz Dreisinger, attests to the ongoing crisis of heterosexual love in our society (2000: 11).

Female friendships, then, have become central in recent indepen-dent romantic comedy scenarios, but it is not easy to determine the extent to which these friendships also reveal an anxiety about lesbian desire. *Desperately Seeking Susan* is certainly ambivalent about it but, as Kelly McWilliam suggests (forthcoming), the genre has become a fertile space for the exploration of lesbian desire, at least since the release in 1994 of *Go Fish* and *Bar Girls*. These and other movies, including *Do I Love You?* (2002), *April's Shower* (2003), *Saving Face* (2004) or *Imagine Me & You* (2005), have started to reveal the specificities of filmic constructions of girl-to-girl love and have, according to McWilliam, developed their own particular conventions within the genre. Other independent movies have explored non-conventional forms of female heterosexual desire. *The Opposite of Sex* and *Secretary* (2002), for example, locate the predicaments of their female heroines within a context of sexual equality between men and women in which more or less explicit sado-masochistic practices acquire new meanings. In general, the narrativisation of multiple forms of female desire and women's experiences in contemporary intimate scenarios within a comic climate has allowed independent cinema to exert a growing influence on more mainstream productions and has contributed to a very large extent to the evolution of romantic comedy in recent years.

This does not mean that male desire and men's difficult adjustments to new social and sexual circumstances have been ignored by the genre, as proven by the recent spate of *hommecoms*, including *The Tao of Steve* (2000), *Hitch* (2005) and *Wedding Crashers* (2005). In the independent sector, films like *Beautiful Girls* and most of Edward Burns's comedies have also catered for the hopes and anxieties of contemporary males but in many other independent romantic comedies the fate of male desire has often been to play second fiddle to the female characters. Even a film like *The Daytrippers*, which features a husband who has come out of the closet and has been having an affair with another man for a year, presents almost exclusively the wife's perspective and the spectator only finds out about the recent changes in the man's sexual orientation at the very end of the movie, at the same time as his wife. Independent cinema has also explored the vicissitudes of gay love and desire from a comic perspective in films like *The Wedding Banquet* (1993), *Kiss Me, Guido* (1997), *Bedrooms & Hallways* (1998), *Trick* (1999) or *Adam & Steve* (2005). Yet these comedies have had a more limited impact on the genre, while male homosexual love appears to have been served better by other genres – witness the cases of *My Own Private Idaho* (1991), *The Living End* (1992), *The Doom Generation* (1995) or *Brokeback Mountain* (2005). More popular comedies featuring gay characters, like *The Adventures of Priscilla, Queen of the Desert* (1994), *To Wong Foo, Thanks for Everything! Julie Newmar* (1995) or, within the mainstream, *My Best Friend's Wedding*, *The Object of My Affection* and *As Good as It Gets* are not concerned at all with gay love and desire, as if the genre were perfectly comfortable with gay characters in all kinds of social relationships as long as they do not express their sexuality openly.

Various forms of heterosexual desire have remained dominant in the genre, even within an 'indie' context. A case in point is *Next Stop, Wonderland* (1998). Distributed by Miramax when the studio had already become firmly integrated within the Hollywood industrial machine, its differences from equivalent mainstream films are revealing. It is similar, for instance, to *Sleepless in Seattle* in that

the two lovers do not meet until the very end of the story and in
that they both focus on the difficulties of men and women who are
'out there', looking for suitable partners and afraid of loneliness,
immersed in the crisis of heterosex but reluctant to give desire up
altogether. Both texts take very different stylistic and ideological
approaches, which can be summarised in the contrast between the
old-fashioned romanticism of Nora Ephron's film and the anti-
romantic realism with which both lovers approach their own desire
in Brad Anderson's movie.

Realism is, of course, a relative term, a mode which is as dependent on artistic and cultural conventions as others, and one which
does not provide a closer or more faithful perspective on reality
than the rest. Realism is also an artistic form which changes (and
often ages) very fast. In any case, one of the central features of the
contemporary independent discourse, although by no means shared
by all so-called independent movies, is a realistic vocation, which,
in the case of romantic comedy, seeks to guarantee a more immediate, unmediated focus on intimate protocols, probably a legacy of
the 1970s (Jeffers McDonald, 2007: 72–3). Whether individual
independent texts achieve this privileged link with reality is more
problematic. *Sleepless in Seattle*, *My Best Friend's Wedding* or
American Pie (1999), for example, may well have as many important things to say about contemporary love as *Go Fish*, *The Daytrippers* or *Next Stop, Wonderland*. Realism is, however, more
embedded in the independent cinema discourse than fantasy, and
films like *Sliding Doors* (1997), *Eternal Sunshine of the Spotless
Mind* (2004) or *Stranger than Fiction* (2006) are, for the moment,
only exceptions to this rule, although individually just as revealing
about contemporary love and desire as the others.

Eternal Sunshine, for example, uses its science-fictional conceit –
a company that erases the memories of those who have been unhappy
in love so that they can start all over again without the heavy weight
of the past – to reflect on what constitutes identity, the part of our
identity that is formed by past romantic and sexual entanglements
and, ultimately, the 'all-time' romantic theme of the simultaneous
power, inscrutability, resilience and vulnerability of desire. The
fantasy of *Stranger than Fiction* is of a metafictional kind. Revolving
around the conceit of a protagonist who can hear the voice of
the author/narrator of the story he is in, the film thematises genre
theory when the author, after meeting her protagonist in the flesh,

convinces a literary theory professor that comedy can be as worthy and as aesthetically great as tragedy and proceeds to change the ending of her novel accordingly. Finally, *The Science of Sleep* (2006), Michel Gondry's sequel of sorts to his *Eternal Sunshine*, underlines the extreme fragility of the space of comedy when dealing with contemporary relationships and suggests that, in spite of their mutual desire, its young protagonists can finally only get together in their dreams. The fantasy of this film does not exclude reality but, rather, builds its romantic discourse on the frustrations of the everyday. This is what the genre has always done but what is missing here is the transformative power of romantic comedy, its vocation of transforming the everyday rather than escaping from it.

In general, however, in spite of these fantastic incursions, realism as a filmic mode has undoubtedly constituted a more fertile field for independent cinema to explore the vicissitudes of modern love. *Before Sunset* is analysed here as an example of this tendency.

Love in real time: *Before Sunset*

The realism of *Before Sunset* does not exclude metafiction. The film knowingly inscribes itself within the history of cinema by, on the one hand, openly acknowledging the influence of Eric Rohmer's Parisian comedies of manners and Jacques Rivette's *Céline et Julie vont en bateau* (1974) – Céline (Julie Delpy) and Jesse (Ethan Hawke) roam around recognisable but not openly touristic Parisian locations, like Rivette's protagonists (even the actress and the character of Linklater's movie have the same names as Rivette's protagonists!). On the other hand it presents itself as the continuation of Linklater, Delpy and Hawke's earlier *Before Sunrise* (1995). In the earlier film, Céline, a French woman returning to Paris from visiting her grandmother in Budapest, and Jesse, a young U.S. student touring Europe after being dropped by his girlfriend in Madrid, meet by chance on the train, get off at Vienna and spend less than a day together, promising to meet again in six months' time. *Before Sunset* picks up nine years later (the film was also made nine years later). It is 2004 and Jesse is now in Paris, on the last day of the European promotional tour of the novel he has written about their one-day relationship. Céline has heard of his book presentation and comes to the Shakespeare and Company bookshop, where he is finishing a Q&A session with a group of journalists. It is late afternoon and they only have a few minutes before he catches his flight back to the United States. The time they spend together corresponds exactly to the duration of the film, about eighty minutes. While *Before Sunrise* had used ellipses to compress about twenty hours of real time into ninety-five minutes of film, Linklater now imposes on himself the strict discipline of doing away with ellipses altogether and has his camera constantly accompany the two characters in their wanderings around Paris, from the bookshop by the bank of the Seine, where they start, to Céline's apartment. The stringent formal strategies become, beyond the real-time conceit, part of the film's discourse on love, desire and contemporary relationships.

The realities of love

Near the beginning, Jesse confesses, to Céline's embarrassment, that he went to Vienna six months later and was devastated to find that she was not there. This event does not appear in his novel, which ends at the same point as *Before Sunrise*, but he explains that he had initially written a different ending in which both of them turn up for their date, have sex for ten days, then realise that they do not get along and part ways. The editor did not like this ending and persuaded Jesse to change it. Céline likes the original ending better, even if it did not happen, because it is more realistic, but understands the editor because people want to believe in love and love sells.

By turning the plot of *Before Sunrise* into a fictional novel, the filmmakers establish two levels of discourse about love in *Before Sunset*: on the one hand, what happens in the novel, including the characters' comments about it and, later on, about their memories of their 'one-night stand', and, on the other, the actual relationship that is developed between them in the course of the film's narrative. In other words, when assessing the film's view of love and desire we must focus both on what the characters say – their own discourses about love – *and* on what the text says through the narrative of their relationship in their eighty minutes together. Céline and Jesse both verbalise contemporary intimate discourses and enact them, both talk about love and experience it. At this point, for example, Céline criticises the traditional view of love as a powerful passion that transcends time and is always projected towards the future, because that is only something that happens in popular novels to sell books, and prefers what she sees as people's real experience, in which this type of love does not work, precisely because it is not real. Ironically, in *Before Sunrise*, the idealised view of romantic love is the 'real' one, while the 'realistic' one – the two characters spending ten days together and then separating – never actually happened. As the story develops, this polarisation between real and ideal love is questioned in various ways.

In generic terms, several things can be said about this dialogue. In the first place, the ending of the novel does not bring about the union of the lovers. Rather, the two young people have had a few hours of happiness and excitement together and have set up the meeting in the unrealistic hope of prolonging what must now come to an abrupt end. *Before Sunrise* may leave a tiny door open to the 'always and forever' but is by no means committed to that ideology. Rather, as a film of the 1990s, it privileges the momentary excitement of the one-night stand and, therefore, reflects the contingency of contemporary relationships, even though, perhaps because of the age of the characters, this pure relationship is free of the anxieties and compromises which have characterised many examples of the genre in the last three decades. That Céline now takes this open ending as a fantasy of romantic love is, therefore, illustrative of the age of diminishing expectations in which she lives and which she appears to have seamlessly incorporated into her identity.

Secondly, the fantasy of love, however tentative it may have become, is described as part of a popular culture which appropriates people's dreams and desires for monetary profit. Jesse's novel is part of the same popular culture to which the genre of romantic comedy belongs, but the film initially separates itself from this discourse by expressing awareness of its purely capitalistic objectives. However, love (i.e. traditional romantic love) would not sell if it were not still a potent component of how men and women relate to one another. To hear Céline talk, one would infer that she does not believe in romantic love and its influence in people's lives, and that she would never fall for this kind of trap. Nothing is further from the truth. As she gradually discloses, her brief encounter with Jesse nine years before has powerfully affected all the relationships she has had since then. Now, their continuing intimacy, as if their meeting in Vienna had only taken place last week, proves that, in the film's discourse, there is more to love than a manipulative

11 Love as fantasy and reality: Céline and Jesse fictionalise their past.
Julie Delpy and Ethan Hawke in *Before Sunset*.
(dir. Richard Linklater, 2004, Warner Bros.)

fantasy promoted for commercial purposes. It would seem that, rather than not believe in love, Céline is using her anti-romantic discourse as a defensive mechanism against something that, far from being unreal, is, in her construction as a character, very powerful. But this is after all only a film, which will eventually become one of those popular texts that Céline had rejected at the beginning, including itself within the category of 'tiny bestseller' that Jesse calls his book, one more romantic dream that, for all its realistic trappings, eventually fails to depict reality 'as it is', pandering to the greedy designs of the film industry.

A dynamic is established, therefore, whereby reality and fiction/ fantasy are opposed as far as intimate relationships are concerned. The text borrows and sharpens a rhetoric of realism from earlier filmic traditions in order to present itself as an 'innocent' reproduction of real people's experiences, and even when its characters, also adept at the discourse of the superiority of real life over fiction, become embodiments, however tentative or imperfect, of the very fantasy of romantic love they reject, it detaches itself from them through its formal strategies. Yet the film is not particularly to be trusted: in the end, it is not its realism but its use of generic and cultural conventions, its constructedness, that most powerfully and accurately sheds light on contemporary relationships.

As we have seen, romantic comedy, while not being reality, uses its own generic devices in order to construct discourses which represent the boundaries within which real people interact intimately in culturally and historically specific ways. What is relevant is not whether or not the genre manipulates reality – it plainly does – but what those manipulations actually say about that reality. This can be best appreciated in *Before Sunset*'s apparently spontaneous and 'unscripted' dialogues: Céline complains that Jesse's book idealises their relationship but, when she is asked to explain why, she says that her character is sometimes a little neurotic, clearly not a mechanism of idealisation. The film's method of apparently spontaneous improvisation facilitates the proliferation of these moments in which the character, faced with the representation of herself on the written page, discloses her anxieties and fears by denying them. In other words, as is gradually revealed, her own idealisation of that moment has become an important component of her sexual identity, and the failure of all her subsequent relationships to measure up to that idealisation has turned her into the neurotic woman she will soon confess to be. Idealisation and neurosis are more clearly related in the character's psyche and in the contemporary intimate discourse she embodies than in the logic of her words. Through her experience, the film is suggesting that in contemporary relationships the idealisation of romantic love still plays an important part. *Before Sunset*, while positing itself as a 'slice of life' narrative, lifts its romantic discourses above the everyday, but, like other romantic comedies, uses this manipulation in order to return to the same everyday in a more powerful and discursively coherent way. 'Reality' in this film is only one more of the mechanisms employed by the text in order to convey its message.

How is this reality constructed in filmic terms? While Jesse and Céline discuss his book and the way in which their past experience has been fictionalised in it, the film is articulating their present-day relationship through the dialogues, the actors' naturalistic performances and a specific use of film grammar. One of the premises of the formal construction of the film is that the editing must preserve the continuity of real time and space. For example, at this point in the narrative, the two characters have turned away from the Seine, into the streets behind the bookshop. The sequence has been built by means of a series of follow-focus tracking shots which accompany the characters in their walk and shot/reverse shots whenever they stop momentarily. This is a very traditional use of framing and editing that seeks, in these early scenes, to establish a

pattern for the spectator: the various framings and cuts convey a
continuity which is not manipulated but real. The cuts between the
different tracking shots, for example, ensure that the spectator
knows that the narrative is actually covering the whole length of
the streets the characters are walking along, that they are turning
from one real street into another and that no part of their progression has been omitted from view. Now, as they walk along a
narrow street with houses on their right and a fence on their left,
the cut from a follow-focus tracking shot from behind the characters to one that precedes them again confirms that no time or space
has been elided – the background remains strictly constant – and,
as a relative novelty, introduces a two-and-a-half minute-long take,
which covers the time that it takes them to get to the end of this
particular street. This long take, like the rest of the film, risks
making the spectator lose her/his patience (especially the spectator
accustomed to the quick elliptical cutting of most contemporary
movies), but enhances the impression of realism as we feel that we
are simply witnessing a conversation between two real people, in a
real street, in real time, as they walk, stop and continue walking.

The shot covers their dialogue about the book and then her
account of what she does in her job for the Green Cross. It is significant that their conversation about the fictionality of the book
and Céline's comments on the capitalistic manipulations of popular
culture are presented in this openly unobtrusive, 'non-manipulative'
way. It is as if the text is emphasising the difference between
popular culture's tendentious methods of representing reality and
its own more honest methods. Jesse and the editorial industry have
manipulated their previous encounter in the novel he has just
published but the film is not manipulating their new encounter,
limiting itself to discreetly recording it or quietly witnessing their
conversation, thus intensifying the contrast between romantic
constructions of love and the reality of it. As Céline concludes later
on, 'reality and love are contradictory.' This contrast is part of
the film's intimate discourse and the fact that the spectator may
'fall' for the powerful illusion of reality attests to the filmmakers'
success at sorting out their views on relationships along different
ontological levels: fictional, i.e. romantic love vs. real people relat-
ing to one another in real space and real time. This is, as is often
the case with so-called realistic texts, the film's most sophisticated
construction.

Walking and talking

The long take and the other formal devices deployed in *Before Sunset*, then, are not just a neutral way of recording the progression of the love affair. The film's formal construction is more than a realistic method of representing a brief affair between a man and a woman. It uses the brevity of this encounter and the devices that reinforce our impression of it as 'real' in order to put forward a view of contemporary relationships in which the present is preferred over the future, self-analysis and talk of love over action or commitment, talk of sex over sex, walking and talking over bodies and physical intimacy. This is an intellectual type of relationship that affects the characters deeply and becomes as powerful for them as others based on more emotional or carnal exchanges. The film's method of representation feels realistic not because it is objectively so but because it appears to be the most appropriate way – in classical terms, the most decorous way – of constructing this particular type of relationship cinematically.

In this sense, *Before Sunset* becomes an illustration of what David Shumway has called 'relationship stories', the most appropriate type of fiction to represent the discourse of intimacy, with its structure of exposition, analysis and instruction (2003: 149–57). There is a before and after for these two characters, a life outside the plot – her job, her war-photographer partner, Jesse's wife and child in New York, the tiring promotional tour he has just ended – but the spectator is less interested in these than in an affair that, for all the film's open-endedness, is exclusively of the 'here and now' variety and is developed through their penchant for self-analysis. For Nick James, the film's central message is that romance is cool and sex is not (2004: 15). In this, it seems to follow the neo-traditional romantic comedy criticised by Jeffers McDonald for its de-emphasising of sex in favour of a vaguer romantic intensity (2007: 97). But in the course of this film we do not see much of either romance or sex, although both romance and sex, or sex as a more traditional expression of romantic love, may well be waiting in the wings after the film's close. What seems really cool in the romantic world of *Before Sunset* is *to talk about* romance and sex. In an age of heightened awareness of intimate discourses, the film seems to suggest that there is nothing as erotic as talking, and that when talking leads to something else, the romance stops being interesting for the spectator. When words stop, the time has come to switch off the camera. It is not that the film is coy about sex. Rather, it is just not very interested. This is the type of romance of self-analysis inaugurated on the screen by Woody Allen in the 1970s but one which has since then evolved and metamorphosed into something else: a defensive mechanism against the ravages of desire in the contemporary intimate panorama, which has turned, like friendship, into a cultural practice that is revealed to have manifold attractions. Even touching each other as a way to soothe their anxieties about other relationships is, as a later scene inside the car suggests, dangerous and to be avoided at all costs. Talking in *Before Sunset* is not just sexy, it is also much safer. It's sexy because it's safe.

Brian Henderson argued in his famous article that classical romantic comedy was predicated on the suppression of the question 'How come we never fucked?' Once the question could not be suppressed any longer – once sex could not be left out of the structure of the genre – romantic comedy, the critic surmised, could not flourish anymore (1978: 21–2). A good proof of the basic soundness of Henderson's thesis was that the genre did not return to form again until Woody Allen and other filmmakers found a culturally understandable and convincing way of bringing sex into the equation. The dialectic between romantic love and sex became part of the thematic structure of *Annie Hall*, *The Goodbye Girl* and the other nervous romances, and even if explicit representations of sexual desire did not always figure prominently in the romantic comedies of the 1980s and 1990s, its role in the new intimate spaces of the genre was never seriously challenged. Sex may not have always been there but neither was it constantly denied or postponed any more.

On the other hand, the ever-growing presence of more or less explicit sex in mainstream films, the recent blurring of boundaries between commercial and pornographic movies as far as the representation of sex on the screen was concerned, and its consequent normalisation as one of the most obvious attractions of the contemporary mainstream may have produced a saturation that the independent cinema of those decades was quick to capitalise on. *sex, lies, and videotape* (1989) caused a sensation not because of the exploitation tactics suggested in its title but precisely because it did not deliver its promise. Before the pleasures of visible sex reached their 1990s mainstream apogee with Paul Verhoeven's

Basic Instinct (1992) and *Showgirls* (1995) and, later, Stanley Kubrick's *Eyes Wide Shut* (1999), Steven Soderbergh's film already anticipated an exhaustion that affected both cinematic spectatorship and cultural discourses. There is some sex on the screen in *sex, lies, and videotape* but both characters and spectators are much more interested in what the protagonists have to say about it to the psychoanalyst, to each other or to the videocamera than in seeing it on the screen. Ann Mullany (Andy McDowell)'s initial frigidity does not prevent her from talking about sex and it is eventually this talk of sex that leads her to enjoy it again, although for the spectator sex in the long climactic scene happens offscreen, and remains only accessible through what she says about it. The voyeuristic expectations are frustrated when the sex scene is abruptly interrupted before physical contact between the protagonists is initiated, but we do not really mind, enthralled as we are by their confessional chat. The recorded interviews reveal the characters' capacity for intense contact. In the end, these interviews – formalised dialogues about sex – become a viable substitute for physical arousal.

Soderbergh's film inaugurates what can be considered one of the most important lines of development of independent cinema in the 1990s: the confessional comedy, a group of 'serious' comedies about intimate relationships, love and romance, which favour word over action and emotion over irony (Levy, 1999: 273). Films like *Rambling Rose* (1991), *The Wedding Banquet, Ruby in Paradise* (1993), *Clerks* (1994), *The Brothers McMullen* (1995), *Smoke* (1995), *Walking and Talking, Beautiful Girls, Box of Moonlight* (1997) and many others constitute an alternative to mainstream Hollywood not because they take the spectator to places where other films do not dare to go. Rather, the daring consists in apparently not going anywhere, staying with the everyday lives of their mostly young protagonists, more or less recognisable contemporary types, rather than visiting special-effects-ridden fantasy worlds or spaces of radical otherness. This low-key vocation is not only reflected in the generally very simple formal strategies employed to visualise the stories but also in the predominance of dialogues over action. The sexual dimension of romance is ever-present in the characters' conversations because sex has, after decades of pushing cultural boundaries, become normalised as part of the construction of contemporary relationships, but, in most of these films, rather than the fulfilment of desire, it becomes a problem to be solved, a source of anxiety, and much more pleasurable as a topic of conversation than as an actual activity in which the characters are longing to engage. *Walking and Talking* is paradigmatic in this respect: like the protagonists of *Sex and the City*, the two heroines enjoy their talks about their heterosexual partners much better than their relationships with them. The sex is seen as, at best, an uneventful activity but the real excitement lies in discussing it before or afterwards, with your friends or even with your partners.

The title of *Before Sunset* could have easily been *Walking and Talking*. After all, this is, almost exclusively, what Céline and Jesse do throughout the film and what they had also done in the previous *Before Sunrise*. In fact, since the 'indie' breakthrough success of *Slacker* (1991), the pleasures provided by Richard Linklater's films have basically consisted in listening to the characters talking to one another: from the apparently inane talk of the slackers endlessly hanging out at the shopping mall in *SubUrbia* (1997), through the pseudo-philosophical conversations of *Waking Life* (2001) and the intense theatrical dialogues of *Tape* (2001), in which past actions are conjured up out of apparent nothingness through words, to his adaptation of Philip S. Dick's discursive *A Scanner Darkly* (2006), the director has shown that, in his fictional world, the word always takes centre stage. In a review of *A Scanner Darkly*, Tim Robey has dismissively referred to Linklater's directorial style as 'chat, chat, narrative box-ticking, chat' (2006: 66), a description which, whether we like the films or not, can hardly be disputed. By the time he made *Before Sunset* the centrality of dialogues was so firmly established in his *oeuvre* that it felt almost natural that the action consisted in no more than two characters talking as they walked through the streets of Paris.

As has been argued before, the filmmakers' stylistic and narrative choices define the boundaries of the central relationship and the thematic lines along which it can be developed. Because of these choices, the characters are forced to live out their relationship in less than eighty minutes of walking and talking. That this eighty-minute affair may be felt to be culturally relevant by the spectator, however, is not only a function of the film's style: the relationship can only work from the perspective of the spectator if it relates to her/his experience of contemporary love and desire. Céline, for example, admits that when she is in a relationship and the other person is around all the time, she feels suffocated, even nauseous. From this perspective, an anxiety-free chat with someone who has to catch the next flight to the other side of the Atlantic has much to recommend itself. Other dimensions of the text's take on intimate matters are equally adapted to the film's narrative frame and formal requirements while remaining culturally pertinent. Delpy, co-writer of the screenplay with Linklater and Hawke, has emphasised the historical immediacy of the film's discourse in an interview which is worth quoting at some length:

> I wrote [the screenplay] after years of talking with girls and guys my age. Since sexual liberation, there has been a need to redefine how relationships are handled. Is it easier or harder to love someone now? What role does the man have to take? I have a lot of single girlfriends who'd like to fall in love with the right guy. They'd like to find someone who will accept the fact that they are a strong woman. [. . .] The idea that they felt numb, that they were not capable of being connected to someone. [. . .] People don't want to open up these days. Showing emotions is seen as a sign of weakness. (Julie Delpy, in Goodridge, 2004: 20)

If the sexiness of its dialogues can be seen as symptomatic of the text's position on intimate matters, Delpy's words guide us quite proficiently through its more explicit sexual discourse, a discourse which deals with the construction of contemporary heterosexuality and with the difficult and painful rearrangement of sexual and social roles in relationships between men and women after the second wave of feminism, a historical moment whose consequences do not seem to have been completely assimilated by men and women several decades later. The romantic comedy's attempts to smooth over these apparently irreconcilable differences and to construct currents of desire on the basis of these differences are classically carried out through the presence of Paris not only as a recognisable geographical background but also as the fictional space of romantic comedy *par excellence*.

Sex and the city

The confessional comedy derives part of its energy from its capacity to incorporate into its fiction believable anxieties that the audience may find it easy to identify with while, at the same time, hoping

that, at least in the fictional world of the film, those anxieties will
be confronted and overcome. But any final resolution of the conflict, if the comic text finally posits one, will not feel relevant or
artistically powerful if the problems to be resolved are not felt to
be close to real people's experience: no convincing conflict, no
believable resolution. As Jesse confesses that his marriage is disin-
tegrating and Céline reveals that she has been unhappy in all her
relationships with other men, including the present one with an
almost-always-absent war photographer, the rift between men and
women becomes apparent. Their Vienna romance gradually emerges
as the root of their present dissatisfaction but the dissatisfaction
itself has wider resonances, as Delpy's words in the interview
suggest. Vienna or no Vienna, contemporary couples are, in Céline's
words, very confused because men still have the need to feel socially
superior and women cannot accept that deeply ingrained male
superiority anymore. On the other hand, demands of social equality, even feminist militancy, do not stop many heterosexual women
from desiring intimacy with men, but it is not easy to find men who
will accept women who are both feminine and strong, that is, the
basic combination of what Jacinda Read has described as contemporary popular feminism (2000: 48–9). At the same time, commitment is felt to be repressive or, at least, not too high on people's
wish lists. Jesse's ostensible mistake is that he married because he
felt that being an adult meant commiting himself to a person – the
person herself did not matter much – and acquiring responsibilities.
That past urge to commit is about to end in disaster now, while
for Céline even the thought of 'the day-to-day life of a relationship'
is insufferable.

Freedom is felt to be essential but it does not make men and
women happy. Romance still occupies an important part in constructions of love even though the 'love of your life' idea is absurd,
even evil, according to Céline. Romance is generally identified with
sex – passion and consuming desire – and that cannot be hoped to
last for very long in stable relationships, but the traditional idea
that something deeper comes to replace the initial passion seems to
have lost ground. Jesse's sex life has been so poor since his child
was born that he feels that if somebody – a woman, it is assumed
– were to even touch him he would dissolve into molecules. Céline
has become numb because every time she has felt passionately
about somebody it has taken something irrecoverable away from

her. She says she does not romanticise things too much nowadays but her cynicism is a thin defence mechanism which quickly crumbles down once the conversation becomes honest and personal. Descriptions of what her love life has turned her into range from deadened to manic depressive. In general, both their attitudes to the link between love and sex are recognisably modern but they are still separated along the gender divide: for Céline, sex, like love, has been harmful and inhibiting; for Jesse, the 'horny' U.S. American man, women still seem to be mainly in the business of setting obstacles to men's sexual pleasure. Céline initially denies that they had sex in Vienna, because 'that is what women do', while Jesse fantasises about having uninterrupted sex with her for ten days and dreams of lying naked next to her and reaching out to touch her (admittedly, a rather tame sexual dream).

What ultimately emerges from these dialogues is that the distance between men and women is so great, and the difference between people's fantasies and what they are ready to give up for love in real life so pronounced, that any compromise seems difficult to envisage. That anything positive may come out of this intimate climate would seem unlikely, except that the talk of sexual and gender conflict between Céline and Jesse is, as has already been pointed out, also the engine of desire, and desire in romantic comedy will not be stopped, however slim the odds, however dismal the prospects. Frank Krutnik has argued that postmodern romantic comedy lovers are perfectly aware of the chasm that has been created by recent cultural developments and they know that love is a fabrication, but that does not stop them from once again engaging in the same sexual games as before (1998: 33). Both the awareness and the readiness to once again fall in the trap are there in *Before Sunset*. Although the transition from real to comic space seems even more difficult here because the characters are so articulate in the presentation of the crisis, and therefore hard to convince that the effort is worth it, this is no *Crimes and Misdemeanors*: the genre of romantic comedy is doing its work by once again deploying the comic space to help them overcome their inhibitions and frustrations. This comic space is geographically identified in the film with the city of Paris, the city most often associated with romantic love in the history of cinema. *Before Sunset* takes full advantage of the cliché and deftly relates the lovers' desire for one another with the background against which it develops. At the same time, however, the city's romantic aura contrasts ironically with the text's realism and its concern with showing, through the characters' wanderings, a more mundane Paris. Paradoxically, Paris becomes a very realistic space of comedy, one that transforms the reality of love without itself abandoning its own reality. In this respect, the use of real locations in this movie bears certain similarities with the way in which the United States as a mythical space was constructed in *North by Northwest*.

By mixing generic conventions of romantic comedy, the adventure and the romance film, Hitchcock provided in *North by Northwest* a type of pleasure that his suspense thrillers had not anticipated: the pleasure of a geographically recognisable magical land in which love can flourish and defeat the most formidable enemies. The famous locations in which the action takes place, especially in the climactic scene on Mount Rushmore, are spectacularly transformed into the space of comedy. These are real spaces but they are not reality, and the United States of the film is not the real United States but a mythical filmic space which has replaced the dangers of the escape narrative by the amenities of love and marriage. Stanley Cavell concludes in his analysis of the movie that 'the achievement of true marriage might ratify something called America as a place in which to seek it' (1986: 263). The U.S. is the special place where love can happen, not because that has any resemblance to reality but because through the generic cocktail created by Hitchcock, love and desire become part of the discourse of America as the land of plenty. *North by Northwest* turns the modern dream of love and romance into a very American Dream. The process of spiritual death and revival undergone by the protagonist couple is facilitated by their desire and ratified by the United States as the ultimate Hollywood space of romantic comedy. It is as if Hitchcock, the European cynic, had, like Ernst Lubitsch or Billy Wilder, finally given up on his scepticism and had been transformed into an 'American romantic', positing his adopted country as the necessary scenario for the development of modern love.

Several decades later, a reverse process is at work in *Before Sunrise* and *Before Sunset*. These two films have their lovers meet during a trip in Europe, spend a few hours together in Vienna and, then, several years later, get together again, for a brief time, in Paris. It is not only that, as we have seen, the length of romantic liaisons has been drastically reduced with respect to more traditional representations of romance but also that, for them to work, they need to take place 'elsewhere'. Europe is, of course, not elsewhere for Europeans and the crises and diminishing expectations in modern intimate discourses are similar both sides of the Atlantic, but these are U.S. films which provide a U.S. perspective. Accordingly, they posit the two European cities as places where love and desire, however fragile and problematic, can, unlike in the U.S., still flourish. Significantly we learn, in the course of *Before Sunset*, that both characters lived in New York at the same time for several years but they never came across each other then. New York, in spite of its cosmopolitanism, would not have done as a place of reunion because it would have been too close to home, not so much the home of the characters (Céline is from Paris) but the home of the film's U.S.-centred discourse. Paris, for all its cultural centrality, has different connotations within the text's imaginary: it is not only the home of Rivette's Céline and Julie and their invigorating narrative fantasies but also of many of Rohmer's lovers and their recognisably 'French', i.e. different, approach to intimate matters.

It may be speculated that for Linklater, the independent film-maker, Rohmer's comedies of manners represent a much needed release from the conventionality of mainstream American romantic comedy. Rohmer provides the model but also, indirectly, the location for the story. This is not Rohmer's Paris, either, but rather what could perhaps be described as a realistic myth of Paris, a location which, because of its *nouvelle vague* credentials, may seem, within the text's cultural construction, more believable as the setting of postmodern desire. Besides, there is one more requirement that Paris fulfils in the 'American imaginary' of the film: it is the ideal place for the narrative of a transnational romance. Again, it is not that young men and women from different nationalities cannot meet in the United States, but the country's 'melting pot' potential may mean that, once transported to the U.S., lovers and intimate matters become automatically Americanised. On the other hand, the U.S. traveller in Europe remains quintessentially 'American' and while his contact with other national identities may give him a distance with respect to his own 'Americanness', it will not threaten it in any essential way.

At the time of release of *Before Sunset* France was not the most popular country in the United States. In the wake of the U.S.

invasion of Iraq and France's initial opposition to it, anti-French sentiment was running high in George Bush's country while anti-Americanism was also widespread throughout Europe, including in those countries whose governments had backed the invasion. In this context, Linklater, Hawke and Delpy's story of international romance could not have been timelier and more deeply committed to the egalitarian and tolerant ethos of the genre. Both *Before Sunrise* and *Before Sunset* excel at the construction of Jesse and Céline as recognisably U.S. American and French, respectively. Popular clichés are undoubtedly used and even turned into elements of the plot – U.S. optimism and individualism, French political commitment and cynicism, French women's sexuality, U.S. men's 'healthy horniness', French (and European) conventional bashing of U.S. foreign policy and U.S. fear of communism, etc. – but they never feel impoverishing or tendentious. If screwball comedy often turned class difference into one more ingredient of the sexual dynamic (Lent, 1995: 315), here national difference is at the heart of the sexual attraction. Gender difference appears to be as wide as ever, but national difference may be seen here as the supplement that is needed to turn distance into attraction. In other words, their national identities are not so much what is protected by the comic space but part of that space. What Céline and Jesse like about each other is so linked with their respective national identities that their desire can only grow in a space that protects and nurtures their difference. Without this protective space, in a world governed by irrational incomprehension and intolerance, the conventions of melodrama would have predominated. Paris in particular and Europe in general become, from a U.S. perspective, this protective space, a place where both characters can remain themselves while being affected by the other in important ways.

In *Before Sunset*, then, not only walking and talking but also national identity become eroticised, while the film openly escapes from the technological sophistication associated with the postmodern era, and its old-fashioned preference for physical travel and face-to-face communication brings forth a more humane side of globalisation which contemporary cinema, particularly mainstream productions, appears to have forgotten. The simplicity associated with independent cinema, therefore, feeds not only into the specific development of the genre of romantic comedy posited in this film but also into its ideological discourse on the cultural conditions of postmodern romance. Céline and Jesse have enough things in common to give them endless topics of conversation through which to play out their desire, but this desire is considerably energised by their national difference, not only because it almost guarantees quick separation but, more importantly, because it places them in a typical romantic comedy scenario in which the acceptance of engaging difference becomes the condition and origin of attraction. That this difference is conceptualised as national difference in *Before Sunset* both identifies the film as a cultural text of its time and places it within a particularly active line of development of contemporary romantic comedy. The use of a 'realistic' version of Paris as the comic space to protect and transform the lovers makes the film's discourse of tolerance and international romance more powerful and believable.

The final scene takes the characters to the end of their pilgrimage in Céline's apartment, one more location constructed with a realistic vocation, deep in the heart of off-the-beaten-track but still tourist-cute Paris. The characters, particularly Jesse, have strung one excuse after another to prolong their time together and, eventually, he misses his flight back to the U.S. How many more flights he will miss after this one remains open but the ending strikes the same blend of pure relationship and escape from compromise that has constituted the film's particular 'translation' of cultural discourses on intimate matters. The two characters, after their abstract and personal conversations, seem to have reached a stage of contentment in each other's company that makes his immediate return to New York (and to his wife and child) less pressing. In this final stage of their mutual seduction, music takes centre stage: not only the music of the love song Céline has written for Jesse but, just as significantly, the music of Nina Simone, who had recently died in France after a long period of self-exile from her country, the United States. Simone, who had always been outspoken in her critique of U.S. politics and racism, represents a different type of U.S. transnationalism, one that links Céline's political commitment with Jesse's European travels but one that could finally not be absorbed by the system. It is an index of the film's defence of tolerance that Simone's more abrasive side is ignored now, while the open sensuality of some of her concerts is comically impersonated by Céline who, still performing, becomes more sexually forward than she had been so far. Temporary contentment and impending

12 Will Nina make them stop talking? The open ending and the future
of relationships. Julie Delpy in *Before Sunset* (dir. Richard Linklater,
2004, Warner Bros.)

physicality, conjured up by the presence of a cultural icon from
another age, mark the end of a film that, even in its apparently
rushed closure, remains reluctant to turn its discourse of crisis of
intimacy and sexy talk into something else. What the future will
bring has never been the concern of romantic comedy as a genre
but it is particularly foreign to a film so 'naturally' committed to
the brevity and volatility, but also continuing allure, of modern
love.

To conclude, the combination of romantic comedy with realism
and the discourse of independence in *Before Sunset* is of a different
kind from the more straightforward intergeneric encounters
explored in previous chapters, but, like them, it allows a glimpse
of the complexity and tortuous paths through which romantic
comedy, like other genres, has developed in the course of its
cinematic history and is still developing at the beginning of the
twenty-first century. In general, the view of romantic comedy as
an ever-evolving genre directly linked with – although not the direct
result of – social changes in intimate matters has allowed us to
start telling a different story: while the purer instances of the genre
during the various ups and downs of its Hollywood history may
be an important part of that story, it is in the interstices of the
genre's frequent crosses with other comic or non-comic genres and
with modes and traditions not usually associated with it that the

most challenging developments have taken place. The critically established cycles of romantic comedy – De Mille's divorce comedies and Lubitsch's silent film interventions, the screwball era, the sophisticated and sex comedies of the 1950s, the nervous and new romances of the 1970s and 1980s – have encapsulated and attempted to resolve narratively historical moments of crisis and transition in the institution of marriage, the role of sexuality in romantic love, the validity of the concept of romantic love itself and its replacement by modified versions, and the construction of gender and sexual identities. At the same time, the secret life of the genre, which the specific examples analysed in this book have attempted to unearth, has often engaged with the same social crises in more unexpected ways, paving the way for more immediate changes in the mainstream or pointing to discourses which would not become socially and generically consolidated until some decades later, even sometimes, as in the case of *Kiss Me, Stupid*, leading nowhere.

In generic terms, the secret life of romantic comedy has constituted a cinematic laboratory in which conventions, discourses and definitions have been tested, sometimes accepted and sometimes discarded, before moving into the genre's more consolidated and universally acknowledged representatives. And this is only a small part of the story: Hollywood and its satellites have perhaps been the centre of romantic comedy in modern times but by no means its only space. The genre has existed, in very diverse ways, in other national cinemas and traditions, not to mention its active life outside the cinema, even though all of these have fallen outside the necessarily restricted scope of this book. It has been my contention that only a more flexible and less deterministic approach to the genre's main characteristics, one that moves beyond compulsory heterosexuality and monogamy and the happy ending, can begin to do justice to and to explain this variety and richness. Given the contrast between romantic comedy's capacity for endlessly transforming itself and the immobility and repetitiveness of contemporary theories and, further, the still firmly established critical disregard for one of the genres more consistently associated with popular culture and the feminine, a lot of work remains to be done. Desire may be compulsive but never compulsory, in any of its forms – likewise with its representation in romantic comedy. By limiting the genre's role to the perpetuation of romantic love, obligatory monogamous heterosexuality and the always and forever, we have been performing an act of massive repression, similar to what we have been blaming the genre for. In view of the growing visibility of what has been left out, perhaps the time has come to open the door and overcome the fear of being blinded by the light outside.

References

Allen, Richard and Ishii-Gonzalès, S. (eds) 1999. *Alfred Hitchcock: Centenary Essays*. London: British Film Institute.

Altman, Rick 1999. *Film/Genre*. London: British Film Institute.

Armstrong, Richard 2000. *Billy Wilder: American Film Realist*. Jefferson, NC and London: McFarland.

Azcona, María del Mar 2007. 'All Together Now: The Rise of the U.S. Multi-Protagonist Film in the 1990s'. Unpublished PhD dissertation. University of Zaragoza.

Babington, Bruce and Evans, Peter William 1989. *Affairs to Remember: The Hollywood Comedy of the Sexes*. Manchester: Manchester University Press.

Bakhtin, Mikhail 1984. *Rabelais and His World*. Bloomington: Indiana University Press.

Barber, C.L. 1959. *Shakespeare's Festive Comedy: A Study of Dramatic Form and Its Relation to Social Custom*. Princeton: Princeton University Press.

Barnes, Peter 2002. *To Be or Not to Be*. London: British Film Institute.

Bates, Catherine. 'Love and Courtship'. In Leggatt (ed), 102–22.

Belton, John 1988. '*Rio Bravo*'. In Edward Buscombe (ed). *The BFI Companion to the Western*. London: Andre Deutsch/BFI, 294.

Belton, John (ed) 2000. *Alfred Hitchcock's* Rear Window. Cambridge: Cambridge University Press.

Berry, Edward 2002. 'Laughing at "Others".' In Leggatt (ed), 123–38.

Bonacci, Anna 2001 (1944). *L'ora della fantasia*. Pesaro: Metauro.

Bordwell, David 1985. *Narration in the Fiction Film*. London: Routledge.

Briggs, John and Peat, David 1999. *Seven Life Lessons of Chaos: Timeless Wisdom from the Science of Change*. New York: HarperCollins.

Brill, Lesley 1988. *The Hitchcock Romance: Love and Irony in Hitchcock's Films*. Princeton, NJ: Princeton University Press.

Brill, Lesley 1999. 'Redemptive Comedy in the Films of Alfred Hitchcock and Preston Sturges: "Are Snakes Necessary?"'. In Allen and Ishii-Gonzalès (eds), 205–19.

Brooks, Peter 1984. *Reading for the Plot: Design and Intention in Narrative*. New York: Knopf.

Butler, Judith 1990. *Gender Trouble: Feminism and the Subversion of Identity*. New York and London: Routledge.

Cavell, Stanley 1981. *Pursuits of Happiness: The Hollywood Comedy of Remarriage*. Cambridge, Mass.: Harvard University Press.

Cavell, Stanley 1986. 'North by Northwest'. In Deutelbaum and Poague (eds), 249–61.

Charlton, H.B. *Shakespearean Comedy* 1966 (1938). London: Methuen.

Clubb, Louise George 2002. 'Italian Stories on the Stage'. In Leggatt (ed), 32–46.

Corrigan, Robert W. (ed) 1981. *Comedy: Meaning and Form*. New York: Harper & Row.

Cowie, Elizabeth 1984. 'Fantasia'. *M/f*, 9, 70–105.

Deleyto, Celestino 1998. 'They Lived Happily Ever After: Ending Contemporary Romantic Comedy'. *Miscelánea* 19, 39–55.

Deleyto, Celestino 2003. 'Between Friends: Love and Friendship in Contemporary Hollywood Romantic Comedy'. *Screen*, 44.2, 167–82.

Derrida, Jacques 1980. 'La loie du genre/The Law of Genre'. *Glyph: Textual Studies*, 7, 176–232.

Deutelbaum, Marshall and Poague, Leland (eds) 1986. *A Hithcock Reader*. Ames: Iowa State University Press.

Douchet, Jean 1960. 'Hitch et son public'. *Cahiers du Cinéma*, 113 (November), 7–15.

Dreisinger, Baz 2000. 'The Queen in Shining Armor: Safe Eroticism and the Gay Friend'. *Journal of Popular Film & Television*, 28.1, 2–11.

Durgnat, Raymond 1965. 'Kiss Me, Stupid'. *Films and Filming*, 11, 7 (April), 27.

Dyer, Richard 1986. *Heavenly Bodies: Film Stars and Society*. New York: St. Martin's Press.

Ehrenreich, Barbara 1983. *The Hearts of Men: American Dreams and the Flight from Commitment*. New York: Pluto Press.

Evans, Peter W. and Deleyto, Celestino 1998. 'Introduction: Surviving Love'. In Evans and Deleyto, eds. *Terms of Endearment: Hollywood Romantic Comedy of the 1980s and 1990s*. Edinburgh: Edinburgh University Press, 1–14.

Eyman, Scott 1993. *Ernst Lubitsch: Laughter in Paradise*. New York: Simon & Schuster.

Fallon, Lee 2001. 'The Nebbish King: Spiritual Renewal in Woody Allen's *Manhattan*'. In Kimball King (ed). *Woody Allen: A Casebook*. New York and London: Routledge, 47–54.

Faludi, Susan 1992. *Backlash: The Undeclared War against Women*. London: Vintage.

References   179

Fawell, John 2001. *Hitchcock's* Rear Window: *The Well-Made Film.* Carbondale & Edwardsville: Southern Illinois University Press.

Foucault, Michel 1981 (1976). *The History of Sexuality. Volume 1: An Introduction.* Trans. Robert Hurley. Harmondsworth: Penguin.

Freud, Sigmund 1983 (1905). *Jokes and their Relation to the Unconscious.* Trans. James Strachey. *The Penguin Freud Library*, vol. 6. Harmondsworth: Penguin.

Freud, Sigmund 1985 (1927). 'Humour'. In *Art and Literature*. Trans. James Strachey. *The Penguin Freud Library*, vol. 14. Harmondsworth: Penguin, 422–33.

Frye, Northrop 1957. *Anatomy of Criticism: Four Essays.* Princeton: Princeton University Press.

Galbraith, David 2002. 'Theories of Comedy'. In Leggatt (ed), 3–17.

Gauchée, Mark 2004. 'De qui se moque-t-on?' *L'avant-scène cinema*, 5, 33, 3–5.

Girgus, Sam B. 2002 (1993). *The Films of Woody Allen.* Cambridge: Cambridge University Press.

Goodridge, Mike 2004. 'Delpy Writes her Own Destiny'. *Screen International* 1478 (6 November), 20.

Greenblatt, Stephen 1988. *Shakespearean Negotiations.* Oxford: Clarendon Press.

Grindon, Leger 2007. 'From the Grotesque to the Ambivalent: Recent Developments in the Hollywood Romantic Comedy, 1997–2007'. Paper read at the Chicago SCMS Conference, 8–11 March.

Harvey, James 1998 (1987). *Romantic Comedy in Hollywood: From Lubitsch to Sturges.* New York: Da Capo Press.

Henderson, Brian 1978. 'Romantic Comedy Today: Semi-Tough or Impossible?' *Film Quarterly*, 31, 4 (Summer), 11–22.

Holmlund, Chris 2005. 'Introduction: From the Margins to the Mainstream'. In Holmlund, Chris and Wyatt, Justin (eds). *Contemporary American Independent Film: From the Margins to the Mainstream.* London and New York: Routledge, 1–19.

Horton, Andrew S. (ed) 1991. Introduction to *Comedy/Cinema/Theory*. Berkeley, Los Angeles and Oxford: University of California Press, 1–21.

James, Nick 2004. 'Debrief Encounter'. *Sight & Sound.* 14, 8 (August), 12–15.

James, Nick 2005. 'Integrity Bites'. *Sight & Sound.* 15, 3 (March), 3.

Jeffers McDonald, Tamar 2007. *Romantic Comedy: Boy Meets Girl Meets Genre.* London and New York: Wallflower.

Jenkins, Henry 1992. *What Made Pistachio Nuts? Early Sound Comedy and the Vaudeville Aesthetic.* New York: Columbia University Press.

Karnick, Kristine 1995. 'Commitment and Reaffirmation in Hollywood Romantic Comedy'. In Karnick and Jenkins (eds), 123–46.

Karnick, Kristine Brunovska and Jenkins, Henry (eds) 1995. *Classical Hollywood Comedy*. New York and London: Routledge.

King, Geoff 2002. *Film Comedy*. London and New York: Wallflower Press.

King, Geoff 2005. *American Independent Cinema*. London and New York: I.B. Tauris.

Krutnik, Frank 1990. 'The Faint Aroma of Performing Seals: The "Nervous" Romance and the Comedy of the Sexes'. *The Velvet Light Trap*, 26 (Autumn), 57–72.

Krutnik, Frank 1995. 'A Spanner in the Works? Genre, Narrative and the Hollywood Comedian'. In Karnick and Jenkins (eds), 17–38.

Krutnik, Frank 1998. 'Love Lies: Romantic Fabrication in Contemporary Romantic Comedy'. In Evans and Deleyto (eds), 15–36.

Krutnik, Frank 2002. 'Conforming Passions? Contemporary Romantic Comedy'. In Steve Neale (ed). *Genre and Contemporary Hollywood*, London: British Film Institute, 130–47.

Lakoff, George 1987. *Women, Fire, and Dangerous Things: What Categories Reveal about the Mind*. Chicago and London: The University of Chicago Press.

Lee, Sander H. 1988. 'Escape and Commitment in Hitchcock's *Rear Window*'. *PostScript*, 7, 2 (Winter), 18–28.

Lee, Sander H. 1997. *Woody Allen's Angst: Philosophical Commentaries on His Serious Films*. Jefferson, NC and London: McFarland.

Leggatt, Alexander (ed) 2002. *The Cambridge Companion to Shakespearean Comedy*. Cambridge: Cambridge University Press.

Lehman, Benjamin 1981. 'Comedy and Laughter'. In Corrigan (ed), 100–11.

Lemire, Elise 2000. 'Voyeurism and the Postwar Crisis of Masculinity'. In Belton (ed), 57–90.

Lemon, Richard 2001 (1966). 'The Message in Billy Wilder's Fortune Cookie: "Well, Nobody's Perfect..."' In Robert Horton (ed). *Billy Wilder Interview*. Jackson: University Press of Mississippi, 38–48.

Lent, Tina Olsin 1995. 'Love and Friendship: The Redefinition of Gender Relations in Screwball Comedy'. In Karnick and Jenkins (eds), 314–31.

Levin, Richard 1985. *Love and Society in Shakespearean Comedy: A Study of Dramatic Form and Content*. Newark: University of Delaware Press, and London: Associated University Presses.

Levy, Emmanuel 1999. *Cinema of Outsiders: The Rise of American Independent Film*. New York and London: New York University Press.

Lippe, Richard 1971/72. '*Kiss Me, Stupid*: A Comedy Dilemma'. *The Velvet Light Trap*, 3 (Winter), 33–5.

McWilliam, Kelly Ann, forthcoming. *When Carrie Met Sally: Lesbian Romantic Comedies and the Public Sphere*. London: I.B. Tauris.

Melehy, Hassan 2001/2002. 'Lubitsch's *To Be or Not to Be*: The Question of Simulation in the Cinema'. *Film Criticism*, 26, 2 (Winter), 19–40.

Mernit, Billy 2000. *Writing the Romantic Comedy*. New York: HarperCollins.

Miola, Robert S. 2002. 'Roman Comedy'. In Leggatt (ed), 18–31.

Modleski, Tania 1988. *The Women Who Knew Too Much: Hitchcock and Feminist Theory*. New York and London: Methuen.

Morson, Gary Saul and Emerson, Caryl 1990. *Mikhail Bakhtin: Creation of a Prosaics*. Stanford, CA: Stanford University Press.

Mulvey, Laura 1989 (1975). 'Visual Pleasure and Narrative Cinema'. In *Visual and Other Pleasures*. Bloomington and Indianapolis: Indiana University Press, 14–26.

Musser, Charles 1995. 'Divorce, DeMille, and the Comedy of Remarriage'. In Karnick and Jenkins (eds), 282–313.

Naremore, James O. 1998. *More than Night: Film Noir and Its Contexts*. Berkeley, Los Angeles and London: University of California Press.

Naremore, James 2004. 'Hitchcock and Humour'. In Richard Allen and Sam Ishii-Gonzalès (eds). *Past and Future Hitchcock*. London and New York: Routledge, 22–36.

Neale, Steve 1992. 'The Big Romance or Something wild? Romantic Comedy Today'. *Screen*, 33, 3 (Autumn), 284–99.

Neale, Steve 2000. *Genre and Hollywood*. London and New York: Routledge.

Neale, Steve and Krutnik, Frank 1990. *Popular Film and Television Comedy*. London and New York: Routledge.

Nelson, T.G.A. 1990. *The Theory of Comedy in Literature, Drama, and Cinema*. Oxford and New York: Oxford University Press.

Nichols, Mary 1998. *Reconstructing Woody: Art, Love, and Life in the Films of Woody Allen*. Lanham, Boulder, New York and Oxford: Rowman & Littlefield.

Opacki, Ireneusz 2000 (1987). 'Royal Genres'. In David Duff (ed). *Modern Genre Theory*. Trans. David Malcolm. Harlow: Longman, 118–26.

Palmer, Jerry 1987. *The Logic of the Absurd: On Film and Television Comedy*. London: British Film Institute.

Pamerleau, William C. 2000. 'Rethinking Raskolnikov: Exploring Contemporary Horizons in Woody Allen's *Crimes and Misdemeanors*'. *Film and Philosophy*, special issue on Woody Allen, 102–14.

Paul, William 1983. *Ernst Lubitsch's American Comedy*. New York: Columbia University Press.

Paul, William 2002. 'The Impossibility of Romance: Hollywood Comedy, 1978–1999'. In Steve Neale (ed). *Genre and Contemporary Hollywood*. London: British Film Institute, 117–29.

Poague, Leland 1978. *The Cinema of Ernst Lubitsch*. New York: Barnes.

Polan, Dana 1991. 'The Light Side of Genius: Hitchcock's *Mr. and Mrs. Smith* in the Screwball Tradition'. In Horton (ed), 131–52.

Powers, James 1964. 'Advanced Pub Will Make Film Big B.O.' *Hollywood Reporter*, 27 (16 December), 3.

Read, Jacinda 2000. *The New Avengers: Feminism, Femininity and the Rape-Revenge Cycle*. Manchester and New York: Manchester University Press.

Robey, Tim 2006. '*A Scanner Darkly*'. *Sight & Sound* 16, 9 (September), 66–8.

Rose, Mary Beth 1988. *The Expense of Spirit: Love and Sexuality in English Renaissance Drama*. Ithaca and London: Cornell University Press.

Rowe, Kathleen 1995. *The Unruly Woman: Gender and the Genres of Laughter*. Austin: University of Texas Press.

Ryall, Tom 1998. 'Genre and Hollywood'. In Hill, John and Gibson, Pamela Church (eds). *The Oxford Guide to Film Studies*. Oxford: Oxford University Press, 327–41.

Salingar, Leo 1974. *Shakespeare and the Traditions of Comedy*. Cambridge: Cambridge University Press.

Samuels, Robert 1998. *Hitchcock's Bi-Textuality: Lacan, Feminisms, and Queer Theory*. New York: State University of New York Press.

Schatz, Thomas 1981. *Hollywood Genres: Formulas, Filmmaking and the Studio System*. New York: McGraw-Hill.

Sedgwick, Eve Kosofsky 1985. *Between Men: English Literature and Male Homosocial Desire*. New York: Columbia University Press.

Seidman, Steve 1981. *Comedian Comedy: A Tradition in Hollywood Film*. Ann Arbor: UMI Research Press.

Seidman, Steven 1991. *Romantic Longings: Love in America, 1830–1980*. London and New York: Routledge.

Seidman, Steven 1992. *Embattled Eros: Sexual Politics and Ethics in Contemporary America*. London and New York: Routledge.

Shakespeare, William 1975 (1601). *Twelfth Night. The Arden Shakespeare*. Ed. J.M. Lothian and T.W. Craik. London and New York: Methuen.

Shakespeare, William 1985 (1603). *Hamlet, Prince of Denmark. The New Cambridge Shakespeare*. Ed. Philip Edwards. Cambridge: Cambridge University Press.

Shumway, David O. 2003. *Modern Love: Romance, Intimacy and the Marriage Crisis*. New York and London: New York University Press.

Sikov, Ed 1994. *Laughing Hysterically: American Screen Comedy of the 1950s*. New York: Columbia University Press.

Sikov, Ed 1998. *On Sunset Boulevard: The Life and Times of Billy Wilder*. New York: Hyperion.

Simon, William 1996. *Postmodern Sexualities*. London and New York: Routledge.

Smith, Susan 2000. *Hitchcock: Suspense, Humour and Tone*. London: British Film Institute.

Staiger, Janet 1997. 'Hybrid or Inbred: The Purity Hypothesis and Hollywood Genre History'. *Film Criticism*, 22, 1 (1997), 5–20.

Stam, Robert and Pearson, Roberta 1986. 'Hitchcock's *Rear Window*: Reflexivity and the Critique of Voyeurism'. In Deutelbaum and Poague (eds), 193–206.

Street, Sarah 2000. ' "The Dresses Had Told Me": Fashion and Femininity in *Rear Window*'. In Belton (ed), 91–109.

Suárez, Juan A. 1996. 'The Rear View: Paranoia and Homosocial Desire in Alfred Hitchcock's *Rear Window*'. In Cornut-Gentille D'Arcy, Chantal and García Landa, José Ángel (eds). *Gender, I-deology: Essays on Theory, Fiction and Film*. Amsterdam and New York: Rodopi, 359–69.

Taves, Brian 1993. *The Romance of Adventure: The Genre of Historical Adventure Movies*. Jackson, MS: Mississippi University Press.

Thackeray, William Makepeace 1968 (1848). *Vanity Fair*. Harmondsworth: Penguin.

Thomas, Deborah 1998. '*Murphy's Romance*: Romantic Love and the Everyday'. In Evans, Peter William and Deleyto, Celestino (eds), 57–74.

Thomas, Deborah 2000. *Beyond Genre: Melodrama, Comedy and Romance in Hollywood*. Moffat: Cameron & Hollis.

Truffaut, François 1986 (1968). *Hitchcock by Truffaut: The Definitive Study*. London: Paladin and Grafton.

Tzioumakis, Yannis 2006. *American Independent Cinema*. Edinburgh: Edinburgh University Press.

Vincendeau, Ginette 2001. 'Café Society'. *Sight & Sound*, 11, 8 (August), 22–5.

Whitaker, Sheila 1976/77. 'To Be or Not to Be'. *Framework*, 5 (winter), 12–14.

Williams, Linda Ruth 2005. *The Erotic Thriller in Contemporary Cinema*. Edinburgh: Edinburgh University Press.

Wittgenstein, Ludwig 1963 (1953). *Philosophical Investigations*. Oxford: Blackwell.

Wood, Robin 1983 (1968). *Howard Hawks*. London: British Film Institute.

Wood, Robin 1989 (1960). *Hitchcock's Films Revisited*. New York: Columbia University Press.

Wood, Robin 1999. 'Looking at *The Birds* and *Marnie* through the *Rear Window*'. *CineAction!*, 50 (September), 80–5.

Zizek, Slavoj 1999. 'The Hitchcockian Blot'. In Allen and Ishii-Gonzalès (eds), 123–39.

Index

Allen, Woody 48, 51, 54, 128–47, 151–2, 164
Altman, Rick 3, 5–6, 7, 11, 14
American President, The 38–45, 152
Annie Hall 130, 151, 164
Apartment, The 22, 83, 95, 97, 127
Aristotelian categorisation 7–8, 9, 10
Aristotelian comedy 19, 25, 35, 61, 84
    see also satire; black comedy
Awful Truth, The 59, 68

Babington, Bruce 40, 64, 65, 82, 83, 134
Bakhtin, Mikhail 8, 21, 33–5, 37
Ball of Fire 15, 58, 69
Beautiful Girls 145, 155, 165
Before Sunrise 157–9, 166, 170, 172
Before Sunset 2, 3, 53, 54, 157–74
Benny, Jack 59, 61, 66–7, 70, 77
Big 25, 50
Birds, The 104, 105
black comedy 43, 60–1, 75
    see also Aristotelian comedy; satire
Bluebeard's Eighth Wife 67
Break-Up, The 25, 144, 152
Brill, Lesley 103, 104, 107

Bringing Up Baby 15, 50, 59, 68, 127
Brooks, Peter 24
Burns, Edward 155
Butler, Judith 79–81

Capra, Frank 55, 67
carnivalesque comedy 21, 32, 33, 37
Cavell, Stanley 48, 64, 103–4, 109, 170
chaos theory 8–9, 10, 52
Christmas in July 49
Cluny Brown 57, 68
comedian comedy 19–21, 23, 34, 37, 48, 51, 53, 59, 66, 129
comic space 18, 30–8, 39–46, 52, 75–6, 85, 92–5, 98–9, 108–10, 118–22, 126–8, 130–1, 132–4, 139–47, 169–74
confessional comedy 165–6, 167–8
Conte d'hiver 133
Crimes and Misdemeanors 54, 128–47, 169
Cukor, George 49

Dave 39
Daytrippers, The 151, 155, 156
de Mille, Cecil B. 48, 57, 175
Decameron 26–7, 30–1
Delpy, Julie 157, 167–8, 172
Derrida 9–11, 12, 16, 52, 60

Design for Living 59, 63, 64, 67, 68
Desperately Seeking Susan 151, 153–4
divorce comedies 48, 61, 65, 175
Dyer, Richard 83, 97

Ephron, Nora 50, 156
Eternal Sunshine of the Spotless Mind 156
Evans, Peter 40, 48, 64–5, 82, 83, 134
Everyone Says I Love You 145

Faludi, Susan 42, 138
fantasy 20, 34, 45, 71, 74, 79, 83, 86, 88–90, 92–6, 97, 98, 100, 119, 134, 153–7, 159–60
female sexuality 76, 80, 84, 88, 89, 94, 97, 115, 123, 126–8, 172
feminism 40, 42, 43, 44, 45, 51, 68, 78, 104, 138, 146, 167–8
femininity 29, 43, 69, 81, 109, 122, 124, 128, 146
film noir 7, 11, 58, 68, 120
Foucault, Michel 79, 81
Freud, Sigmund 21, 131, 136–7, 147
friendship 18, 36, 47, 117, 144, 149, 153–4, 164
Friends with Money 153–4
Frye, Northrop 1, 19, 22, 28, 31, 37, 86

Gentlemen Prefer Blondes 13, 97
Girl Can't Help It, The 13, 121
Greenblatt, Stephen 34–5, 70, 122
Grindon, Leger 148–9

happy ending 18, 20, 23, 24–5, 27–9, 33, 35, 101, 126–7, 140, 144, 175

Hatari! 4, 13
Hawke, Ethan 157, 167, 172
Hawks, Howard 3–6, 13, 15–16, 49, 55, 58, 69, 82, 97
Henderson, Brian 82, 84, 164
heterosexual desire 36, 43, 51, 64, 115, 122, 124, 128, 138, 154, 155
heterosexuality 18, 20, 25–6, 27–9, 44, 47, 68, 97, 107, 108, 111, 112, 113, 115, 123, 126, 127, 128, 137, 144, 147, 148, 149, 150, 151, 153, 154, 166–8, 175–6
His Girl Friday 15, 68
Hitchcock, Alfred 53–4, 58, 67, 82, 103–28, 129–30, 170
Holmlund, Christine 150–1
homoerotic desire 107, 114, 116, 123, 128
homosexuality 78, 112–16, 124, 149, 153–5
homosocial desire 16, 31, 51, 64, 115, 153
humour 18, 20–4, 30, 33–6, 40–1, 44, 46, 71, 86, 103, 106, 130, 131, 135, 136–7, 138, 144, 146, 147
  see also jokes; laughter
Husbands and Wives 46, 129, 135, 143

independent cinema 50–1, 54, 150–7, 164, 165, 172–3, 174
In Good Company 25, 144
intimacy 1, 24, 28–9, 40, 117–18, 152, 163, 168, 174
It Happened One Night 59, 67, 68
I Was a Male War Bride 13, 15, 97

Jeffers McDonald, Tamar 1, 7, 22–3, 82, 84, 150, 153, 156, 163
jokes 20, 23–4, 35, 40–1, 71, 74–5, 135, 136–7, 138
see also humour; laughter

King, Geoff 85–6, 151–2
Kiss Me, Stupid 53, 81–102, 175
Krutnik, Frank 20, 21, 22, 27, 29–30, 48, 50, 62, 82, 84, 129–30, 148, 152, 169

Lady Eve, The 48, 57–8, 68, 127
laughter 19–24, 30, 33, 34, 35
see also humour; jokes
Linklater, Richard 157–75
Lombard, Carole 56, 58–9, 61, 67, 77, 80
L'ora della fantasia 93
Love in the Afternoon 88, 121
love triangle 56, 58, 60, 61–6, 71, 76, 130
Lubitsch, Ernst 35, 48, 53, 55–81, 82, 101, 170, 175
Lubitschean comedy 57–8, 61, 65, 67, 68, 70

Maid in Manhattan 2, 50, 151
male anxiety 43, 123–8
male desire 106, 113, 155
Manhattan 130, 143–5, 152
Man's Favorite Sport? 13, 15, 83, 97
marriage 18, 22, 25–6, 27–8, 29, 48, 56, 61, 63, 64–5, 68, 70, 73, 83, 84, 88–9, 91, 96, 97, 109, 110, 112–18, 120–8, 135–6, 138, 140, 145, 170, 175
Marriage Circle, The 63, 65, 68
marriage comedy 51, 53, 56, 57, 61, 63, 71, 89, 93, 98, 101

masculinity 16, 29, 43, 45, 81, 112, 114–15, 122, 124, 128, 137, 146
melodrama 6, 11, 34, 36, 56, 60, 62, 75, 95, 102, 131, 172
Mernit, Billy 25, 29, 36, 51
metafiction 51, 53, 75, 105, 106, 156, 157, 164
Mr. and Mrs. Smith 58, 67, 104
Moglie per una notte 93
Much Ado About Nothing (play) 31
multi-protagonist films 37, 52, 129, 131, 149
My Best Friend's Wedding 25, 42, 144, 152, 154, 155, 156

Naremore, James 7, 103–4
Neale, Steve 1, 4, 5, 11, 14, 20, 21, 22, 40, 82, 108–9, 148
neo-conservative discourses 138, 143, 146, 148
nervous romances 17, 38, 48, 129, 148, 164
new romances 17, 38, 48, 148–9, 175
Next Stop, Wonderland 155–6
Ninotchka 35–6, 66, 68
North by Northwest 103–4, 109, 170

Object of My Affection, The 25, 144, 152, 154, 155
Opposite of Sex, The 151, 154
Out of Sight 1–3, 50, 51, 152

Palm Beach Story, The 48, 58
Paul, William 59, 61, 62, 64, 66, 74, 75–6, 149
performance 2, 43, 67, 69, 71–5, 75–81, 89, 91, 95, 98, 112, 115, 122, 135, 161
Philadelphia Story, The 58, 68

Pillow Talk 13, 50, 118, 121, 127
Play It to the Bone 1, 6
Portrait of Jenny 145
Pretty Woman 2, 50, 151
Prime 25, 144

realism 2, 19, 21, 60, 64, 77, 94, 98, 107, 153, 156–63, 170–1, 173–4
Rear Window 54, 103–28, 129
relationship stories 28, 29, 163
Rio Bravo 3–6, 12–17, 50
Rivette, Jacques 2, 157, 171
Rohmer, Eric 2, 103, 133, 157, 171
romantic love 25, 33, 47, 97, 116–19, 122, 123, 144–7, 149, 153, 159–62, 163–4, 169, 175

Sabrina 88
Sartrean philosophy 130, 140, 141
satire 19, 27, 51, 53, 60–2, 66, 69–70, 83, 85–7, 89–91, 94–8, 100–1, 138, 146
  see also Aristotelian comedy; black comedy
Schatz, Thomas 12
Science of Sleep, The 157
screwball comedy 15, 17, 48–9, 50, 57–9, 61, 64–5, 66–9, 70–2, 78, 80, 97, 103, 104, 123, 128, 172, 175
Searchers, The 13, 16
Sedgwick, Eve Kosofsky 51, 64, 153
sex comedy 82, 84, 113
sex, lies, and videotape 164–5
sexual desire 27, 44, 45, 76, 83, 93, 95, 97–8, 116–17, 122, 123, 136, 137, 143–6, 164

  see also female desire; heterosexual desire; homoerotic desire; sexuality
sexuality 27–9, 34, 36, 38, 40, 45, 52, 62, 65, 77, 79, 81, 83, 97, 99, 104, 107, 117, 121, 128, 131, 136, 137, 143, 144, 155, 175
Shakespeare, William 19, 26–7, 28, 32, 33, 34, 37, 62, 70, 72–4, 92, 95, 97, 99, 123, 142
Shakespearean comedy 1, 19, 28, 31–4, 37, 70
Shop Around the Corner, The 66, 68
Shumway, David 28, 40, 117, 163
Sikov, Ed 53–4, 82, 85, 94, 96
Simone, Nina 173
Sleepless in Seattle 2, 42, 50, 151, 155–6
Smiles of a Summer Night 97
Some Like it Hot 13, 35, 83, 97
Speed 51, 152
Staiger, Janet 14
Stranger than Fiction 156–7
Sturges, Preston 48–9, 50, 57–8, 103
Sullivan's Travels 48, 50, 57–8

Take a Letter, Darling 58
Thomas, Deborah 20, 34, 37, 62, 92
thriller 1, 43, 45, 53, 60, 75, 102, 103–5, 106, 110–11, 122–4, 126, 128, 129–30, 143, 147
To Be or Not to Be 53, 55–81, 82, 85, 88, 92, 100, 101, 105
To Catch a Thief 104, 121
transnational romance 149, 171
Truffaut, François 103, 105
Tzioumakis, Yannis 151–2

Unfaithfully Yours 49

Walking and Talking 144, 151, 153, 165–6
western 4–6, 11, 12–13, 15–16
White Men Can't Jump 25, 144, 152
Wilder, Billy 35, 53, 81–102, 170

Wittgenstein, Ludwig 7, 9, 10, 52
Woman of Paris, A 57
Wood, Robin 5, 15, 103, 105–6, 107, 110
Working Girl 42, 129

Zizek, Slavoj 109–110